NATIONAL INSTITUTE SOCIAL SERVICES LIBRARY

NO. 33

GROUP WORK: LEARNING AND PRACTICE

National Institute Social Services Library

2 INTRODUCTION TO A SOCIAL WORKER
3 SOCIAL POLICY AND ADMINISTRATION REVISITED
Studies in the Development of Social Services at the Local Level
by David Donnison and others
4 SOCIAL WORK WITH FAMILIES
Readings in Social Work, Volume I
Compiled by Eileen Younghusband
6 NEW DEVELOPMENTS IN CASEWORK
Readings in Social Work, Volume II
Compiled by Eileen Younghusband
14 EDUCATION FOR SOCIAL WORK
Readings in Social Work, Volume IV
Compiled by Eileen Younghusband
15 CHILD CARE: NEEDS AND NUMBERS
by Jean Packman
17 A PLACE LIKE HOME
A Hostel for Disturbed Adolescents
by W. David Wills
18 ADOPTION OF NON-WHITE CHILDREN
The Experience of a British Adoption Project
by Lois Rayner
19 HELPING THE AGED
A Field Experiment in Social Work
by E. Matilda Goldberg and others
20 VOLUNTEERS IN PRISON AFTER-CARE
The Report of the Teamwork Associates Pilot Project
by Hugh Barr
21 HOMELESS NEAR A THOUSAND HOMES
A Study of Families Without Homes in South Wales and the West of England
by Bryan Glastonbury
22 HUMAN DEVELOPMENT
An Introduction to the Psychodynamics of Growth, Maturity and Ageing
by Eric Rayner
23 PLANS AND PROVISIONS FOR THE MENTALLY HANDICAPPED
by Margaret Bone, Bernie Spain and F. M. Martin
24 SOCIAL WORK IN GENERAL PRACTICE
by E. Matilda Goldberg and June E. Neill
25 CLAIMANT OR CLIENT?
A Social Worker's View of the Supplementary Benefits Commission
by Olive Stevenson
26 COMMON HUMAN NEEDS
by Charlotte Towle
27 THE POINT OF ENTRY
A Study of Client Reception in the Social Services
by Anthony S. Hall
28 ACROSS THE GENERATIONS
Old People and Young Volunteers
by Roger Hadley, Adrian Webb and Christine Farrell
29 CHILDREN AND DECENT PEOPLE
Edited by Alvin L. Schorr
30 ORGANISING FOR SOCIAL CHANGE
A Study in the Theory and Practice of Community Work
by David N. Thomas
31 INTEGRATING SOCIAL WORK METHODS
Edited by Harry Specht and Anne Vickery
32 COMMUNITY WORK: LEARNING AND SUPERVISION
Edited by Catherine Briscoe and David N. Thomas

GROUP WORK: LEARNING AND PRACTICE

Edited by
NANO McCAUGHAN

Lecturer in Group Work
National Institute for Social Work

London
GEORGE ALLEN & UNWIN
Boston Sydney

First published in 1978

ISBN 0 04 361029 3 papercase
0 04 361030 7 paperback

Printed in Great Britain in 10 on 11 point Times by
Willmer Brothers Limited, Birkenhead

FOREWORD

The National Institute for Social Work is an independent centre for the promotion and development of the personal social services and the training of social workers. It attempts this through a varied but mutually reinforcing programme which includes post-professional education, short courses, consultancy, library and information service, publications and research. The improvement of social work practice has always been a basic concern. This particular volume was a natural development from the exploration of unitary methods of social work reported in *Integrating Social Work Methods* (Specht and Vickery, 1977) and is a companion to *Community Work: Learning and Supervision* (Briscoe and Thomas, 1977).

Group work is so central to social work, whether it be work with individuals and families, residential work, day care, community work, management or social work education, that the relative lack of development in this aspect of social work method must be reckoned among the most serious deficiencies in the field.

This was recognised by the Younghusband Report as far back as 1959, and in urging the establishment of the National Institute the report recommended that training for group work should be one of its major areas of activity. Despite this long-standing commitment, it is only in recent years that significant progress has been made in this aspect of the Institute's work and the credit for this must go to Nano McCaughan.

Many of the clients of social workers are people whose links with society through primary group membership are weak or non-existent. In residential institutions, in family and community settings, the initial task of the social worker is often to attempt to provide a 'corrective' experience of group life for such people. As a result it is hoped that they can learn to make more effective use of the normal opportunities offered by society to achieve their individual purposes, be they institutional change, practical assistance or emotional satisfaction.

This reader brings together a selection of papers by experienced group workers as an aid to teachers, practitioners and students engaged in this onerous task.

DAVID JONES
Principal of the National Institute for Social Work

ACKNOWLEDGEMENTS

I am very grateful to my colleagues at the National Institute for Social Work for their editorial help on the papers; Anne Vickery, David Thomas, Kate Griffiths, David Jones; also to Sheila Feld, visiting scholar from the University of Michigan; to Jenny McElhinney for patiently typing and retyping numerous drafts; also to Ruby Woodman and Margaret Theodore; to Oula Jones for her careful indexing; and most of all to those who contributed papers and generously accepted my editorial suggestions and deletions.

CONTENTS

NOTES ON CONTRIBUTORS

ALICE BRESLIN is Officer in Charge of a Hostel for the Mentally Handicapped, Hertfordshire Social Services Department.

CATHERINE BRISCOE is Visiting Lecturer in Social Work, University of Singapore.

HILARY DAVIES is now a Lecturer in Social Work at Glasgow University – was formerly a fieldwork teacher in a Family Service Unit.

TOM DOUGLAS is Senior Lecturer in Social Work, Department of Social Policy and Social Work, University of Keele.

HERBERT LAMING is Director of Social Services Department, Hertfordshire.

NANO McCAUGHAN is Lecturer in Group Work, National Institute for Social Work.

BARRY PALMER is a Senior Consultant with the Grubb Institute.

CHRIS PAYNE is Lecturer in Residential Social Work, National Institute for Social Work.

CHARLOTTE RAWCLIFFE is a Social Worker, with the London Borough of Lewisham Social Services Department; formerly Good Neighbourhood Worker, Peckham Settlement.

PETER B. SMITH is Lecturer in Social Psychology, School of Social Sciences, University of Sussex.

SHEILA STURTON was formerly Group Work Adviser to Hertfordshire County Council, Social Services Department.

DAVID N. THOMAS is Lecturer in Community Work, National Institute for Social Work.

ANNE VICKERY is Senior Lecturer in Social Work, National Institute for Social Work.

LORNA WALKER is now part-time Lecturer in Social Work, University of Liverpool, Institute of Extension Studies, was formerly Unit Organiser, Bradford Family Service Unit.

VERONICA WARD is a part-time Administrative Secretary of the Association of Community Workers; formerly Community Worker, London Borough of Southwark Social Services Department.

ROSEMARY WHIFFEN is Co-Chairman of the Family Therapy Programme, Department of Children and Parents, Tavistock Clinic.

PART I

FRAMEWORKS FOR PRACTICE

The papers in this section reflect different ways of establishing a context for group work. To undertake this intellectual task implies that the group worker must answer questions about the nature of the particular function of the social welfare agency which the group work will hopefully implement. A useful way to concretise thinking is to enumerate the task or tasks which the group worker and clients should be engaged in together. If one establishes clearly enough the context of the intervention, it is then more evident what knowledge, theories, skill and activities can be 'selected' in, for guidance in the group project.

In my paper 'Continuing Themes in Social Group Work' I have listed and discussed what I take to be enduring principles guiding the practice of group workers during the last one hundred years. These principles have been elaborated and altered by changing social philosophy and mores in society, but still connect group work practice theory with its historical roots. It is comforting to note that problematic issues such as 'leadership' and 'control' are by no means resolved.

Anne Vickery, Charlotte Rawcliffe and Veronica Ward trace the formation and career of a self-help group of elderly people, who resided on the same housing estate. The context of this group illustrates the use of a unitary approach to social work practice, and how the group work is chosen as a feasible and effective solution to discovered need. Alternative responses or intervention could have been made; in fact different 'models' of group work introduced. As I stated, the framework used by the workers in exploring and assessing the need led logically to the choice they made and no doubt ensured the consistency of their actions in the group.

Peter Smith extrapolates from social psychological research some theories and conceptualisations which illuminate various aspects of group work practice. His emphasis is on the influence possibilities in group work: both that exerted by worker on members (and vice versa) and that likely to be exerted among the members. The two aspects of 'support' and 'confrontation' are explored as necessary concomitants of change and factors affecting their appropriate use discussed.

Chris Payne analyses tasks which residential workers are faced with, whatever their setting. He discusses how group work interventions might enhance the work, suggesting the desirability of forming some groups for special purposes in an institution, as well as developing skill in exploiting the natural group living situation on behalf of residents. Payne implies that it is important and possible to attempt to 'boundary' both forms of group intervention.

Chapter 1

INTRODUCTION: A FRAMEWORK FOR THINKING ABOUT GROUP WORK

Nano McCaughan

I PURPOSE OF THE READER

The purpose of this reader is to enlarge the scanty resource of British publications about social group work. The design was created to emphasise the complex skills that are required from the formal leaders in social work groups, skills which have many different purposes. The authors were selected because of the concern manifested in their teaching, thinking and practice for this element. The first two sections include the work of social work teachers and trainers who are aware that education should be designed for the development of competence in action as well as for the acquisition of knowledge. The last section includes some accounts of social work practice in a variety of groups.

I make the assumption that the development of group work skills would be a useful addition to the repertoire of activities of social workers, and that clients might actually be better helped by their peers in a group setting in some situations, than by other forms of intervention. The evidence for this assumption is difficult to come by in any rigorous form. I would have liked to include a paper on recent researches on the outcomes of group work. A preliminary search of the literature revealed a dearth of material, apart from studies into psychotherapy groups. (Some useful references can be found in Yalom, 1970, and in the Tavistock Publications List (Tavistock Institute of Human Relations, 1975).) However, some positive evidence for the effectiveness of group work, or of a multi-method approach, can be found in studies such as *The Canford Families* (*Sociological Review*, 1962), *Girls at Vocational High* (Meyer *et al.*, 1965), and the *Wincroft Youth Project* (Smith *et al.*, 1972). Although there are many accounts of group work practice in British and American journals in recent years, the analysis of outcomes is either based on the group worker's subjective judgement, or left for the reader to judge for himself.

Content

All but two of the papers have been written especially for this Reader. In commissioning the papers I decided to omit papers on areas of work that have been very adequately dealt with elsewhere. For example, in the first section, 'Frameworks for Practice', the contribution of the work of social psychologists to the understanding of groups has been limited to Peter Smith's paper – who naturally could only touch on a few relevant findings, and chose those which inform his particular view of the group worker's role. The ever-increasing body of knowledge about small groups drawn from 'laboratory' studies will be found summarised in most recent group work texts (see Northen, 1969; Hartford, 1972). A supplement to Smith's paper is my own chapter summarising some group behaviour theories for community workers (McCaughan, 1977a). The usefulness of these laboratory studies for practitioners can be questioned, as well as the validity of applying the results to the general population. However, the information exists and its richness and diversity create a problem for teachers of group behaviour when they attempt to select content for their seminars.

In this book the authors demonstrate an approach to their work which has been formed by theoretical viewpoints drawn variously from psychoanalytic theories, behavioural psychological theories and theories of social role. One must turn to the relevant source for a more detailed discussion of these approaches, and their derivations which have been translated into the newer therapies used in groups, such as transactional analysis, gestalt therapy.

Social work courses increasingly provide students with opportunities to develop in self-awareness and sensitivity through a consciously examined group experience. Accounts of these experiences and their outcomes for the individuals who take part can be found in some recent journals (Papell, 1972; Hunt *et al.*, 1974; Smith, 1975). In this book Barry Palmer and Tom Douglas have contributed papers which will add to this small store. They demonstrate models of learning and teaching about groups which attempt to integrate intellect, feeling and action.

It was not appropriate to include detailed discussion of such aspects of group work as composition, size, group development stages, recording, etc. These have been very adequately written about in the group work texts over the years (for example, see Konopka, 1963; Northen, 1969; Trecker, 1972; Hartford, 1972; Douglas, 1976). The use of activities in groups discussed in Catherine Briscoe's paper is one exception, as this has not been covered very fully in these writings.

The authors who describe their practice in this book are eclectic in their use of theories, drawing from various sources concepts, frameworks and principles of action which appeared useful to them in understanding and enhancing the work they had undertaken. The intention was to demonstrate by this small selection the wide range of possible consumers of group work and the difference in goal setting, and formal leadership role that follows.

II A FRAMEWORK FOR THINKING ABOUT GROUP WORK

As a framework for planning the book I have used four crucial concepts, an elaboration of which may be useful in helping the reader find some common ground in the different approaches to group work. The first is the understanding of the group as a small social *system*, and the consequences that flow from regarding it in that dynamic way. The majority of the contributors have in the forefront or background of their minds a systems model as a useful framework for planning, organising and evaluating the outcomes of group work (see Vickery, Whiffen, Thomas, Breslin and Sturton).

The other three concepts that are also derived from this model are notions about *boundary*, *task* and *role*. A system is defined by a *boundary*, which is permeable in terms of admitting the ideas, attitudes and feelings which the members carry with them from other meaningful groups. A human or social system is largely defined by its goals which must be put into operation by the members engaging together in appropriate *tasks*. This work provides opportunity for members to take up different *roles*, which serve to reinforce familiar behaviours or cause the member to develop new repertoires of behaviour. As much as any other member the group worker, or formal leader, will have to struggle to find an appropriate role for himself, and constantly re-examine the authority he has in his role.

In its present state of development the systems approach in social work intervention is probably more useful in planning and initiating group work intervention than it is in guiding the worker through the actual process of face-to-face interaction with the group members. The following vignette may illustrate this statement.

> A social worker employed by a voluntary agency stands anxiously awaiting the arrival (or perhaps non-arrival) of some students to the first of a series of literacy tutorials she has organised. There had been months of preparatory work. It was necessary to gain the approval of her agency director for this venture. Suitable voluntary tutors had to be recruited and briefed. The target population – illiterate adults with a motivation to acquire skills in reading and writing – had to be identified, informed of the project and invited or persuaded to attend. The setting is a 'drop-in' centre owned by the agency – shabby but homely, the walls hung with posters depicting the activities of the centre.
>
> The middle-aged men in working clothes arrive, looking extremely sheepish. As the worker greets them and identifies them as students, the door is flung open and heralds the arrival of Bill, the aggressive but indispensable caretaker. Bill was an ex-client and is now a part-time employee of the agency. Within a minute the atmosphere the social

worker was attempting to create is destroyed by Bill demanding 'Are you the chaps who can't read or write – what happened to you – didn't go to school I expect when you should of'.

The social worker attempts to intervene as one of the students begins to move towards the street door. To be successful her intervention must achieve several purposes in a brief period of time: a definition of group purpose and her own attitude to it; expression in word or body language of her awareness of the feelings of the students as they stand on the edge of a venture which requires new role behaviour and risks a loss of self-esteem; some form of reparation to Bill who she realises was not fully informed about this invasion of territory she knows he feels is his; and the exercise of authority in refusing to permit him to sabotage the project because of *his* feelings.

An examination of this group encounter and the events that led up to it reveals tasks, attitudes, needs and problems that require a special kind of synthesis in order for the worker to intervene with skill. She must not focus solely on Bill's needs to assert his power and ownership of territory by claiming superiority over the incipient group; neither should she concentrate on the group members' problems in experiencing a no doubt familiar jeering comment on their inadequacies. She must focus on those two in interaction and at the same time monitor her own inner experience and attitudes to the participants. She has to work out the balance between authenticity and expected role behaviour; probably she has to control a very human response to the affront to her authority as project leader. If she demonstrates too forcibly 'I'm the person in charge here', will she later convince the students of her belief that the centre is for their use as members of the local community? The success of the project will rest on *their* efforts and motivation, and not solely on the skill of the tutors.

If the social worker concerned had used a systems model, she would have commenced her thinking about a new group project from a somewhat global conception of two systems in interaction – her *agency* with its primary task of giving service to the disadvantaged members of the local *community*. When the problems the residents faced had been discovered, among many other instances of unmet need, illiteracy with its effect on employment and recreational opportunities, as well as the self-esteem of some citizens, was selected as a target. To work towards meeting this *felt* need could enhance the material and emotional opportunities for a potential group.

Resources to work on this problem could be identified both in the agency and in the community: herself as organiser, a friendly and appropriate environment, financial aid for equipment in the former; potential voluntary 'teachers' in the latter. Working together in this way would demonstrate the reciprocity and interdependence of a caring agency and its local community. But even 'caring agencies' require some leverage to persuade them to liberate their resources – particularly if the project is an innovatory or unusual one. The social worker must grasp the dynamics of her organisational system sufficiently accurately to assess the amount of change needed there to sustain the growth of a new project. Likewise in the local community: it would be necessary to promote the project in a variety of 'systems' in the hope of recruiting both teachers and students for it, gaining goodwill and a change of attitude locally towards illiteracy. Organisations the social worker would choose as a preliminary target might include schools, local libraries, tenants' associations and community centres, the local press, etc.

Thinking systemically encourages one to anticipate the likely outcomes and the location of future tasks. For example, it would be likely that such a literacy project would be devised as a pilot scheme, which hopefully would be taken over on a permanent basis by another organisation with clearer adult education responsibilities. From the initiation of the project the worker would consider the appropriate involvement of, say, a local settlement or adult education department. Given the complexity of these different tasks, no wonder our social worker neglected to spend some time with the caretaker, who emerged as a potentially destructive subsystem!

But although a systems approach could help our worker map out a course of action in broad terms, it will not necessarily provide her with guidelines for the fine detail of intervention in these different groups. The use of a systems model in social work has produced useful frameworks, terminology that can be used to describe the similarities of interventive strategies at individual, group and community levels. It describes the complex inter-relationships between individual, groups, organisation, etc., in the maintenance of social problems, but does not as yet provide a causal theory which might intimate how things got the way they were. Neither does a systems model guide one in the choice of which theories-for-action to use.

To enrich practice experience, the group worker must turn to the developing models of group work practice. Crudely these are organised around differences about what is regarded as the *focal system* in group work: the individual in the group, the group as a whole, or some other systemic aspect of society (see Papell and Rothman, 1966; Schwartz and Zalba, 1971). There are difficulties inherent in selecting even that rough analysis of difference. For example, theories of group developmental phases (Tuckman, 1965; Sarri and Galinsky, 1974) suggest we should pay more attention to the experiences of individuals in the beginning stages of an artificially formed group; and to the time needed for individuals to be able to co-operate with each other, giving up some of their own needs in the service of group purposes. It may be appropriate in the beginning stages of

Table 1

	Social Goals Model	*Remedial Model*	*Reciprocal Model*
Primary task of social work function seen as:	*Provision* of resources and *prevention* of social breakdown (informal political and social action).	*Restoration and rehabilitation* of social casualties (introduce treatment via group medium).	Combination of first two aims (creation of mutual aid systems for the solution of problems).
Long-term aims of intervention and proponents of models	A more democratic *society* (verging on community work methods). G. Coyle Wilson and Ryland J. Klein	*Individual* social adaptation. Fritz Redl (institutional treatment of children) Robert Vinter Foulkes and Anthony	Individual, *group* and society. W. Schwartz – reflects work of many non social work theorists – W. R. Bion, E. Tropp, K. Lewin
Major assumptions about society and social work	Social consciousness and responsibility can be taught and developed in individuals. Aim is to create a broader base of knowledgeable citizens.	Society creates casualties, and social work should direct its efforts to those most in need – individuals can be helped to adapt or change current societal norms via medium of individual growth.	Symbiotic relationship between the individual and society – *normally* subject to stress. Social work should be directed to the interface of the individual and society, and attempt to remove obstacles to mutual fulfilment of need.
Group worker role	*'Influence person'* does not dictate political view but inculcates a value system. Acts as a model, reinforces conduct appropriate to citizen responsibility; aims to transfer leadership gradually to 'indigenous' members.	*'Change agent'* creates specially formed groups with composition being a particular skill. Concepts used of diagnosis and treatment indicate closeness to a clinical model. Worker remains in control of the group experience, assigning task and role.	*'Mediator'*. Worker is an enabler, part of the worker/client system and therefore subject to influence himself. Emphasis is on open communication, dispelling professional mysticism; definition of broad tasks exists – but detail left to artistry of individual worker.

most groups, regardless of purpose, to regard the *individual* as the focal system.

Developing models of group work

I have discussed elsewhere (McCaughan, 1977b) how different purposes in group work can be served by the choice of different models. Papell and Rothman (1966) discuss the emergence of clusters of values, assumptions, role behaviour and theoretical underpinnings which serve to guide group work practice. They have labelled their models *social goals*, *remedial* and *reciprocal*. Table 1, a summary of their views, demonstrates some of the different and distinctive features.

In considering how use of these models might influence differentially the actions of the group work practitioner, let use return to our concepts of *boundary*, *task* and *role*.

Boundary. As stated before, the boundary around a group is often formed by its acknowledged purpose. Other concepts related to boundary are composition (who is in the group), environment (the territory on which the group meets) and timing (the intensity of meetings, and their duration).

Task. Questions about task and sub-task naturally arise in considering the work of a group. Decisions are made about: (1) who controls the process of goal setting; (2) what is the primary task of each meeting – i.e. work without which the group would not survive at least within the boundary as originally defined (see Miller and Rice, 1967, pp. 25–8); (3) what are appropriate activities or programme for the group to be engaged in; and finally (4) how the group is controlled, and who wields normative sanctions.

Role. The group worker's role can be looked at from two main aspects. First, it can be looked at in terms of the source of the group worker's mandate or authority for acting. This may stem from his *professional expertise*, from his *agency's objectives*, from the *group members' acceptance and approbation*, or from his *personal charism*, drive or vision to achieve change. It is quite natural that those sources will be mixed, but most group workers would regard one mandate as more important than the others. This will powerfully influence leadership behaviour.

The second aspect of role is the behavioural one: one can categorise a group worker's leadership style as directive, democratic or passive. The role behaviour of the worker can also be clearly described in words such as 'therapist', 'organiser', 'social skills trainer' or 'facilitor'.

In applying these concepts and questions to the three models – Social Goals, Remedial and Reciprocal – it becomes clearer how the group work practitioner might differentiate his actions, and regard the parameters of

Table 2

Social goals		
Purpose	*Remedial*	*Reciprocal*
(1) To increase belongingness and train in democratic participation.	(1) To improve social functioning of individuals via group interaction. Group work directed towards social casualties as defined by the agency.	(1) Identifying unmet needs – particularly those caused by obstacles between organisational resource holders and the supposed beneficiaries of the resources.
(2) Purpose initially decided by worker, later responsibility handed to group.	(2) Worker decides on specific purposes and shares with potential members before group commences.	(2) Purpose is initially left vague, and elaborated in encounter. Shared with both resource holders and clients.
Composition		
(1) People who live in proximity or who are in common 'categories' (age, disability, etc.).	(1) Members are selected by worker to ensure a careful balance of personality and a similar problem.	(1) Members in a common situation – likely to be heterogeneous group. No individual assessment.
(2) Size can vary from 3 to 25.	(2) Clearly identifiable membership 7–10.	(2) Size flexible, varies according to the current transactions.
(3) 'Friends' encouraged to join.	(3) Worker controls inclusion of additional members.	(3) Significant outsiders join group at request of member or worker.
Environment		
Use natural settings – meeting place may vary from street to community centre to a member's home.	Recognised and stable meeting place, usually on agency territory. Worker feels responsible for creating the environment.	Meet where clients are to be found – hospital ward, residential home, etc. Meeting place varies according to current purpose.
Time/Timing		
Time flexible – pre-group work may be substantial, contact will vary throughout group.	Number of sessions agreed before group commences. Regular and frequent contact. Conscious use of time boundary in treatment.	Time is flexible, used within the limits of the engagement between the group and target system. Recognition that 'work' will have taken place between meetings.

the group. If we take first the concepts I outlined under *boundary* – purpose, composition, environment and timing – Table 2 indicates the variations.

A careful study of the literature relevant to each model will enable the interested reader to carry the analysis further through the nature of defining and encouraging 'work' in the group, and worker mandate and role taking. Apart from American writings which are referenced in the Papell and Rothman paper (1966), there are some British sources to explore. The Social Goals model appears to fit well with the writings of

Batten (1967), Button (1974), Davies (1975), FSU Publications (1974, 1975). It is illustrated in this book (Vickery *et al.*). The Remedial model is less easy to distinguish, possibly because there are so few published accounts by British group workers. Perhaps the nearest source is the work by Foulkes and Anthony (1965) in psychotherapy and the approach described by McCullough and Ely (1968) in their introductory text. The Reciprocal model has been used by Breslin and Sturton, Laming and Sturton (this Reader), both in running a group and in attempting to develop group work in an agency.

Chapter 2

CONTINUING THEMES IN SOCIAL GROUP WORK

Nano McCaughan

In their struggles to develop theoretical models to guide practice, social workers share a long tradition of ideas and values, deriving from a variety of social movements in the last two centuries. This heritage contains conflicts. For example, in a recent discussion about the purposes and management of groups in intermediate treatment schemes, the social workers who participated disagreed heatedly, and it became clear that two basic ideologies were in conflict: the first was that the major guiding value of such groups of young people in trouble should be to offer *treatment* or therapy in an attempt to change delinquent behaviour; and the second was that they should attempt to *develop social consciousness* and an awareness of the nature of the deprivation suffered by the members. A decision on that question would naturally lead to very different arrangements by the worker, from the act of composing the group to the manner and timing of terminating it.

This particular conflict is, of course, not a new one. One hundred years ago one might have found the same heated discussion among teachers in a Ragged School although the terminology used would have been different. Later on the founders of the various young people's movements – the Boys' Clubs Federation, for example – disagreed quite strongly about the relative merits of focusing on the individual in the group, or the groups as a whole (Young and Ashton, 1956).

The development of social work can be broadly viewed as a social movement (Seed, 1973).

As such it has gathered to itself an increasingly large number of identified tasks or responsibilities carried on behalf of society; it is not easy to identify the limits it imposes (or should impose) on itself, or to define any clear boundary with other professions or individuals who intervene in the lives of others to produce change, and the betterment of an individual or a neighbourhood. John Haines (1975) reminds us that the aims of social work are similar to the aims of man in society: 'The very existence of man in society rather than in isolation involves him in a mutual process of interchange with other human beings. This is essential to ensure the continuation of the basic necessities of life, such as food, warmth, shelter and also as part of the process of regulating behaviour that is represented by law and tradition.' However, social workers (as well as others in society) strive to add quality to the life pursuit of basic needs, and are concerned with emotional and philosophical values. They aim to provide warmth and friendliness as well as social justice. They attempt to increase the self-esteem of deprived individuals, to help such individuals find a purpose in living by locating themselves more firmly in their society, endeavouring to compensate for the inevitable unhappiness consequent on being unloved, ill or poor. Social work as a professional body concerned with these obviously desirable but difficult to implement values has emerged comparatively recently. However, since the industrial revolution changed the basic structure and qualities of the society we live in, numerous individuals, groups and organisations have worked with similar aims, and it is to a brief examination of the principles underlying this work that we turn, particularly to those principles that have relevance to the crude practice models employed today by aspiring group workers. They are crude in the sense that we simply do not have enough detailed knowledge to set about effectively translating principles into action with a group, or how to resolve the problems posed by working with unique and disparate individuals in interaction, or to evaluate in any rigorous way the results of our interventions.

There is a growing interest among social workers to develop skills and initiatives in working with groups. Opportunities are there, quite naturally, in the settings in which they work. But in considering the difficulties in actually beginning to practise group work the social worker is hampered by lack of the firm base a specialist training in this method provides if it is part of a basic training course. In the USA those teachers who are working on integrating group work with casework and community work, do start with the advantage of having had a specialist two years group work training on their Master's programme followed by relevant experience. They may now feel dissatisfied with the particular group work model they were presented with but presumably they will have a clearer conception of what needs to be changed; of which aspects of their knowledge and practice are similar and may be used as underpinnings to skill development in other methods; and which require special study and attention, and are unique to that special situation of being a social worker in interaction with a small, defined group of clients.

HISTORICAL INFLUENCES ON THE PRACTICE OF GROUP WORK

It is important to understand the varying motives of different social reformers, philanthropists and social workers. We will examine those which still appear to have strong relevance to the practice and the vision of group workers today. Constellations of these purposes tend to appear in the practice models now in process of development and labelled Social Goals, Remedial and Reciprocal models (Papell and Rothman, 1966). It is likely that other models are in process of development, and given the changes in society which create new needs, the models will spring from motives not discussed here. We will briefly examine five themes which are still of concern to group workers.

Rescue

First, there is the theme of rescue, a motivation which strongly influences group workers who see their clients as victims of themselves, or of their environment – social casualties. Hannah More, the founder of the Sunday School movement, attempted to offer both education and moral and religious training to poor children in the early nineteenth century, because she believed she was rescuing the children from the dangers of becoming vandals or delinquents by keeping them occupied on their only free day. Incidentally she appeared to use quite consciously what we might now term behaviour modification principles. In her pamphlet 'Hints on how to run a Sunday School' (More, *undated*) she wrote: 'I encourage them by little bribes of a penny a chapter to get by heart certain fundamental parts of Scripture . . . those who attend four Sundays without intermission receive a penny.'

The Ragged Schools were set up in the 1840s and appear to have used small group principles. They were designed only for the children of vagrants, drunkards, etc., children already deserted and on the streets. Initially founded by philanthropic volunteers, they provided in their structure some inspiration to those considering the problems of the alienated young truants of today. The 'school'–usually a warehouse or even a railway arch–was sited where the children were to be located. Their clothing, manners and ways were accepted, and the numbers attending were small. The teachers gradually hoped to encourage cleanliness, an interest in industrial training and more conformity to the expected morals of the time. One observable fact was that 'everything depended on the character and quality of the leader' (Young and Ashton, 1956, p. 246). It was recognised that the aims of the school and qualities of the teachers had of necessity to be quite dramatically opposed to the prevailing culture of National and Industrial Schools–if the purpose of 'rescue' was to be achieved.

The theme of rescue was repeated in the founding during the late nineteenth century of many befriending organisations such as the Girls' Friendly Society, the Temperance Society, etc. The hidden agenda was to prevent worse evil befalling the vulnerable and unfortunate. These societies were often founded by members of the evangelical movement–philanthropy was a way of life–'a bridge between the business man and his

Christian conscience' (Young and Ashton, 1956, p. 38). The flaws in the social system may have been needed by some Christians to provide an opportunity for charity and good works. A strict mode of conduct was demanded from the poor to whom the opportunities of rescue were given (see Owen, 1965, pt 3).

The puritanical religious conscience has almost disappeared as a force in social work. However, if social workers are strongly motivated by a need to rescue others one can find that conformity to the leader's notion of appropriate behaviour in the group is the implicit price for help, or access to the group's resources. The demand for conformity is sometimes consciously used as treatment technique – in Phoenix House and the Synanon Centres in the treatment of young addicts, for example. But it is often manifested at a more subconscious level by group leaders who, invaded by anxiety, may retreat behind the defences of control and authoritarianism. Professional expertise then becomes a new religion whose dictates must not be questioned. We will now turn to a less controversial theme.

Mutual Aid

One movement which exemplified the aspirations of creating mutual aid systems was that of the development of settlements. This was created by the collaboration of very different men – Edward Denison, Arnold Toynbee and Canon Barnett. It is in the writings of the last that one can note the growing understanding that people will not radically change or improve through having things done for or to them by those more fortunate than themselves. Barnett believed that educated men would have a more direct influence on deprived people by living and sharing their lives and ideas with them and by providing an example of higher standards and the leadership that would inspire them to seek these standards for themselves (see Seed, 1973; Young and Ashton, 1956, p. 226). Barnett learned that it was important for the members of one social class to know the members of another by close physical contact before they could share their advantages of education, skills in recreation and in organisation. He came to realise that poverty and degradation were not the result of weakness of character but the necessary consequences of the social structure and cultural transmission. He sought to develop a sense of belongingness by forming clubs and groups for a great variety of purposes, based on neighbourhood centres.

Barnett did not fail to appreciate the formative influence of participant group life and his work was carried further by other settlement wardens. An important feature was the work for youth – the founding of clubs and camps for purely recreational purposes. Neighbourhood Clubs were started with the belief that in a centre of political and religious neutrality, all those living in the neighbourhood might experience warmth and friendship and an opportunity to develop by sharing the problems of group life. It was also hoped that club members would become better informed of the nature of the society they were living in, by studying empirical data about it, and that this information would produce a desire for leadership and change.

This thinking was shared by progressive educators – notably first the Quakers, whose model school at Ackworth, founded in 1779, was followed by many others. An important factor of change was the use of monitors (older children) to teach the younger ones. This lessened the dependency and subservience on middle class teachers/reformers and showed a trust in the ability of the poor to help themselves.

Barnett recognised the indivisibility of the individual from the community in which he lived, and the necessity to bring about change through attraction, satisfaction and collective work. The settlement movement leaders impressed on their voluntary workers the notion that giving money was not enough and would not make any real impact on poverty and its attendant evils. One had to give oneself in service, and this giving was encouraged to be thoughtful non-partisan, and accepting of community norms.

Canon Barnett recorded his assumptions and objectives in settlement work in various tracts. For example, he wrote:

> [A settlement is] an association of persons with different opinions and different tasks. Its unity is that of variety, its methods are spiritual (in the widest sense) rather than material in its aims at permeation rather than conversion and its trust is in friends linked to friends rather than in organisation. Each man was made to feel he could make a worth while contribution to the group, whether club, class or party. (Barnett, 1919)

Settlements for a period waned as an important force, particularly after the second world war because of the advent of new needs, created by the dispersal of slum dwellers into distant and unfamiliar housing estates. The recognition of these needs had led to the growth of community centres, but the interest in neighbourhood, community and mutual aid in the inner city has produced something of a renaissance in the settlement movement in the last few years. There has also been a neo-settlement movement in groups of professionals and the better educated, establishing communal living arrangements in deprived areas with the intention of participating in local life and changing it (for discussion see Kuenstler, 1954, pp. 29–48).

The redevelopment of cities has led to a need for association via common residence rather than common class. New housing estates have created problems to which group work might be a response. This is coupled with a greater awareness and sensitivity to the complex reasons behind isolation and loneliness. The growth of community centres and their variety of purposes is interesting – some wardens take an interest only in the 'joiners' – others seek to acquire knowledge of the area as a whole and to develop appropriate group formation based on that knowledge. This leads to a conflict as to whether mutual aid should be encouraged in the members already known to one another, or whether they as a group should be helped to develop an interest and responsibility for their neighbourhood as a whole, and thus learn to solve their own problems by attempting to engage and aid others.

The concept of mutual aid was the motivating force behind the formation of many societies and movements: the Co-operative Societies, Mutual Insurance Societies, Trade Unions, Workers' Educational Association (Beveridge, 1948). It is clear that for many members the experience of belonging and opportunities to learn and practise the social skills of organisation, teaching, reaching out to others, and acquiring information were as enriching as the financial benefits and insurance against personal economic disaster. Membership created an opportunity to find a place for oneself in the community, to have experience of power and learn the discipline of self-government. There are echoes of these advantages in the creation of therapeutic communities, in the formation of women's groups, and other self-help groups such as Alcoholics Anonymous. These vary in the opportunity they provide in learning how to negotiate with other systems, some of necessity remaining more inward-looking than others because of the depth of personal problems experienced by the members.

Social Action

This leads us to consider another concept in group formation. Here the group is formed primarily with the intention of bringing about some social change. The advantages to individuals derived from belonging to the group participating in action are of secondary importance. Historically, many of these groups came about through the vision and determination of individual reformers. One can fruitfully study the work of Octavia Hill, Elizabeth Fry, Robert Owen, and today of David Wills, Des Wilson and Group Captain Leonard Cheshire. On the whole these individuals ignored the legislative process as a means of bringing about social change. It so happened that many had politically important figures among their friends, and used their influence via their private relations.

Earlier reformers believed strongly that change came about through groups of people making personal relationships with one another in order to meet a common need. One can often sense an emotional closeness between the initiators of change and their target groups – the initiators are perhaps psychologically identified with the handicaps of the people to be helped.

Philip Seed (1973, p. 30) writes of Octavia Hill's view that both people and their environment needed to be changed. In working on the latter she founded the National Trust and was influential in promoting the open space movement. Her actions in these spheres were motivated by a close knowledge of the needs of people on the housing estates she managed, and of those she encountered as individual 'cases' in her work with the Charity Organisation Society. She attempted to involve poor tenants in the housing schemes by forming groups to develop responsibility for the use and management of the recreational facilities in the deprived community. This form of social action may now seem paternalistic, but it suggests that people deprived of education, pleasure and enjoyment may need to receive social education in a primary group before they can feel inspired to become involved in a process of change (Brager and Specht, 1973). The leader must initially take responsibility for the 'looking outwards' of the group, and at the same time take care not to create dependence and false consensus for his aims. Today workers in activity-based intermediate treatment groups give testimony to the need for a subtle transformation in leadership in order to promote the active involvement of group members in working towards the solution of their own problems (Paley and Thorpe, 1974).

Developing Leadership
An overlapping motivation in much of the work already described has been that of developing leadership, or increasing self-responsibility and enhancing individual potential.

Describing her initial work (at age 14) with Ragged School children, in which she mobilised poor children to create and work in a co-operative toy furniture business, Octavia Hill shows a sophisticated awareness of the process of encouraging leadership. 'I have to study how to interest each. I comment on all they say, do or look into one whole, I get to know the things they really care for' (Bell, 1942). She organised parties and social outings and got to know their names. 'Modelling behaviour' and 'Training in social skills' were concepts she understood in practice. She comments that in her supervisory work with voluntary visitors in COS she struggled not to intervene but to give each his own court to be responsible for (Woodroofe, 1962, Ch. 2). On her work with housing estate tenants, she insisted that they become responsible for their own repairs and for the management of the property (Seed, 1973, p. 31). In this instance the training for leadership came about by giving responsibility and refusing to take it away when failure occurred. She dealt with failure by authentic confrontation and suggestion, rather than by command.

Canon Barnett thought that the development of individual potential would be brought about by the example (modelling) of the rich and well-educated young men he gathered around him in the settlements. But, as well as example, he continually emphasised the necessity for friendship or the development of a personal relation if transformation was to be achieved. One could say his approach bore the seeds of the Reciprocal model (see Schwartz and Zalba, 1971). His twofold purpose was the awakening of the conscience of the rich – the so-called 'born' leaders – to the deprivation around them, and to training the poor to deal more effectively with the social systems that oppressed them, by forming informal educational small groups.

In youth work the concept of training for leadership was given serious consideration – and influenced the structure of many youth organisations. For example, the Scout Movement and the Boys' Brigade are structured so as to permit one young person to lead and be responsible (under supervision) for the management of others. By contrast T. W. H. Pelham, an influential chairman of the London Federation of Boys' Clubs, placed more importance on the character and personal relations of the formal adult leader. In 1889 (Young and Ashton, 1956, p. 251), he argued that the clubs should be kept small and never outgrow the personal influence of the leader, that activities attractive in themselves would soon cease to be effective and that only personal relations would have a lasting effect. He was, however, in favour of the boys helping to run their own clubs. On the other hand, in 1908 C. E. B. Russell, writing a manual on Working Lads' Clubs, profoundly disagreed with the personal relation theory. He thought clubs should be large, and organised completely by adults who knew what they were intending to do; and he stressed the need for discipline, and presumably subservience, to authority as the best training milieu.

Liberation

One last concept, which in this context has a more recent twentieth-century origin, is that of liberation of the individual from oppressive cultural norms. The influence behind this movement is not very clear – it has its origins in philosophical thinking and in the humanist psychologies. Certainly the aversion of many people in the Western world to the rise of fascism and totalitarian state control has had an effect. Educators, religious leaders, and community workers, have recognised the importance of not taking for granted the permanence of democratic principles in the state. In education, therapy and the church there has been a movement to affirm the individual, and support his desire to manage his affairs for himself, and become more adventuresome and confronting in his negotiations with collectivities, while accepting the needs of others and the potent influence of the group on the individual.

Mary Follett states in her introduction to *The New State* (Follett, 1918):

> The twentieth century must find a new principle of association. Crowd philosophy, crowd government, crowd patriotism must go. The herd is no longer sufficient to enfold us.
>
> Group organisation is to be the new method in politics, the basis of our

future industrial system, the foundation of international order. Group organisation will create the new world we are now blindly feeling after, for creative force comes from the group, creative power is evolved through the activities of group life.

We have had many examples in the United Kingdom in the last fifty years of practitioners and thinkers who have attempted to evolve in practice and concept some principles for action. The work of Homer Lane (Wills, 1964), David Wills (Wills, 1970, 1971) and A. S. Neill (Neill, 1962), in the field of education and residential care of disadvantaged youth is one example. Others are the growth of therapeutic communities in the treatment of mental disorder (see, for example, Jones, 1968); the increasing popularity of the Human Relations School in the training of managers, and assessment of organisational problems (see Jacques, 1970; Rice, 1963); the increasing number of consciousness-raising self-help groups, such as women's liberation groups, the Patients' Association, etc. These groups are formed by people personally involved in a situation which they wish to change, but who are prepared to work at examining and changing their own attitudes, and recognising their own contribution to the interactional situation in which they feel oppressed. (An interesting guide to self-help organisations has been produced by Jerman, 1971.) One final example can be found in the numbers of people who enjoy participation in what might still be considered fringe group activities – encounter groups, sensitivity groups, groups formed to enhance self-awareness. It is by no means uncommon to find many of the individuals attending these groups uninvolved in professional counselling roles. These groups are influenced by the 'new' therapies – gestalt, transactional analysis, etc., and appear to meet a need for intimacy, the development of self-understanding, and legitimate expression of profound interpersonal emotions.

One common notion underlying these varied activities is that only by accepting openly and honestly all the aspects of himself, both public and private, can a man come to understand the 'reality' of the world and thus learn to make his own unique contribution to society at his highest level. Consequent to this is the notion that the self can only be understood and revealed in relationships with others. In many instances this implies a painful re-examination of one's role-taking behaviour in the light of the goals of the particular role relationship. Myths about therapist/patient relationships are uncovered (Bion, 1961). Messages from the past about one's gender or sexual role are disentangled. The teacher/learner relationship is studied in the light of commonly held fantasies about expertise and the dubious value of the transmission of 'banked' knowledge (Illich, 1971; Freire, 1972). Group life explored in this way may be a liberating experience but often proves to be a dislocating one for individuals when they have to relate to people who have not been exposed to the same liberating experience, and have to discover in that context how to be more authentically themselves and transform habitual role behaviours.

CONCLUSION

This paper has traced the development of five commonly held themes or motivations for group formation and the actions of group leaders. The heritage and influence of past and current social movements has been discussed. The paper has indicated that the problems and conflicts social workers face in developing goals for group work and attempts to influence others in groups have been shared by their predecessors in ever-recurrent attempts to create a better world.

Chapter 3

CHOICE OF THE GROUP AS A TARGET OF INTERVENTION

Anne Vickery, Charlotte Rawcliffe and Veronica Ward

INTRODUCTION

Consumers of social work are not often given a choice as to the form in which they are to receive a service. In certain agencies workers seldom ask: 'Can this client be helped best within an individual relationship or would a group offer him a better chance?' The failure to ask this question may be due to at least two inter-relating influences. First, when the social worker's skill is confined to work in one modality, particularly casework; second, when his agency makes explicit or implicit assumptions as to the 'normal' way of offering a service. In recent years many agencies have become 'multi-method' and so need to have sound criteria for deciding what method to use.

Besides choosing whether to work with a client as an individual or in a group, there are other choices to be made as to whom the worker should influence and by what means. An elderly client, for example, might be directly affected by her relatives, neighbours, volunteer, doctor, social security officer, home help, club, local shopkeeper; and indirectly, but crucially, affected by the local authority's social services, housing, and planning departments, Age Concern, the Department of Health and Social Security, and District Health Authority. While intervention with any of these people and organisations is not usually thought of as 'group work', successful influence may often depend on the worker's ability to compose a group and work with it, to become attached to an existing group and work with it, to act as a catalyst in a group on a short-term basis. For example, on behalf of elderly clients it might be crucial to work supportively with a group of volunteers, work with a tenants' association committee in regard to bad housing maintenance, join and work with an inter-professional team concerned with geriatric care, argue a case with an agency's top management group for an increase in day-care provision.

To consider intervention in such a wide range of groups on behalf of actual and potential clients is one of the features of a unitary approach to social work practice, and is unlikely to happen if the agency has no group work skills.

Features of a unitary approach

Authors who have conceptualised a unitary approach to social work practice differ in the emphasis they give to the various possible ingredients of a unitary model (see, for example, Pincus and Minahan, 1973; Goldstein, 1973; Whittaker, 1974; Middleman and Goldberg, 1974). But despite variations, all the models make similar assumptions about at least two aspects of social work practice. First, that the assessment of a social situation, and the planning of interventions should take account of and be prepared to consider intervention in a sizeable number of influential and interacting social phenomena. These may range from individual consumers of the service, through various kinds of small group, to organisations and the interactions between organisations that determine the nature of service delivery. The second essential assumption is that social work methodology is based on a rational problem-solving process embracing the establishment of a need for change, assessment of need, the examination of alternative goals and ways of achieving them, the determination of goals and how to achieve them, the change effort itself, the stabilisation of change, evaluation of outcome. The whole process is mediated through relationships between social workers and various types of consumers in which working agreements have to be established, ends and means agreed, progress and outcome mutually assessed, and a termination of the relationship achieved. This process is applicable, whether the social worker is engaging with individual clients, families, small groups, community groups, or organisations.

Working with groups

In a sense, groups occupy the central position in a unitary approach. This is because in assessing problem situations the unitary approach worker always looks beyond the individual sufferer to see if the problem is held in common with other sufferers. If so, the worker has first to examine whether they share any common environmental pressures that perpetuate the problem and what implications they may have for choice of intervention; and second, to assess whether the individual sufferers might be best helped with their common problems by working on them together.

This paper gives an account of a particular piece of work with old people living on the same housing estate. The work took the form it did because of the workers' adherence to the above criteria for deciding whom they needed to influence, or in other words, whom they needed to choose as targets of intervention. Most of the targets were groups. The work was not consciously conceived as a unitary approach and does not fit the model in every respect. Nor, from a group work perspective, do we think it to have been at all sophisticated. We have selected it because it illustrates the necessity and the merits of choosing to work with groups when the logic of the clients' problem demands that choice; and it also highlights the need for social workers to have the ability to work with groups.

Interacting Personality and Social Systems
In order to capture the unitary perspective of this piece of work we are using the same terminology as Pincus and Minahan (1970, 1973) to denote the nature of the various interacting social systems that affected it. Their concepts 'change-agent' and 'client system' were borrowed from Lippitt *et al.* (1958), and 'action system' from Warren (1963). 'Target system' has been used by many authors including Burns and Glasser (1963).

> The 'change-agent system' is the organisation employing the helping worker. In our example there are two workers, each employed by a different organisation.
>
> The 'client system' is the person, family, group or organisation that engages the services of the worker and is the expected beneficiary.
>
> The 'target system' is the person, family, group, organisation, or community that the client has agreed should be influenced towards some change. This system may or may not include the client system.
>
> The 'action system' comprises the people and organisations who have to be mobilised as resources in bringing about change in the target system.

THE CHANGE-AGENT SYSTEMS

The Settlement. One of the workers was a 'Good Neighbour Worker' employed by a settlement that, as well as work with children and young people, had a long tradition of work with the elderly. It ran four afternoon clubs, a lunch club and an annual seaside holiday for the housebound. For many years it had provided some kind of individual visiting service. Although more recently the settlement had been trying to develop neighbourhood community work, it had not substantially succeeded in relating its work with the elderly to their geographically common environmental circumstances. This was due partly to the difficulty of changing programmes that relied heavily on very part-time voluntary workers; but mainly to an inability to obtain funding to employ a community worker.

In 1972 a trust that had refused the settlement's application for help with a three-year community work project took a different view of a second application formulating the need for a 'Friend and Neighbour Service' to the elderly and handicapped. Verbal backing for the service was given by the recently reorganised local authority social services department who were well aware that their individual service to the elderly and handicapped had declined since the demise of the old welfare department, and the implementation of the 1969 Children and Young Persons Act.

In the light of changed circumstances and funding, the settlement, in appointing a Good Neighbour Worker, had to compromise on its intention to engage in community work. The new worker was to get to know the circumstances of the physically handicapped and the elderly living in a defined area surrounding the settlement. Besides offering help in cases of need, she was to identify the lonely and those in danger of becoming isolated, and to try and keep them in touch with the community. She was to do this by working with existing agencies, churches, tenants' associations and clubs; and also by recruiting, supporting and co-ordinating volunteers. Where possible, the volunteers would be near-neighbours, or members of a neighbourhood group. Although typical of a unitary approach in aiming to strengthen the helping capacity of the client's immediate environment, rather than introducing volunteers from outside, the project, as far as the elderly and handicapped were concerned, was essentially aimed at the individual as the long-term target for change, and not the group.

The social services department area office. The new social services department had a community worker attached to each area team. For a time, the community worker for the area nearest to the settlement was based in the settlement and became an integral part of the settlement staff group. She worked hand in hand with the good neighbour worker on the project we describe, and brought to it a strong community work orientation.

CHOOSING THE CLIENT SYSTEM

After her appointment, the settlement good neighbour worker, henceforth called 'settlement worker', surveyed the streets of terrace houses surrounding the settlement, but did not uncover the loneliness and isolation which had been judged to exist. Many of the inhabitants had lived there for years, knew each other, and kept an eye on one another; and many attended clubs and were well known to the voluntary workers. Although the settlement worker continued the tradition of working with local schools in their schemes involving pupils in gardening, decorating and doing odd jobs for pensioners, the more 'organic' approach hoped for by the settlement staff and committee came to fruition, not in the streets of terrace houses around the settlement, but in a new Greater London Council housing estate situated just beyond the geographical boundary that the settlement had drawn for its activities.

The estate was then about five years old, and might be described as an island bordered by factories to the north, a main trunk road to the south, gasworks to the west, and a railway line to the east. It consisted of three seventeen-floor tower blocks, some houses with gardens, two large four-storey blocks of flats and maisonettes, two blocks of flats reserved for pensioners. It totalled about 400 housing units. Many of them had no outlook except on to a wall or on to the gas works. Everywhere was brick and concrete. One only had to wander round the estate to experience its dehumanising influence. During the day, with many people out at work, it had the appearance of being deserted. On the same site was an old peoples' home and a sheltered housing unit, a primary school, a play group, and a purpose-built youth club. The estate was very cut off from the rest of the community. The shopping centre was a long way, as were other kinds of social amenities such as clubs and day centres.

The area social services department's community worker, henceforth called 'community worker', had her attention drawn to this estate by a senior social worker who wondered why the incidence of family problems was especially high in one of the estate's tower blocks. This was early in 1972 during the first year of the community worker's appointment when she was doing a general survey of her whole area. Besides the influence of the social worker's view that a lot of problems emanated from one out of the three tower blocks, there were other reasons why the community worker paid attention to that particular estate.

She was concerned to learn about the estate as a whole, rather than the 'problems' of individual families; and when she knocked on doors and informally interviewed people in another tower block, the problems she identified were common problems stemming from life on the estate, and not peculiar to the individuals concerned.

Nearly all the tenants had been rehoused from other areas, and many felt they were 'camping out' far away from familiar surroundings. Hardly any knew the neighbourhood. A high proportion of the tenants she spoke to happened to be elderly. That was because they were always in when she called, but younger people who were a long way from parents, friends and shops were also sadly affected. A retired docker seemed to the community worker to epitomise the negation of the individual person wrought by removal from familiar surroundings to an alien world. He lived with his wife on the seventeenth floor, isolated 'in the clouds', unable to relate to anyone. Life had dealt him a double blow. Normally retired dockers in his area of London would go to the dock every day to have lunch with their old workmates. This man's dock had closed down. That too seemed to negate his whole life. He had no other interests. In desperation he had visited the neighbourhood in which he used to live, a redevelopment area. But it had all 'gone'; and he could find no one he knew. He did not seem to have anything left.

Mothers who were not working also complained of isolation, but at least they could meet each other at the school and the play group. Young people had the youth club. Gradually the elderly emerged as being especially vulnerable to the effects of the estate. It contained a borough old people's home and sheltered housing, but for the elderly living on the Greater London Council part of the estate there was no easily accessible club or day centre to mitigate their isolation. The need for a club became apparent to the community worker. However, while many elderly people on the estate were isolated, it did not follow that they would welcome a club as a solution. It was necessary to find out whether there were enough old people willing to attend a club to get it started, and whether adequate facilities and manpower were available to make it a feasible method of intervention.

Although for the sake of the unitary model we have called this section 'choosing the client system', the elderly as a collectivity on the estate were in no sense then a social system. As individual personality systems they were starved of transactions with their fellow human beings, and starved of the stimulus of creative activity, and aesthetic surroundings.

WORKING WITH ACTION SYSTEMS THAT DID NOT INITIALLY INCLUDE THE CLIENT SYSTEM

The School Girls

In the summer of 1972 one of the local schools affiliated to the settlement expressed a wish to undertake a project under the auspices of the settlement. They wanted it to be more exacting than just visiting the elderly or helping with a play group. The settlement worker was already interested in the problems of the estate and among other things suggested the school girls undertake a survey of its elderly population. This suggestion was accepted, and seven 15-year-old girls came every week and did most of the interviewing.

The work with this group of girls would make an interesting study in itself, but space does not allow us to do more than note that as well as the outcome of their project in terms of information collected and services given, the project was successful in terms of what these future citizens learnt about working with the elderly, and the problems of new housing schemes.

In the autumn of 1972, using a questionnaire, they conducted sixty interviews with individuals and couples. Among other things they asked what social activities the elderly enjoyed, and whether or not they would attend an old people's club if one were started on the estate. Out of the sixty interviews, sixteen people had some outside social activity ranging from attendance at a day centre, club or lunch club to involvement in church activities or pub life. Thirty-eight said they did not participate in any social activity whatsoever. Thirty-nine said they would like to go to a club, and a number of these were very enthusiastic about the idea. Of the thirty-nine wanting a club, twenty-one said they would welcome help with getting to it. Sixteen said they were not interested, partly because of illness, but mainly because they 'did not go to clubs'.

Of particular interest is what the old people felt about the estate. Fifteen liked it, and these included people in the sheltered housing block, people on the ground floor who were glad to have no stairs, and one person who had been born in the area. Several people liked their flats, but not the 'surrounds'. In general they had been glad to leave bad housing but felt they had had no choice but to move to this estate. Quite strong critical comments covered:

lack of telephone kiosks and post boxes
poor caretaking
rent office being too far away
lack of 'scenery'
too much concrete
depressing surroundings
the cold
rough and dirty neighbourhood
noisy children
noisy lifts
lifts not working
poor shopping
unfriendly estate.

As we shall see, the group of school girls who did the survey continued as part of the action system which set the club up.

Tenants' Association

Long before the girls did their survey, the community worker had been relating as closely as she could to the estate's tenants' association. Apart from the interest she later developed in working with the elderly, she wanted to do whatever she could to enable the tenants' association to become more effective. This tenants' association was no exception in being polite, but initially very suspicious of the attention of an outside worker. It took her a long time to gain their confidence. The committee consisted of a group of middle-aged men who were not very imaginative. They were doing little else but communicate with the Greater London Council about blocked drains and other requirements for maintenance, and the worker found it difficult to help them widen their horizons. As her interest in the elderly developed she hoped that the tenants' association would become the main force in enabling the elderly to start a club. Both workers discussed every move in the process with the committee: the proposal for the survey, the draft questionnaire, the notes to the elderly telling them about the survey and when the girls would visit, the survey's findings. They emphasised how much the association's help was needed, and how impossible it would be to do anything without them. But although the association clearly recognised the special difficulties of the elderly, the workers were left with the impression that the association agreed to all the moves because they felt they had to.

Because of its potential influence on the estate, the group that formed the tenants' association was an important target of intervention in its own right. But it never became an action system with the elderly in any real sense. Nevertheless, working with it was crucial. The workers valued community participation very highly; and also knew that their efforts might be sabotaged unless their plans received at least notional assent.

Education Authority

Lack of premises to run a club on the estate appeared to be an insuperable difficulty. The workers thought they would be able to have the education authority's purpose-built youth club which was unused in the daytime. It was the only suitable building on the estate available throughout the year. When the workers approached the education officer they were told they might hire the building as an outside body at an economic rate. This was far beyond what an old people's club could raise, and the workers were in despair. Rescue came through the head of a local adult education institute who was also chairman of the youth club committee and well known to the settlement as a resource person and a settlement committee member. He advised the workers to register the proposed old people's club as a class with a voluntary tutor under the education authority who would then pay for the hire of its premises. This they did.

The fruitful relationship that built up between the club and the adult education institute might well have developed anyway. But the fact that it was a requirement at the outset was probably important. Although the club was registered as a class for 'Living in Retirement', this did not interfere with it developing according to the wishes of its members. As a 'presence' in the wings, the resources of the education system stood ready to come on stage whenever it was required to play a part in the club's action system.

THE FRIENDS AND NEIGHBOURS CLUB: CLIENT AND ACTION SYSTEMS

Gaining confidence

The workers' objective in starting the club was not only to look at ways in which isolation among the elderly on this estate could be alleviated, but also, using community work methods, to enable a group of elderly people to take charge, run the club in their own way and develop their own social links on the estate in the way that suited them best.

The club met for the first time in March 1973. All the people who had said they were interested had been invited. Fifteen came.

Apart from the normal anxieties attaching to the initial stage of group life, the workers were anxious about the need to find an accommodation between their purposes for the group, the expectations of its members, and the requirement of the education authority for it to be a 'class'. This weighed heavily on them. Their aim at the first meeting was to find out what the old people wanted to do so that appropriate teachers might be requested from the education institute. The group spent a long time discussing this, but in fact there were some vital resources within the group itself. Some members had experience of other clubs and knew the kind of thing clubs did. A pianist emerged from the group quite quickly and community singing soon began.

What the club should be called seemed to be a more important question than what it should do. Several suggestions were made. One of the songs they sang was 'Friends and Neighbours', and when they came to take a vote on a name, 'Friends and Neighbours Club' gained overwhelming support.

Looking back on the development of the club it is clear that the workers' energies were exercised far more by the discrepancy between their purposes and the expectations of the group, than by the discrepancy between both of these and the education requirement. The name 'Friends and Neighbours Club', chosen so early, was uncannily congruent with their main purpose. But they had yet to grapple with differences between the members' expectations of how the club would be run, and their own. Given their objectives, they were naturally anxious to relinquish the leadership role as quickly as possible, and to avoid doing things that club members could do for themselves.

The early meetings, with a gradually increasing membership, built on the members' liking for singing. A singing teacher was soon brought in. She came once a month and clearly had difficulties about the old people's failure to behave like a class. However, there was sufficient tolerance on both sides to overcome them.

Besides wanting to sing, members expressed preferences for different topics; and various speakers were arranged. An important one was a supervisor from the local Department of Health and Social Security office. Two very successful entertainments were provided, one by a piano accordion player, the other by the brass band of a local boys' school.

Meanwhile members were undertaking certain tasks such as collecting membership fees, tea and raffle money. Two members played the piano and provided much spontaneous entertainment. But the workers were the main organisers of the beetle and bingo sessions, and the small fund-raising bring-and-buy sales, and the very successful outing to Kew Gardens in May. The school girls continued to come, and besides escorting the disabled, they made and served the tea. As long as they were there, no one helped with it. After the school timetable was changed and the girls could not come, the old people took on the tea-making without hesitation. However, the workers considered this a very small gain. Despite much prodding they had not succeeded in getting the group to form a committee.

The breakthrough came in the summer school holiday when the club meeting place had to be transferred to the primary school because the youth club building was in use during the day as a play centre. In the school it was possible for the education institute to make video equipment available to the club. The members had themselves filmed. Some of them were filmed singing or dancing or reciting poetry; and one was filmed interviewing each of the other members, eliciting from them how pleased they were to be at the club. The effect of seeing themselves on video was dramatic. Even the inactive members were delighted just to catch sight of themselves as the camera roamed round the entire group. The workers could see the members' confidence in themselves growing by leaps and bounds as they became more and more impressed by how good they looked on the screen. At this point, with no prompting from the workers, the club elected its committee.

BUILDING THE CLUB

The committee met regularly and consisted of a chairman, secretary, treasurer, tea organiser, and organisers for outings. At their second meeting they took their first real decision: to have bingo every week. The workers were dismayed but fortunately for them some committee members did not want bingo to crowd out other activities, and it was agreed that bingo should last only half-an-hour.

The committee worked steadily on through the autumn and gradually the club members took more responsibility for deciding what the club would do and how it should be run. But it was a slow process. The workers were no longer the leaders but rather naturally were still seen as the people who had a powerful command over external resources; a command which the old people clearly did not believe they could exercise themselves. An example of this was the organising of the Christmas Party. They seemed to think it would fall from the sky. It was an understandable expectation. It is what appeared to happen in other old people's clubs, and they saw no reason why theirs would be an exception. However, when the workers explained that there would be no party unless the members organised it themselves the committee willingly contributed food and drinks, and they organised similar contributions from other members as well as the preparation and provision of entertainment. By Christmas 1974, the committee was much stronger. They had been told that the borough provided Christmas dinners to old people's clubs, and on their own initiative they ordered one for themselves.

It was also some time before the committee felt able to make known the members' wish to change things that had been established by the workers. For example, the workers at the very first meeting had arranged the chairs in a big circle. When, half apologetically, the committee told them that the members wanted tables to sit round, the workers realised that, unknown to them, the wish had been present in the club for a long time.

As the club got into its stride the workers sensed increasingly the culture of the group. The members' decisions about what to do and how were based on their common assumptions about what was correct in social relations and what clubs normally did. Whatever the workers felt about the group's decisions, they were scrupulously careful to respect cultural norms and to work within them. Any conflict that existed between members and workers was about who should do various tasks, and this arose because of the members' initial lack of confidence and experience.

The chairman of the committee was both a strength and a source of anxiety. He was an energetic enthusiast who did many things on his own initiative. But his ideas for the club, though given tacit approval, were not often generated by discussion in the committee; they were self-generated. The workers feared the club might become a 'one-man show'. But the steady strength of the other committee members was later to become apparent after the chairman died suddenly during a club meeting.

Meanwhile, by 1974 life was expanding to offer much more to club members in the way of interest, choice and companionship. The club had fifty members of whom twenty-five to thirty-five attended weekly. Classes in handicrafts and indoor gardening legitimised the education department's sponsorship of the club. But the classes were held on different days from the main club meeting, thereby expanding the time that the old people might meet in the youth club building.

A GOOD NEIGHBOUR SCHEME FOR THE ESTATE

In the course of a recruiting drive for club members the chairman visited a great number of elderly people in the tower blocks. Each of the blocks' seventeen floors had one small flat for an elderly person. As a result of finding many frail people at risk he initiated the kind of good neighbour scheme that the settlement had envisaged. In each tower block a club committee member was designated as the person to be called upon to help with individual problems. In this way many needs were made known to social services which might otherwise have been neglected. Most of the referrals were made by committee members via the community worker who passed them on to the appropriate social work team. Some were made direct.

EFFECTS ON OTHER SYSTEMS

The club related to a considerable number of other systems including the old people's home and sheltered housing, the shopkeepers who provided fruit for raffle prizes, the Greater London Council housing estates office.

Here we identify a few of the systems upon which the effects of their relationship were most interesting.

The Youth Club

It could not be expected that the 'ripple' effect of the old people's club would be all sweetness and light. But at first it seemed to be so. The rather Scrooge-like attitude of the education authority regarding the use of the youth club building was quite soon undermined by the youth leader who started to encourage the community at large to feel free to use it as they wished. Furthermore he helped a few members of the old people's club to buy meat at Smithfield market and package it. They then sold it to the other old people at a much lower price than the local shop. This scheme was very successful and lasted until the government beef-token scheme began. However, as usually happens, difficulties over 'territory' began to develop. As the old people's chairman became increasingly involved and his club's activities expanded, so the youth leader felt the chairman to be 'taking over' his building. Somewhat naturally he retreated behind the rules laid down by his authority about the use of premises, and rows between him and the chairman ensued. But eventually, by keeping their distance, the two leaders and their respective groups were able to co-exist.

Tenants' Association

We have noted how the association acquiesced, but played no active part, in establishing the club. Eventually they invited the club's chairman to join their committee, but only after this had been suggested to them by the community worker. Somewhat to the workers' amusement the committee was then in a position to claim all of the work with the elderly as theirs. It became a 'section' of the tenants' association, thereby giving the association a strength it had not had before.

The Social Services Department

It is difficult to gauge the effect of the club on the social services department area team. At the outset of the project the area had a 'patch' worker covering the estate, i.e. one social worker's work was confined geographically to the population of the estate. This particular worker was as much concerned about the social isolation of the elderly as were the community worker and the settlement worker. They involved her in consultations about the survey and speculations as to what might follow. However, by the time the club was established she had left, and the area team was no longer operating a 'patch' system. Cases of elderly people on the estate were being handled by several different workers. As we have noted already the department had not been giving the elderly high priority as far as *social workers* were concerned, and it is unlikely that the social workers were able to devote any significant attention to the old people's isolation. Therefore the work of the club did not relieve them of a problem that they were already trying to tackle. As far as numbers of cases were concerned, many old people with so-called individual problems were now being helped by informal resource systems. But decreased work for these cases was probably balanced by the greater amount of genuine individual need that was identified through the good neighbour scheme. However, the weight of these individual problems probably fell more heavily on staff providing domiciliary services than on social work staff.

As a group, the club dealt effectively with problems such as the need for welfare rights information and difficulties with electricity and gas boards. This must have diminished some of the work of the social service department. On the other hand, as the club became stronger it was able to make demands for other kinds of service such as the provision of a luncheon club on the estate. In financial terms the club probably made little difference to the department, but in terms of client benefit, the club was a crucial resource in promoting social well-being.

EVALUATING THE CHOICE OF THE GROUP AS A TARGET OF INTERVENTION

By 1975 the community worker and the settlement worker had both left. The club continues without professional help and is as active as ever. It has gained a good reputation for itself and become a force to be reckoned with. What were the most important things to come out of the decision of the workers to make the group the target of intervention?

The central achievement was the establishment of friendship networks throughout the estate. Some club members admitted they had not known anyone for the seven years before the club started. It had transformed the sorrow of an arid lonely existence into the joy of living among caring friends. Everything else stemmed from that: mutual help, creative activity, companionship in all the ordinary events of life. People who had previously done little else than 'survive' in their flats entered into a wholly new range of activities. Some activities were within the context of the club. Many more were outside it, but dependent on the friendships that the club had nurtured.

Another vital achievement was the personal development of individual club members, especially some of its committee. They developed considerable knowledge of the social services and knew whom to contact about what on whose behalf. They also developed new skills in such things as fund raising for the club. In dealing with formal and informal organisations they discovered within themselves talents they had not known they had. Their growth in confidence and self-esteem was a joy both to them and to others. The energy generated by the old people allowed many other things to happen. Not only did the old people attract the caring capacities of other tenants, they also gave other tenants an example of what could be achieved by a self-help group.

The workers would not claim to have affected every single old person on the estate. Some were too frail to come to the club, even in a wheel-chair; others were unclubbable. The need for individual help remains, but no longer because of the lack of opportunity for normal social relations. Before they left, the workers argued strongly for an urban aid application to support a social worker who would be appointed to work on the estate specifically with old people who had individual problems. At the same time the social worker would liaise closely with the club and its multifarious activities. Because of the club and the network of social relations it has created, the social worker would be able to devote much greater attention to the people really needing an individual service; and in doing so, would be able to draw on the resources now existing in this previously alienated community.

Conclusion

The success of the work must have depended on a large number of factors over which the workers had no control, such as the talents of the old people themselves and the willingness of other people to contribute time and energy to it. But of the factors over which the workers were able to exercise control, it is important to identify the things they did that arose from their theoretical orientation and philosophy, and that crucially affected the nature of the whole project.

(1) Their decision to work with the elderly on that particular estate was based on an adequate survey of need.
(2) They were concerned that the work would result in a permanent development of the whole community and not be a 'patching up' of problems stemming from the community's alienation. For this reason they chose to form the elderly into an action system rather than flood the estate with volunteers working with the elderly as individuals.
(3) Having succeeded in forming the group, they allowed it to develop spontaneously, going at the pace dictated by its members.
(4) When the members were ready, the workers relinquished their roles as leaders and became enablers and suppliers of information.
(5) In all their planning they consulted and tried to involve other vital workers and groups.

Chapter 4

GROUP WORK AS A PROCESS OF SOCIAL INFLUENCE

Peter B. Smith

At first sight social psychology and social group work appear to have an obvious relevance to each other. Social psychologists' most enduring research topic has been the study of social influence, while social group workers have been attempting to create particular influence effects amongst their groups of clients. But this mutual relevance has often been clouded over by other equally important attributes of the two fields. Kurt Lewin has been quoted as having said, 'there's nothing so practical as a good theory'. Many of the theories developed by social psychologists since Lewin's time do not have very clear practical implications, so that if we wish to adhere to Lewin's notion we shall have to consider such theories to be poor theories. They are theories which have been developed to account for behaviour in simplified laboratory settings where many of the social influences of everyday life are attenuated.

Social group workers for their part have not shunned everyday life experience, but some at least of them would hesitate to describe themselves as attempting to create particular influence effects. The literature of social work lays stress on client self-determination and does not linger on such questions as the role of the group worker as an agent of social control or the limitations on the client's consent to the worker's intervention.

In this chapter I shall attempt to show that social psychological conceptions of social influence can nonetheless illuminate various aspects of social group work practice. The social psychologist's conception of human nature stresses the manner in which not only our behaviour but even the way we think is profoundly influenced by the company we keep. Our everyday experience is seen as continuingly ambiguous, necessitating frequent reference to others to determine the most appropriate response. According to Festinger's (1954) theory of social comparison processes, we prefer impersonal, objective criteria (such as testing how good one is at driving a car by actually driving it), but in the many situations where no such impersonal criteria are available we fall back on the opinions of others (such as testing how good a parent one is by talking to others facing similar situations).

SOCIAL INFLUENCE PROCESSES

Early research in social psychology suggested that the outcome of such comparisons was a pressure to conform to majority opinion. If one came well out of such a comparison one's existing behaviours and life style were supported, whereas if one did not then one was confronted by a choice between changing one's responses or accepting the majority view that one was wrong, lacking in some quality or in some other way undesirable. While such an analysis has its usefulness, more recent thinking has enriched our knowledge of the process of social comparison. Hollander and Willis (1967) have shown how conformity is only one of the several possible responses to social comparison. Another possible response is *anticonformity*, i.e. discerning what the group wants from one and then doing the opposite. Such a process is unlikely to be frequent in laboratory experiments where a single group is studied, but in real settings, people tend to belong concurrently to several different groups. In such circumstances anticonforming to one group may be the price of acceptance in a second group. Examples of such effects may frequently be observed in settings where age or social class differences are important factors.

The usefulness of this type of formulation of social influence processes is that it emphasises both that the individual *does* have some choice as to who shall influence him and that that choice is quite severely bounded by the particular groups available to him. In terms of the possibilities for group work it argues against the fatalistic position that the individual's experience is so heavily determined by his existing group loyalties that intervention oriented toward change has little hope of success. Equally it argues against the conceptualisation of group work as a magical process which achieves its effects regardless of the context from which clients are drawn. Group work must be seen as an attempt to create a temporary additional group in the client's life, from which he obtains some satisfaction but whose effects are also felt in the other groups which are salient in the client's life.

The problem of creating influence which extends beyond the actual group in which it initially occurs is a key one, not just in group work but throughout social work, psychotherapy and indeed education. To express it in terms of the previous analysis of conformity, if someone changes his behaviour in a group we cannot be sure whether that change is a 'real' change or merely a temporary expedient. If a group has the ability to reward or punish members for deviant responses, individuals will be likely to comply with the group's demands. But this does not guarantee that members will accept that their changed behaviour is right for them. When other members of the group are not around they may revert to former behaviours. Thus the important issue in analysing group work as a social influence process is not what factors cause members to comply with the group, but what factors cause them to accept that their changed behaviours have value and are worth preserving.

One social psychologist whose theories bear on this question is Herbert Kelman. Kelman (1958, 1963) differentiates three types of social influence, which he terms compliance, identification and internalisation. Compliance is seen as a process whereby one makes expedient changes in behaviour in response to others who have the power to reward or punish one. Such effects will persist only while those others are around to ensure compliance. Identification is seen as a state where one is in doubt as to how to behave, but there is someone else around who appears less in doubt. One's doubt is resolved by doing what one thinks this attractive figure would like one to do. This influence also is seen as temporary since it is likely only to persist while the attraction is still present. Internalisation is seen as occurring where the individual locates others having similar values or problems as himself and observes that some of these others have ways of coping with these problems which seem to work out better than does one's own current behaviour. This type of influence is accepted not to please others but because it appears that one's own difficulties may be reduced as a result. Whether or not this influence persists should thus depend not on whether others are still present but on whether or not the changed behaviour does in fact work out in one's own life.

Kelman's model has a good deal of usefulness in thinking through the necessary prerequisites for effective group work. Of course it is not the case that all group work is oriented toward internalisation of change. Some groups may be focused toward support of existing behaviours or toward struggle with other groups (see, for example, Vickery, Thomas in this Reader), and in these identification may be a salient process. But many groups are set up with goals which require internalisation and these will be the main focus here. Kelman's conceptualisation of internalisation has three elements. First, one's sources of influence are in some way attractive. Kelman postulates similarity of values as the basis for attraction, but there may well be others. Secondly, these influence sources do something which encourages one to change. This need not necessarily be an overt demand for change. It could equally well be being seen to cope adequately with some problem which was causing one difficulty. The third element in Kelman's definition, though he does not spell it out, is that the attractive person and the stimulus for change must be one and the same person. In this discussion I shall term these two necessary components *support* and *confrontation*, since I believe these words convey more vividly the elements of the internalisation process. Supportive behaviours are those which provide the member with encouragement and reassurance; confronting behaviours are those which challenge or disconfirm him.

Much of the experimental research into attitude change conducted by social psychologists has concerned short-term effects and the findings most likely tell us more about the process of compliance than the process of internalisation. However, some studies have looked at the persistence of change. Collins and Hoyt (1972) found that persistence of changed attitudes depended on whether or not the experimental subjects felt personally responsible for the effects of the changes. Although the terms used in this study were somewhat different, the high changers would appear to resemble internalisers. In a study more directly derived from Kelman's model, Smith (1976) found that among sensitivity training participants those classified as internalisers showed changes still present five months after training, while those classified as identifiers or as compliant showed no such persistence of change. Much more evidence will be required before we can be sure how fruitful Kelman's model is. At present it provides an intriguing but unproven hypothesis.

LEADERSHIP IN GROUPS

The processes of influence within a small group are complex and diverse. Each of the members is likely to have some share in influencing what occurs at one moment or another. Thus the group worker can never expect to be more than one among a number of influential group members. Part of the worker's task may well include attempts to influence the emerging group climate, but another part of the task is often simply letting others take initiatives which also help the growth of the group. In the case of groups oriented toward behaviour change the task may amount to the creation of a climate of supportive and confronting relationships. In other settings there may be more tangible goals such as developing a pattern of activities or maintaining relations with other groups. The group worker's contribution to such climates is usually considered as an instance of leadership. Theories of leadership have shown a gradual evolution over the years away from the notion that the leader is a heroic figure who is somewhat immune to the group's influence, and toward the view of leadership as a two-way influence process. Such an evolution is by no means easily won. We all fall readily into the assumption that it is the leader who causes what happens: the mother raises the child, the foreman achieves high worker productivity, the majority influences the minority. Such beliefs are commonsensical and have also been supported by research findings. But the beliefs have until recently prevented researchers from looking for other types of relationships. We now find that children have marked effects on their parents' behaviour (Danziger, 1971), that workers can influence their supervisors (Lowin and Craig, 1968; Haythorn, 1956) and that minorities can affect the dominant orthodoxy by taking up a consistent position (Moscovici and Faucheux, 1972).

Perhaps the most marked illustration of our predisposition to see leaders as the source of all influence is given by Milgram's (1974) series of experiments on obedience. In these experiments subjects were asked to administer increasingly severe shocks to an innocent victim. The experiment was based on deception and no actual shocks were administered. However, the staging was highly realistic and there is no doubt that the subjects found it convincing. More than 60 per cent of them went along with the instructions. Milgram studied numerous variations in this basic experimental design. The interesting one for present purposes is one in which the naive subject was asked to collaborate with two others in administering the shocks. The two others were actually also accomplices of the experimenter and at a predetermined point they refused to proceed further. Under these circumstances only 10 per cent of the naive subjects were willing to proceed further, even though the experimenter insisted that they should do so. This variant of Milgram's experiment illustrates the manner in which the leader's apparent power rests on the consent of the followers. Where this consent is called in question by other group members the leader's influence is radically curtailed.

Thus the power of the leader is inextricably tied up with the power group members exert over one another and over the leader. The power of the group worker as leader varies a great deal. In residential settings group workers may potentially exercise considerable power, while in non-residential settings this is less likely to be so. In either event the initial climate of the group is likely to be set by the expectations and needs of the clients who attend. The group worker may have a clear conception of the direction which he would like the group to take from this point on, but the process whereby this conception is communicated to the group is probably better thought of as a bargaining process than as the exercise of leadership.

The selection of group members is one action by which the leader may be thought of as controlling the emergent group climate. The leader certainly exercises choice in deciding whose attendance to solicit. He may decide to recruit members all facing a similar problem, for instance. But here too the exercise of the leader's choice is but the first step in a process of negotiation concerning the leader's intentions in setting up the group, who else will be coming, when will it meet, transport problems and so forth. In settings where there is less choice about attendance the same dynamic will be played out but it will focus not on attendance but on willingness to co-operate with the purpose of the group. Leadership in group work is thus, as in other fields, not so much a heroic performance as an ability to show others that both oneself and other members of the group have something which they may find useful in coping with their own difficulties.

THE LEADER'S ROLE IN BUILDING SUPPORT IN THE GROUP

One advantage of the 'transactional' view of leadership advanced above is that it emphasises the manner in which effective leadership of a group will evolve over time. The leader's initial orientation toward the group will be one of several determinants of the initial group climate. This in turn will elicit later leader interventions. One theorist of leadership who has adopted this type of model is Hollander (1960). Hollander stresses three determinants of the leader's initial acceptability to the group: task competence, conformity and manner of appointment. According to Hollander the acceptable leader will be one who is able early on to demonstrate to his group that he has expertise in tasks relevant to the group's purpose, that he respects the norm preferences of group members and that he has legitimate reasons for being the group leader. Such reasons might include election by the group, but in most fields of group work the reasons would more likely be employment by a social work agency with a legitimate interest in whatever is the focus of the group. In a series of laboratory experiments Hollander and Julian (1970) were able to show the importance of each of these variables. Where the leader is able to achieve initial acceptance Hollander suggests that the group will be willing to accord him what he calls 'idiosyncracy credit', i.e. they will be prepared to tolerate a certain amount of subsequent nonconformity or even initiatives to change the norms from him. They will be prepared to do this because his earlier behaviour in the group has generated a certain amount of trust that he does have the interests of the group at heart. Such credit is not likely to be inexhaustible, and if the leader's initiatives lead to members' frustration, embarrassment or humiliation it will be withdrawn.

Hollander's analysis of leadership skills has some interesting parallels with the earlier discussion of social influence processes. It was suggested that the prerequisites for the achievement of internalisation were some support and some confrontation. Hollander can be seen as proposing that the processes of support must necessarily be achieved *before* the processes of confrontation may be fruitfully engaged. All of the initial leader behaviours will need to have a supportive element if there is to *be* a group sufficiently committed to sustain later confrontation. Thus the leader will do his best to explain the purpose of the group to prospective members, he will obtain a setting protected from intrusion wherein the group may meet, he will recruit members whose goals have some relevance to one another, he may propose particular tasks or activities, and he will define the time boundaries of the group's meetings. In all these and many other ways he will foster the growth of supportive processes in the group. If he later proposes activities which confront members' values or accustomed routines, these will be acceptable and useful to the group only insofar as those support processes have been achieved.

There are numerous reasons why the leader may have difficulty in fostering the supportive processes of the group. First among these is likely to be the leader's own deviance from the group. Frequently the leader differs from group members in such aspects as age, sex, social class, colour and occupation. There is some question about the applicability of the findings to longer-term relationships, but for initial acquaintance there is no doubt that the more similar we are to someone the more we like that person (Byrne, 1969; Newcomb, 1961). Thus the leader who differs from his clients starts out with an initial handicap. This handicap will affect the subsequent development of the group, both by way of the group members' initially guarded response to the leader and by way of the leader having to find some way of coping with his needs for acceptance.

A second difficulty the leader may encounter in creating support is the ambivalence of his own feelings toward group members. It is likely that the leader has some positive feeling toward the clients, or he would not seek to set the group up. But he may also feel critical, disapproving, anxious or whatever in relation to the problems his clients face and which provide the rationale for assembling the group. To express such feelings is to confront the group at a time which may be inappropriate, but to withold them is to leave the leader in a state where he will feel less than wholehearted in fostering supportive processes in the group.

A third restraint on the leader as a source of support may be his particular theoretical orientation as a group worker. For instance, workers within the Bion or 'Tavistock' tradition (see Palmer in this Reader) do not conceptualise their role as active creators of group climate, but rather as commentators on the climate which evolves around them. Such an orientation may serve to highlight particular aspects of group functioning, but it renders the growth of supportive processes in groups less likely. Harrow *et al.* (1971) have shown that members of groups with Tavistock-oriented leaders liked one another less than members of matched groups with more participatively oriented leaders, working within the 'T-group' or Rogerian tradition. In the T-group the leader expects to express his own feelings and reactions in much the same way that members do.

The final source of difficulty in creating a supportive group climate may be the particular composition of the group. The leader will most likely seek to exercise some control over this in advance, but such control can never be very precise. By selecting members who are similar to one another the leader will enhance the probability of liking and acceptance. But particular members may elicit from others behaviours which were not evident prior to the group. There may also be long-standing conflicts between particular individuals of which the leader is unaware when he composes the group. Such compositional difficulties will provide the leader with some of his most obvious problems in seeking to influence the direction in which his group develops.

Several difficulties have been delineated which hinder the early development of supportive processes in groups. Such difficulties do not as a rule prove insuperable but they provide some rather more concrete illustration of the manner in which the initial development of the group is more akin to bargaining than to the exercise of heroic leadership. Quite often the bargaining positions, implicity if not explicitly, sound a bit like this:

Group members: 'If we're going to take this seriously you'll have to show us you know what you're doing and that this group can be a safe and homely place. Go ahead, we're waiting.'

Leader: 'I accept that, but what you are asking of me cannot be done by any one individual single-handed. I want each of us to look at what we are contributing to the group's development.'

The manner in which this initial bargaining is elaborated into the complex subsequent history of a particular group is a key problem, to which I now turn.

GROUP DEVELOPMENT

Numerous authors have published descriptions of the development of groups over time. Summarising many of these, Tuckman (1965) suggested that in fact the same sequence of phases occurs in laboratory experimental groups, in naturally occurring groups, in sensitivity training groups and in psychotherapy groups. He delineates four phases of group life which he names 'forming', 'storming', 'norming', and 'performing'. Essentially this reduces to the proposition that after an initial phase where first impressions are formed, a conflict or series of conflicts arise. This is followed by phases in which agreement as to how to proceed is achieved and the group proceeds to carry out its task. The most obvious omission from such a sequence is any reference to the termination of the group, but there are other models, e.g. Mann (1967), which incorporate an additional 'separation' phase.

A good deal of the work on group development is based on descriptions by leaders of how their groups 'usually' develop. Those studies which have actually depended on codings by researchers of tape-recorded groups have usually rested on few groups or on a series of groups all having the same leader. The evidence that there is some pre-ordained sequence of phases through which groups pass is thus tenuous. We have evidence about phases through which groups have sometimes been found to pass, but to assert that they will always do so is far ahead of the evidence. It is a much more plausible hypothesis that the phases in the development of a particular group will arise out of the particular needs of group members, the type of setting in which they meet and the orientation of the leader of that group. For instance, Sherwood (1964) has argued that many of the events upon which a Tavistock-style leader comments are inevitable consequences of his own previous behaviour. Thus, if we take the Sherwood view, the Tavistock leader creates a series of developmental phases, which he then interprets. Such a procedure may have value, but it is important to be clear that the sequence is not inexorable, but is a consequence of the developing history of the group. Another illustration of the manner in which leaders act on the developmental phases of a group is in the contrast between Tavistock groups and T-groups. Even where the membership is held constant (Harrow *et al.*, 1971), T-group leaders achieve a stronger focus on peer relations and problems of affection, while Tavistock leaders achieve a stronger focus on authority relations and problems of power. These differences follow clearly from the theoretical orientations of these two types of leader (Klein and Astrachan, 1971).

I find it most fruitful to think of the phases in group development identified by Tuckman and others as a checklist of issues that are important in any group. Each may be emphasised or passed over lightly. An issue may be thoroughly explored at just one point in the group's history or returned to on many occasions.

THE MANAGEMENT OF CONFRONTATION

I have argued earlier that a group which is to create influence extending beyond its own confines must generate both support and confrontation. Whilst initially the leader needs to build support in the group, later he will be able to encourage members to confront one another's anxieties and to participate in this process himself. In most types of group work, confrontation means no more than providing opportunities for group members to talk openly about feelings which are important to them, which may be strongly held or painful, and which relate to the purpose for which the group has been set up. In some circumstances it can be appropriate to employ non-verbal exercises which enable particular group members to act out such feelings (see, for example, Shutz, 1967), but in many settings where group work is employed the leader's idiosyncrasy credit is somewhat overstretched by such devices. In all circumstances the leader should ensure that whether confrontation be through verbal interchange, non-verbal activity, psychodrama or some other procedure, those involved know what procedure they are entering into and are not coerced into doing so.

The creation of a group having simultaneous support and confrontation rests on such factors as (1) the group's composition, (2) the group's history, (3) the leader's contributions and (4) the leader's awareness of his own contribution. Each of these will be explored in turn.

(1) It was suggested earlier that a homogeneous group enhanced the processes of support. While this is a key factor early in the group's life, subsequent confrontation is aided by some diversity. In an experimental study of brief T-groups, Smith (1974) found that the groups with the widest

range of personalities achieved most internalisation. However, all groups were composed of undergraduate students, so that the heterogeneity was that to be found within a framework of homogeneity. Similar findings, favouring heterogeneous composition within homogeneous populations, have been obtained with various other studies of participants in T-groups (e.g. Smith and Linton, 1975).

(2) These effects of group composition are not achieved automatically. They rest on the historical development of the group. For instance, if a group establishes in its initial meeting a pattern of warm, friendly relations, group standards may develop about 'not rocking the boat', which may overlay the potential for confrontation built into the group's composition. The group may start to satisfy unfulfilled social needs of members, who then become unwilling to undertake what they see as the risk of losing this source of gratification. Here the leader will need to initiate a review as to whether the group is meeting the needs originally specified by members who joined the group.

(3) The leader is himself an important source of confrontation in the group. His presence is often seen as a source of inhibition, even, or perhaps especially, when he chooses to say very little. He most contributes to internalisation where his behaviour is seen as genuine rather than contrived (Cooper, 1969). While the leader's difference from other group members may constitute an initial handicap, it may later prove an advantage, enabling him to confront members with novel perspectives on their behaviour which are less visible to those who are closely similar to themselves. This shift in the significance of particular behaviours as the group evolves is reminiscent of research findings into love and marriage. For instance, Murstein (1971) has found that similarity is a very important factor in determining whether or not a relationship between a couple gets started. But the later progress of the relationship is not at all related to similarity. Later progress is dependent on whether or not the partners are able to satisfy each other's needs.

(4) The success of the group leader will depend in a similar manner on whether he is able to provide the role behaviours required by the directions in which the group evolves. In order to achieve this he will require a considerable awareness of both the behaviour of others in the group and also the manner in which others in the group are responding to him. The development of such skills is discussed elsewhere in this Reader (see chapter by Palmer). This chapter began by stressing the ambiguity of human experience, necessitating frequent references to others. Group leaders are not exempt from such needs, and effective group leadership requires not only skills to be acquired in such training but also other people with whom the progress of a specific group can be discussed. This may require that there be two group leaders, or that the group leader has supervision of his work between sessions.

BALANCE BETWEEN CONFRONTATION AND SUPPORT

In seeking to create a group climate which will maximise the occurrence of internalisation the leader will need to be able to recognise and respond to three types of situation. These are situations in which there is support but no confrontation, situations in which there is confrontation but no support, and situations in which both confrontation and support are present but they are directed toward different members of the group.

In groups with support but no confrontation there will most likely be a pleasant climate, with members enjoying the activities of the group and expressing concern for one another. The leader is likely to find himself reluctant to initiate exploration of sensitive areas, and when he does so may meet with incomprehension or puzzlement. The group will seek to encourage him to share their optimistic view of the proceedings.

In groups with confrontation but no support, the leader faces a variety of problems. Where participation in the group has been influenced by organisational pressures, the leader may find that he is the principal source of confrontation. This may occur, for instance, in groups in residential or therapeutic communities. The leader will find it difficult to create a climate in which members feel sufficiently safe to take responsibility for their own actions. While it will certainly help for him to make clear the nature of his relationship to the organisation which has pressured members into attending, he is likely to find that his attempts to foster support within the group are perceived by the group as manipulative control strategies.

Alternatively, the leader may find that the group has inbuilt confrontation to which he himself is not a major party. For instance, this will be the case where the group spans a wide range of ages, occupations or reasons for attending or where it includes people with long-standing conflict with one another. Here the leader's task is to create the supportive context within which the divergent group members may learn from confronting one another.

Situations where support and confrontation processes are both present in the group but become split off from one another occur frequently. Here a subgroup find one another attractive but blame the fact that they cannot make progress toward their goals on another subgroup whom they denigrate. Where the subgroup is a single member this would amount to scapegoating, but more typically it resembles factional conflict. Such splitting may unwittingly be encouraged by the leader(s), particularly if there are two of them. Some theorists of group processes (e.g. Bennis and Shepard, 1956; Stock Whitaker and Lieberman, 1964) argue that the polarisation and subsequent resolution of such conflicts constitute the principal learning mode of groups. According to the present approach they constitute frequent events on the path toward integrating support processes with confrontation. The leader's task must be to avoid capture by either faction, to show by example that he finds elements worthy of support and of confrontation in each of the factions. Where the factions have some deep-rooted reason to scapegoat one another, such as a split on racial or sexual lines, this may require rather direct and sustained intervention by the leader, but it is vital to the success of such groups that intervention does occur.

SOME CONCLUSIONS

In this chapter I have argued for an analysis of group work as a process of social influence. I have stressed that a group which is to create lasting influence requires an integration of support and confrontation. In picking out such groups for emphasis I may have overemphasised my own interests and experience. As a corrective let it be said that many forms of social group work do not aspire to the creation of lasting influence. Their role is rather more the provision of support in a situation which is difficult if not intolerable. In such settings the worker's task may for long periods be focused on the provision of support and the consequent development of identification.

This analysis has employed terminology which is not widely employed by group workers, parts of which are more fully explored in Smith (1973). However, I believe that the terms I employ are by no means incompatible with those employed elsewhere in this volume. A number of contributors use the concepts of Bion (1961) to analyse group phenomena, and it would not be difficult to relabel the types of group I have delineated in the previous section as those in which processes of pairing, dependency and fight respectively predominate. Where I would diverge from a Bionic approach is not over the usefulness of Bion's diagnostic concepts, but over the actions the leader may then take. My account makes it clear that I favour a more active, interventionist style of leadership. However, there is still far too little research linking leader style to the outcomes of group work. Until such time as we have firmer knowledge of such effects, the best strategy is undoubtedly for group leaders to experience and develop as wide a range of intervention skills as practicable.

Chapter 5

WORKING WITH GROUPS IN THE RESIDENTIAL SETTING

Chris Payne

INTRODUCTION

It is a considerable undertaking to discuss in one short paper the contribution made by group work to a field of social work practice that is as varied as residential care. Over a quarter of a million people are accommodated, on either a temporary or permanent basis, in numerous types of residential centres. They include children in care, who may be placed in different types of community homes or in residential schools; the mentally subnormal, the mentally ill and the physically disabled, living in homes and hostels run by local authorities and voluntary organisations; the residents of probation hostels, homes for the elderly and other accommodation for the needy and disadvantaged.

Although provision has expanded considerably since the second world war, residential care has developed piecemeal, without a common philosophy and without clear aims and objectives. The different branches of residential care have not based their practices on common assumptions and principles. Consequently methods vary considerably from one type of establishment, indeed, from one establishment to another. All that different establishments manifestly have in common is the provision of life's basics, shelter, food, care and protection, for a specified group of people who, for various reasons, cannot maintain themselves or be maintained by members of their families.

In this paper we develop some of the thinking first contained in the report of the Williams Committee (1967) and continued by the Working Party of the Central Council for Education and Training in Social Work (CCETSW) concerning the common tasks and skill requirements for residential work (see Discussion Document: *Training for Residential Work*, 1973).

The CCETSW Working Party placed considerable emphasis on residential workers acquiring a thorough understanding of group processes, and the skills to manage group interactions. Our aim is to outline and discuss a framework that should enable those concerned with the development of residential practice to identify more closely those aspects in which group work knowledge and skills are applied.

THE RESIDENTIAL TASK

Readers may be familiar with William Golding's novel *Lord of the Flies* – a penetrating insight into group behaviour. Golding describes how a party of schoolboys find themselves on a desert island with no adults to provide care, protection and leadership. The boys face the threat to their survival first under the democratic but conservative leadership of one of the senior boys, Ralph. His efforts to provide a modicum of order and stability appear to succeed. Then fears and anxieties rapidly escalate, and the group panics. Ralph finds his position challenged by a rival faction dominated by the aggressive, warlike Jack. Under Jack's autocratic command the group is lured into an exciting but increasingly perilous way of life. Jack destroys any pretence of following the values of civilisation, and substitutes a primitive, tribal mode of living which is inevitably self-destructive. Some children, including Ralph's right-hand man, the clever but ineffectual Piggy, lose their lives. Ralph and a few loyal companions are outlawed and hunted by the mob. Ralph's life is saved only by the arrival on the island of a crew from a passing ship.

The experience of admission to residential care is for many people one of being marooned on a desert island. Their first need is to survive, though physical survival is not the primary consideration. It is true that some physically disabled and elderly people would die without continuous personal care and attention, but for the majority it is much more a matter of their survival as a person. The loss of close relationships, of familiar surroundings, and the stresses felt in adjusting to people who, initially at least, are strangers, can result in considerable personal disorganisation. Reactions vary: some withdraw and insulate themselves from human contact; some, in their anxiety, become demanding of attention, and consequently increase their dependency; whilst others express anger, and fight hard to retain a sense of independence. Without exception, irrespective of whether they are children or adults, they remain vulnerable to inner fears and anxieties, and many experience panic or despair.

The responsibility for helping these vulnerable people not only to survive but to restore and maintain a sense of personal identity, and to develop their capacities to the full, rests heavily on the staff of the residential unit. Indeed, residential workers have to perform many of the functions that would be undertaken by adults had they been present on that island in *Lord of the Flies*. (However, we do not imply that all residents should be treated like children.) First and foremost amongst their numerous tasks is that of developing a satisfactory environment for shared daily living. We would adjudge a 'satisfactory environment' to be one with foundations firm enough to prevent disintegration into anarchy and chaos, but one that is sufficiently flexible and open to allow for the exercise of basic human rights and freedoms.

Many other opportunities are then needed for human potential to develop, and for individuals to work on the life problems that have often precipitated admission to the residential setting. The causes and nature of these 'life problems' are too numerous to discuss fully here, because they clearly vary from one type of residential centre to another, indeed from one resident to another. For example, children in care often suffer from many different forms of deprivation, emotional, social and educational. It is the task of the residential unit to mitigate the effects of deprivation through provision of appropriate remedial and compensatory experiences. Alternatively, physically or mentally handicapped people in residential care may not only require good physical care, but they may also need help to overcome the effects their respective disabilities may have on their personal and social lives and relationships. There are people in hostels for the mentally ill and for offenders, who have spent many years in mental hospitals and prisons, and who need similar forms of help in relearning to live in the community at large. Elderly people in care may need new and stimulating experiences to enrich their otherwise drab daily lives, or to restore their sense of purpose in life.

The essence of residential work thus lies, first, in the development of a 'round the clock' experience that is subjectively satisfying as well as being communally coherent, and, secondly, in the creation of opportunities for personal growth and the resolution of problems of living. In accomplishing any of these tasks it is apparent that an understanding of interpersonal processes and group intervention skills are vital. Indeed, some argue that group work is the 'natural' method for residential work. This is an oversimplification, but there is no doubt that knowledge of group behaviour and skills in group work are needed in many areas of residential practice. We suggest the following to be most important:

(1) in developing and managing the 'natural resources' of group living;
(2) in identifying, managing and mitigating the many tensions and stresses encountered in daily living;
(3) in facilitating the integration of the newcomer to the residential setting, and correspondingly, in helping him to prepare for departure from the setting;
(4) in providing opportunities for personal development and life enrichment;
(5) in helping residents find solutions to the interpersonal and other life problems that have often been the cause of their admission into care;
(6) in helping residential staff to exercise constructive and creative leadership, in particular through a continuous process of appraisal and review of the events and happenings of residential life.

DEVELOPING AND MANAGING THE 'NATURAL RESOURCES' OF GROUP LIVING

Residential living by its very nature generates a multitude of interlocking groups. There are the formal groups for eating, sleeping, work, learning, recreation, discussion, decision making and problem solving. There are the numerous informal groups: the friendship groups, the alliances, and many ephemeral groups forming and reforming for specific events and happenings. Although each group has its own structure, content and dynamics, it has to be evaluated for the contribution it makes to the total residential experience.

Many resources needed for the development of identity and for social learning are contained in these myriad relationship networks. Residential staff need to be able to assess differently the needs and capacities of these groups and those of the individuals within them, and to be able to intervene or not as appropriate. Thus the leadership potential of the 'Ralphs', even the 'Jacks' of the group might be identified and developed through the provision of appropriate opportunities.

The tasks of daily living provide focal points for important emotional interactions and social encounters between members of the residential community. These social situations are sources of satisfaction and dissatisfaction, of pleasure, anger or frustration, and they frequently give rise to intense feelings of love and affection, acceptance or rejection, hurt, fear and jealousy.

The skills of group care lie in the organisation and management of these deceptively simple social situations in order to facilitate personal interaction and the development of meaningful relationships. The vast majority of people give little or no conscious thought to the routine activities of the day – getting out of bed in the morning, washing, dressing, bathing, going to the toilet, eating meals and going to bed at night – or they think of them as rather tiresome and time-consuming chores, like the house cleaning, the shopping, the cooking and preparation of meals and the washing up. But for socially deprived people, who live in residential settings, these taken-for-granted daily events and happenings often assume considerable importance.

ENGAGING RESIDENTS IN THE TASKS OF DAILY LIVING

For some, in particular the disabled and the elderly, the lack or loss of opportunity to do what most people do for themselves, and what they themselves have done most of their lives, is a denial of their freedom of choice, a reflection of their dependence and diminished status as human beings. For others, for example many children in residential care, the lack of opportunities to see how meals are prepared, and how food is bought, deprives them not only of important emotional experiences but also of opportunities to acquire the basic social skills necessary if they are to gain mastery over their lives, and to exercise choice wisely.

One approach is to increase the level of participation of residents in the day-to-day affairs and decisions of the unit. The importance of involving residents in the formulation and implementation of decisions and policies which, after all, affect mainly themselves, and the need for opportunities to exercise choice are already recognised in many areas of residential work. Indeed, methods of 'self-government' were employed in certain nineteenth-century institutions, and throughout the present century there have been many attempts to articulate the concept of 'shared responsibility' in residential schools for emotionally disturbed children, and in hospitals organised as 'therapeutic communities'. In these settings the responsibility for the affairs of the community is invested in the total group of staff and residents, who share concerns and discuss common issues and problems at their daily meetings.

Attempting some form of resident participation makes considerable demands on personal qualities, and on the mediating skills of residential staff. Many residential staff fail to tolerate the idea of resident participation as it constitutes a threat to their authority and status. They are not prepared or able to take the risk of relinquishing power or to assume a different kind of leadership from the authoritarianism to which they are accustomed. Where staff have feelings of anxiety about loss of control and loss of authority they are likely to establish 'token' groups which have neither power nor influence.

Their fears are not entirely without foundation. As one study (Millham *et al.*, 1975) of the former approved schools has shown, delinquent boys are adept at subverting the democratic process, which they interpret as a form of permissiveness and therefore something to be taken advantage of. The writer has observed similar processes operating in a 'halfway' hostel for the mentally ill. Around the house were several notices stuck in different parts of the building of the 'keep out', 'do not do this' variety. They were the work of one of the residents, a paranoid young man, who in his role as secretary to the community meetings had achieved considerable power. The effects of his 'rule' were evident in many ways. There was very little interaction amongst the resident group. One of the problems was that the staff, including the warden, had been in post only a short time. They were clearly concerned, but at this stage their interventions in the daily meeting, which were aimed at securing a redistribution of power within the group, were by and large ineffectual.

MANAGING THE TENSIONS OF DAILY LIVING

The present writer's first job in residential work was that of housemaster in a Classifying School (now known as a Regional Assessment Centre). Admitted to the school were boys, aged 10–16 years, following their committal for approved school training by the Juvenile Court. The boys remained in the school for four to five weeks, whilst an assessment was made of their personal, social and educational needs. They were then transferred to another school, which was selected on the basis of the assessment, for a period of social training and education. The housemaster was responsible for a group of about fifteen or sixteen boys, and through his involvement in their day-to-day care made an important contribution to their assessment.

Permanent instability is one of the main features of living and working in a transitory situation like an assessment centre. Anxiety levels remain constantly high as frightened, bewildered newcomers, who are often experiencing their first protracted separation from home, mingle with others, the newcomers of a week or fortnight previous, who themselves are beginning to turn their thoughts to departure to yet another strange situation. With the steady flow of boys arriving and departing, the group is caught in a maelstrom of 'forming, storming, norming and performing' (Tuckman, 1965). For example, the arrival of a single highly disruptive or very disturbed youngster, or a powerful clique of boys who may have engaged together in delinquent exploits, has a profound effect on the entire group. Within very short spans of time new alliances are made, old ones are re-established, leaders are usurped and new scapegoats found.

In this potentially explosive situation, where reactions of 'fight' through expressions of aggression and violence, or 'flight' (Bion, 1961) in the form of absconding, are common, the management of group interaction becomes an important aspect of the caring task. Elements of stability have to be preserved, but opportunities for the expression of anxieties, and the relief of tension have also to be provided. The weak, the 'little 'uns', as in *Lord of the Flies*, and the scapegoats have to be protected from the would-be tyrants, and the positive forces operating in the group have to be developed not only for the common good, but also as a resource for the more vulnerable members.

In the Classifying School, as in most residential settings, the emotional barometer has to be read constantly. A critically low point was often reached on the Sunday teatime, which for many youngsters was a period of sadness and reflection following visits of parents and girlfriends. Sometimes the entire school could be plunged into a trough of depression, and 'trouble', e.g. through absconding, would often follow unless there was an appropriate vehicle for discharging those tensions.

One suspects that the tensions developing in the Classifying School are distillations of many residential experiences. Residential staff experience these tensions, as a result of having to reconcile many competing and conflicting needs in their work: in preserving order and stability in order to engender a sense of trust and security, whilst also remaining responsive to the fluctuating needs of individuals. They are often in the position of having to respond to demands from individuals for dependent, trusting relationships, but in doing so run the risk of arousing feelings of jealousy and envy from other members of the group. There are occasions when they have to be protectively controlling, but they also have to ensure that residents have sufficient freedom to learn from their own actions, and to discover for themselves their own capacities and limitations. Staff can only become more confident in managing these tensions when given the knowledge and opportunity to understand the processes in which they are engaged.

GROUP WORK TO ASSIST ENTRY INTO CARE AND TO PREPARE FOR DEPARTURE

The newcomer to the residential setting is faced with two major tasks. The first is to overcome the sense of loss that arises from any major change of personal circumstances, and to contain and work on one's anxieties about the past, present and future. The second task is to adjust to a new group care situation. In preparing to leave the setting a similar situation occurs. For either event, opportunities are needed to explore subjective feelings about the realities of one's current life situation. We stress the word 'opportunity' because it is possible for some people to want to engage in this reflective activity alone, while others might prefer individual assistance.

However, many might find the support they need through some form of group activity. An example of the type of group that can be developed in child care is described by Beedell (1970–1) who, as a special project, established an activity group in the cellar of a children's reception centre. The aims of the group were: to provide opportunities for children, who were in a state of crisis as a result of their reception into care, to explore aspects of their inner world, and to work through their uncertainties about the future, and present life situation, *away* from the hurly-burly of daily living. The group thus provided much-needed 'breathing space' for the children, and an opportunity for the adults to demonstrate their capacity for acceptance, by giving the children the focused attention they needed to help them retain pieces of their identity.

Although Beedell is describing an experimental project, in which he acted as a supernumerary member of the reception centre's staff, he firmly maintains that there is nothing *in principle* to prevent residential staff from making similar provision themselves as an integral part of their programme, and to give the same sort of attention to insulation, time boundaries, subgroupings of children, availability of adults and attention to internal circumstances.

Admission and departure are not discrete happenings, but are critical parts of a continuum of experience that need to be kept as live issues throughout a person's period of residence. Unfortunately residential staff are not always aware of the potential use of group situations that arise naturally for discussion of these and other sensitive issues.

GROUP WORK TO ASSIST PERSONAL DEVELOPMENT AND LIFE ENRICHMENT

In the course of their development the majority of people find numerous opportunities for learning through social interaction within the family, in the activities of the classroom, the youth club, in the work place, and in the informal groups of the playground, the street corner, the adolescent gang, and in the social clubs of adult life. These activities serve many different purposes according to the stage of development reached. Some naturally outlive their value and usefulness, while others are sustained or modified throughout life.

Many of the people in residential care have not always had or been able to take full advantage of the opportunities presented to the population at large, and their personal development and quality of experience has sometimes suffered in consequence. In some instances this is due to the impoverishment of their previous environment, in others it might arise because of intrinsic handicaps or disabilities. Therefore an important aspect of the residential task is to find ways and means of providing compensatory or supplementary experiences for people who have experienced these different forms of deprivation.

We should add that this is an area of residential care which is often neglected, for many reasons. One problem is that focused attention on the social and educational aspects of residential care makes considerable demands on staff resources. They do not always have the time, or indeed the ingenuity, to plan, prepare and manage a full programme of activities in addition to their other responsibilities. Nevertheless, as far as possible we would always encourage and hope to educate residential staff to make creative use of the opportunities for group activity that develop throughout the course of the day, and to make optimum use of the resources to be found in the immediate neighbourhood and community for these purposes.

The nature of group living, however, sometimes prevents the development of experiences that are commonly found in families or independent living arrangements. An obvious example is the preparation and costing of food, which we have already said are important sources of experimentation and learning for young and old alike. If we consider fully the problems presented by the handicaps and disabilities of the people who enter residential care, then alternative ways of providing these experiences need to be found. Activity groups of various kinds can thus serve useful educational, social and therapeutic purposes by stimulating interest and relieving boredom and apathy. For example, elderly people in care can often regain the use of their bodies and become more alert and aware of their environment if given the appropriate encouragement through group activity.

GROUP WORK TO HELP RESIDENTS FIND SOLUTIONS TO THEIR 'PROBLEMS OF LIVING'

People in residential care continue to experience many besetting problems: of personality, of handicap, of social adjustment, and of interpersonal relationships. Some difficulties arise directly from the nature of the residential experience itself; others are related to the circumstances surrounding their admission to care. We have already discussed and illustrated how a carefully constructed and managed residential experience can enable them to cope more effectively with some of these problems. In this process we have placed considerable emphasis on the development of the 'here and now' as an effective learning experience.

Nevertheless, group work can also serve specific therapeutic aims. Clearly the precise purpose and nature of such activity must vary according to the specific needs of the residential clientele. For example, we would not advocate the establishment of residents' meetings in a residential nursery, although we would consider the development of an activity or play group there. We might suggest that the residents of a hostel for the physically disabled be given the opportunities to discuss and share the difficulties they encounter in their personal and social relationships, and for those in homes for the mentally handicapped to develop skills in social interaction, for example, through role play and various forms of simulation.

Group therapy and group counselling have been important therapeutic tools in institutional treatment, particularly in prisons and hospitals, for many years. It is not our intention to discuss the relative merits of different methods that can be employed, except to agree with Maier (1965) that the principles underlying their application (and by implication, problems regarding their usefulness and effectiveness) remain the same whether they form part of a residential programme or not.

However, the establishment of specially constituted groups in residential settings always requires careful consideration. First, the aims of the group need to be clarified with all those who are likely to be affected by its development. This includes residential staff who continue to work with the members outside the context of the group. As Whitaker points out, an important condition for effective group work in any context is the creation of a 'sympathetic and trusting' environment (Whitaker, 1976). It is important, therefore, to obtain the consent and co-operation of the primary care staff, who may fear, not always unreasonably, that the group may cause trouble for them by bringing to the surface false hopes and expectations. Thus failure to obtain the co-operation of staff may engender considerable resistance, which often manifests itself in insidious ways. Again, when considering the aims of the group it is important not to see it as a means of remedying the deficiencies of the primary care situation, but rather as an additional resource.

Also, it must be remembered that group work is not a panacea for the difficulties experienced by people in residential care. Treatment goals, therefore, should be modest rather than over-ambitious. For example, Tutt (1974) in his evaluation of a group counselling programme for the boys of an approved school stresses that radical changes of behaviour and personality could not have been expected from the group experience. But he considered his groups to serve more limited, nonetheless useful purposes, of improving verbal skills, of facilitating communication between staff and residents' cultures, and of securing some degree of attitude change.

THE NEED FOR CONSTRUCTIVE AND CREATIVE LEADERSHIP

In *Lord of the Flies* we see in the repressive regime developed by the tyrannical Jack the consequences of Ralph's inability to govern by democracy. Events analogous to this are found in residential work, and for similar reasons. Jane Sparrow records a series of episodes in an approved school for girls, following which the headmistress, the artistic and gentle Miss Gracey, loses almost total control. She has to leave, with the school in a state of chaos. Her successor, the authoritarian Miss Strang, extinguishes by harsh methods any spark of creativity and vitality remaining in the place, leaving the staff group perhaps more demoralised than before (Sparrow, 1976).

We might ask, then, what leadership qualities are required for residential work. It is doubtful whether a satisfactory answer can be given. Few people would be in agreement about the characteristics required; in general we perhaps seek people who are sufficiently flexible to be decisive when the need arises, but who provide opportunities for others to use their initiative and to assume responsibility themselves whenever appropriate.

We can also state that leadership skills are required by everyone appointed to work in the residential setting, irrespective of status or levels of responsibility. For example, we might examine a typical activity undertaken by a young assistant residential child care worker, left in charge of a group of youngsters for the afternoon. She decides to go to the local park. Once at the park the children scatter and engage in a number of different pursuits. Some take to the swings, others gambol on the grass. Two children demand to be pushed on the swings. The assistant complies with their request, but has to keep an eye on two youngsters who are threatening to quarrel. In anticipation of trouble she leaves the swings and engages the two antagonists in a game of ball. But then a fight does break out, and the worker has to separate them. As she does so one boy turns aggressively on to her. She tries to calm him, but he loses his temper completely, strikes out wildly, runs away, and starts throwing stones indiscriminately. Made anxious by the spectators gathering to view the spectacle, she hurriedly rounds up her group and they all troop back to the home feeling dejected and frustrated. The problems do not end there, as her colleagues express their displeasure at having to pick up the pieces of a shattered and discontented group.

In any subsequent discussion on the events of the afternoon we might ask a number of questions about how that worker used her understanding of the group to cope with the situations she encountered. We might ask questions about the *social context* chosen for the afternoon's activities. Remembering that the coping capacities of very disturbed youngsters, particularly in exposed social situations, may be very weak, we might ask why the park? Is there a more suitable venue available? Then there are questions about the *composition* of the group. Who chose who to go with whom? Knowledge of personal preferences in relationships is important, as it enables the worker to assess the likely effect of A accompanying B, again remembering that quite intense emotional conflicts and rivalries may be acted out in the group. We might ask about the content of the afternoon's activity, and whether the worker used the time effectively or succeeded in her efforts to maintain the interests of the group. Finally, we might discuss her *management* of the different interactions occurring in the group. On what basis did she respond to one child rather than another? Was it a question of he who shouts loudest receives most attention? By moving from one subgroup to another, would it have been possible to prevent the crisis from erupting?

The tasks (a) of helping this young worker, not only to deal with her anxieties, but also to learn from any mistakes made, and (b) of repairing any damage caused to working relationships would usually belong to the senior staff at the home. We might of course question how it was that a young and inexperienced worker was left to deal with a group of potentially difficult youngsters unaided. But this leads to another aspect of the leadership issue, namely the knowledge and skills required for staff development and supervision. Senior staff in residential settings transact much of their business in groups: in staff meetings, case conferences and in supervision groups, in addition to any involvement they may have in the group activities of residents.

It is regrettable that too few opportunities exist for residential workers to receive appropriate training and to be given the support and supervision needed to develop the skills required for these important areas of their work. It may be that the group work consultants now being employed in many social work agencies have an important role to play in the provision of such support.

CONCLUSION

In this paper we have analysed various aspects of the residential task and discussed how knowledge and skills in working with groups could enhance the quality of the residential experience. In addition to the need to develop interventive skills in natural group situations, there has also been discussion of special purpose groups.

PART II

ASPECTS OF TRAINING

God guard me from those thoughts men think
In the mind alone;
He that sings a lasting song
Thinks in a marrow bone.
W. B. Yeats

Training for group work must include opportunities for the learner to use and extend his 'marrow-bone' knowledge of group processes, and the meaning of his experience in relation to the work of the group. Knowledge 'about' derived from models and theories may be the screen against which that more intimate 'knowledge how' will be reviewed, accepted and revised. Knowledge 'about' can be all too easily blocked off in the intellect and discarded as a source of enrichment for action.

In this section the four papers describe different ways of helping novices in group work to integrate knowledge and skill.

Tom Douglas describes his particular way of teaching group work: enabling students to learn about group processes and the means of influencing them is perhaps a better way to describe the sequence. Douglas links the informational and experiential aspects of his course in such a way that the whole teaching/learning process within the group work sessions exemplifies aspects of a group work approach. As he states, three levels of learning are established at the outset, informational, experiential and exemplary.

Barry Palmer describes a model of group relations training that assumes group members are influenced by unconscious intentions as well as their perceptions and feelings about 'here and now' events. The group is viewed in its institutional context, and the dynamic relationship between the group and its environment is kept in view. The training workshops he describes are designed to further the understanding of organisational behaviour, and of the complex patterns of intra- and inter-group relationships which evolve. He discusses the special significance for social workers of this kind of understanding, faced, as they so frequently are, with a conflict between the needs of the individual and the needs of a group.

Palmer recognises that this approach to learning about group behaviour brings some themes into prominence and leaves others relatively unexamined: he outlines the elements of group life most frequently highlighted. As he states, this choice does not denigrate existing theories of group behaviour. The courses he describes are planned to enable the participants to become more aware of the theories with which they are already working.

Douglas and Palmer describe ways of learning about groups, and about the various roles one plays in them. Hilary Davies describes how one helps social workers to learn to develop their work using a group experience. Through case discussions in group supervision, the individual is helped both to enlarge his personal framework for acting in one-to-one situations, and to become more sophisticated in using the resources of a group. As most social workers operate in a team context this method seems a good means of preparation.

Hilary Davies in discussing the objectives of group supervision brings together some useful theories about the nature of adult learning. She suggests some guidelines of composition and size for fieldwork teachers who are planning to start group supervision. The paper concludes with a discussion of the advantages and disadvantages of group supervision, and includes the comments of students who have been involved in placements where it has been used.

Herbert Laming and Sheila Sturton point out that for most social services departments group work is still a peripheral activity. In their paper they describe the attempt made by one department to promote the use of group work as an alternative or addition to casework intervention. The development of group work became the responsibility of a newly appointed group work adviser, whose developing role is described, and could usefully act as a model for those taking up a similar post. The progress rested mainly on the regular in-service training sessions offered. The results achieved both in field and residential care encouraged the authors to believe that a wider use of group work would be beneficial to many clients.

Chapter 6

A MODEL FOR TEACHING GROUP WORK

Tom Douglas

Group work as a method of social work is a fairly recent importation to this country. This means in effect that few workers have received a training in the use of group methods which is as rooted in tradition, practice and ethos as other social work teaching, or have been offered practical experience in placements long established and fairly certain of their purpose. Obviously this situation has far-reaching effects, not least in the area of social work education.

What needs to be clearly stated at the outset is that there is a considerable confusion, which is very general, about group methods which are primarily directed at the personal growth of the members, and those which are primarily directed to acquiring an understanding of group processes with a view to being able to influence those processes for beneficial ends. There is also added complication of a straight intellectual appreciation of experimental data about groups and about the dynamics of groups. All three areas are valid in their own right, but it is my opinion that to subject students to one under the guise of the others is at best deceitful and insincere and at the worst is possibly dangerous. If a teacher of group work believes implicitly that the only way for students to become group workers is by continuing exposure to a sensitivity training group of their peers, i.e. attempting to enhance personal awareness, then this should be clearly stated as the objective and not disguised as either a course in group work methods or group dynamics. Above all, students would then be given the choice of opting out, especially if the group pressures involved in taking this action were made explicit and worked through.

What follows is an attempt to explain the basic ideas which lie behind my courses in group work for social work students, bearing in mind that these basic ideas are used in different combinations and sequences to meet the needs of different groups of students. This approach is eclectic and attempts to eschew theoretical bias, but I am well aware that concentrating on the area of understanding group processes and the means of influencing them does not and should not eliminate any spin-off in terms of enhanced personal growth for the student members of the group. Equally, experience without the informational inputs which are relevant and timely suffers greatly. Role playing, drama, exercises, games, audio and visual recording processes, as well as the more ordinary forms of learning reinforcement, are used, but students are offered the opportunity of not taking part in any of the activities offered, and such refusals serve to throw light on the group pressures involved and the fallacy of free choice. Above all, great care is taken to ensure that as far as is humanly possible all students are aware at all stages of what is happening, all unclear plans are discussed and the course proceeds on the basis of general consensus.

Social work students need to discover in what ways a group can be a useful social work tool; they also need to discover whether it is a tool which is compatible with their outlook, personality and abilities. Obviously there are many ways in which such a learning process can take place and there are many alternative ideas and experiences which can be offered. What is written here is a personal approach based upon consciously selected elements accepted because of their proven value, and which is in no way meant to suggest that other approaches are less valid or less effective.

PLAN OF GROUP WORK COURSE

The group work courses referred to here are confined to one academic year. In the case of one-year postgraduates this is roughly one hour a week throughout their course, i.e. twenty-seven hours; for the two-year course the time amounts to two hours per week throughout the first and last terms of their second year, i.e. thirty-six hours. Thus both courses are in a position to bring to the sessions some experience of social work practice and a grasp of basic foundation knowledge. The postgraduate group is usually small enough to work with as a unit, i.e. ten to twelve members; the two-year course second year is usually split into three to four work groups probably identical in composition to seminar groups used in the first year. The two-year course therefore starts with a fairly large number of contact hours to their credit and the postgraduate course starts from scratch as strangers.

It seems axiomatic that in the process of learning about social group work an excellent point of departure should be the questions 'what is a group?' and 'why are groups used in social work?' My assumption is that the theoretical concepts about groups which derive from social psychology and sociology are multi-dimensional and usually confusing when offered as information unrelated to any form of experience. By starting from the questions given above we are making certain that the information about groups in general and social work groups in particular which is already in the possession of the student group is expressed and discussed. It will be, for instance, immediately apparent that there is a multiplicity of views about what constitutes a group and these can be compared to the kind of groupings observable amongst the members of the course, so that they can examine whether they constitute a group and, if so, in what sense.

Shortly after this point, two things become evident. One is that information which is related to a perceived need on the part of the course members is information which is readily absorbed and equally readily used. Its purposes and relationships to factual existence are clear. Two is that the whole teaching/learning process within the group work sessions exemplifies aspects of a group work approach. Thus three levels of learning are established at the outset, informational, experiential and exemplary.

As information about different kinds of groups is accepted it becomes necessary to understand why groups can have such an enormous influence upon human behaviour. At this stage the course members are asked to visualise with closed eyes the worst thing that can happen to them. Inevitably all these 'horrors' are concerned with some form of isolation, either by being cut off physically, being deprived of senses or being subjected to intense loss. Other visualisation experiences emphasise these points about isolation, and lead directly to informational inputs from the tutor and from literature about the formation of self-concepts and the dependent state of the individual on personal contact and confirmation of himself and his ideas by others, in order to efface the basic fear of having to accept the terrifying fact of separateness. This is the common well from which authors, poets and dramatists have drawn inspiration for centuries; for example:

> deep within every man lies the dread of being alone in the world, forgotten by God, overlooked among the tremendous household of millions and millions. That fear is kept away by looking upon all those about one who are bound to one as friends or family, but the dread is nevertheless there and one hardly dares think of what would happen to one of us if all the rest were taken away. (Kierkegaard, 1938)

This leads indisputably to an examination of the need of human beings for confirmation and affirmation and the recognition that this can only be done by contact with others. In turn this produces recognition that all human beings have existed in and been influenced by groups from the moment of birth. Here exercises about reference groups and their influence are used and material about conformity and group pressure is sought and discussed. Some analysis of the pressures operating within the course group is made. Most of this material has integrative links with matter which is being discussed in other parts of the social work course.

Now it becomes possible to assert the first of several general propositions, which is *that groups have influenced people all their lives and the power of the group to influence is in direct proportion to the need of the individual to be accepted by it.*

This is quickly followed by a second general proposition which forms the basis of the answer to question two, from which the learning process started. It is, *if group pressures have created the current situation in which every human being exists, is it not feasible that other group pressures consciously directed can be used to change that current state, however slightly, especially if it is not a well functioning one*?

At this stage, course members have become aware of the variety of groups, of their essential nature, of the power of groups and finally of the reasons for using groups in social work practice.

The next development most naturally stems from the fact that the course members, having become aware of group pressure both intellectually and experientially within their own group, express a desire to know how such pressure can be used to modify behaviour. Now we have to discuss whether pressure to conform and the need to be accepted are the sum total of processes within a group. Quite obviously they are not. Members of a group influence one another as individuals, the group grows and changes, standards of behaviour are outlined and positions of authority and power change hands. In short, through examining the progress within the course group it becomes apparent that something like ten processes seem to be produced whenever a collection of people have operated together over a period of time.

The groups will now be asked to make a tape-recording lasting about thirty minutes of one of their group discussions – the subject of discussion being left to the group's choice. (Frequently the tape seems to be produced of the group discussing what they would like to discuss). This tape is listened to several times by the members who made it, and they then individually write an analysis of it in terms of the group processes they can identify and in what way they think these processes are being influenced, if at all, and by whom. Comparison of these documents usually reveals wide discrepancies in perception, but it also reveals remarkably consistent recognition of the major processes and attempts at influencing them. We are now in a position to assert a third proposition which is *group processes are identifiable and attempts to influence them can be recognised.*

It is noted at this stage that the usual theories of behaviour which are normally associated with learning about groups and almost exclusively oriented toward the individual have been bypassed in favour of seeing what actually occurs in a group as a functioning entity. Obviously the interpretation of group processes and the choice of those which are to be used depends a great deal upon the kind of theoretical information and understanding possessed by the group worker. Students are now asked to relate their reading and experience outside the group to its current workings.

It then becomes important to discuss the question of leadership. Not only have the group members become aware of the development of their own groups to the point where the use of power has been questioned, but examination of the tapes has revealed many subtle and direct attempts by members to influence decisions. The power of the course tutor is also revealed and challenged as a necessary part of the development of the group as a whole. Exercises are used which require co-operative effort on the part of all group members in order to achieve some fairly complex goal. Socio drama plays a great role here because it combines so many possible learning opportunities.

Each work group is given a group situation usually involving some specific interaction and asked to produce it as a dramatic interlude lasting about five minutes. It is made clear that the production of the play is only one of several objectives, others being the way in which the group works to achieve its ends and the emergence of leaders; the choice or imposition of roles also is stressed as important. An observer from another group is placed with each work group, charged with the task of observing in detail the processes of the group constructing the play and with being able to check explanations given by group members of their behaviour at a later stage.

Beyond the role play experiences this exercise gives us the opportunity to look at the ways in which people attempt to direct the behaviour of their peers in task-oriented or socio-emotional ways. It reveals our general lack of perception about decision making in groups, sharpens observational abilities and introduces the idea that watching people in group situations is an essential skill of the group worker. Socio drama is usually followed by inputs on leadership acts and the concepts of social power, with students being encouraged to examine what forms of social power they are given by others in different situations including a work situation. Observation skills are heightened by the use of 'fish bowl' techniques with one group of students sitting around another group which is holding a discussion. Each student in the outer ring is paired to a student in the inner ring whom he is charged to observe closely. At the end of the allotted period each pair of students discusses between themselves what was seen and what was felt to be done. Later, positions are reversed and the whole process gone through again.

Observation of behaviour becomes easier in this kind of situation because it is removed from those social taboos which would inhibit it. Students quickly learn that the way they feel they are being seen by others does not always bear a very close resemblance to what others see, and the possibility of misunderstanding based on mistaken assumptions tends to become clearer. The learning which takes place here is reinforced by exposure to video-taped group discussions in the audio-visual studio. Here students see themselves as they have not been able to do before. They also see more clearly the group processes because the tape can be stopped and replayed several times when significant movements are taking place.

Each student is now reasonably well aware of group processes and of an enhanced sensitivity to other group members and to his self-image. The stage (about halfway through the course) has been reached when all this newly acquired understanding has to be directed toward the practice use of groups in social work. Usually some students will have attempted to establish groups of clients in their fieldwork placements, and the practical problems of these exercises are fed back into the course group and related to the available information about such problems. What tends to emerge from this is the fact that knowing about groups and being able to establish a viable social work group are two very different things. Another general proposition emerges which is *all social work groups are artificial but exist within an environment which imposes certain constraints upon them.*

APPLICATION TO SOCIAL WORK GROUPS

This is quickly followed by the realisation that social work groups are usually conceived within the mind of the group worker, and that effective conceptualisation requires information about proposed client members which is significantly different from that normally obtained by social workers. Knowing what group processes are and understanding to some degree the possibility of influencing them, the students are now led to see that client needs in a given instance can best be met by a certain kind of group. The process of matching is well on the way to being understood and the selection of clients and the effects of group composition become clearer.

Effective groups are those which are conceived and created so that the processes within the group can be activated or reduced by the group worker and/or the group to meet the assessed needs of the members as nearly as possible. This proposition becomes more clearly understood through the analysis of the creation and design of actual groups and of recorded material, and through the exercise of attempting to create designs for groups to meet explicitly stated client needs. These exercises reveal the need for knowledge about intensity of group experience, about size, timing, frequency, duration and styles of leadership. The obvious fallacy of attempting to influence behaviour over short periods of time, a frequent occurrence in practice, is revealed, and a clear idea of matching what is available in a group situation with what needs to be achieved to enhance client functioning emerges. Eventually students develop forms of instruments which relate the known effects of modifying group processes to the needs of client members.

What also emerges is the continuum of leadership practice from directive to non-directive, with the realisation that the social work philosophy of self-help tends to push social workers towards establishing groups which become self-directing. The concept of responsibility for the creation of groups is studied in the work groups, and a realisation formed that different points on the leadership continuum are necessary at different times in the life of one group as well as for different kinds of groups. Thus responsibility for ensuring that group members have the experience, the level of group sophistication required for their operational ends belongs exclusively to the group worker.

Other factors now emerge, e.g. open and closed groups, groups within institutions and the range of possible activities. Because of the nature of their own learning experience, students tend to accept that talking is only one form of activity which takes place within a group. Using their own learning experience they can usually see quite clearly the benefit of all kinds of activities including games, sports, hobbies, drama, work, role play, etc. Button (1974) gives examples of role play being used with groups of adolescents to prepare them for situations which they will have to meet and of which they have either no previous experience or have had a bad experience, e.g. job applications and interviews. Activities like these can be seen to produce a basis for discussion of difficulties which is relevant, related to immediate experience and recent.

The student groups are closed groups in the sense that they are not added to during the period of the course. Course members are asked to analyse what effect this seems to have had upon them, and to compare this with any group of which they have had experience where members arrived and departed, but the group continued on its way. They learn that closed groups tend to intensify interpersonal relationships, show the phases of group development clearly and to produce norms and standards of behaviour quickly and firmly. Open groups on the other hand are less intense, become very aware of the difficulties of arrival and departure and have problems of the transmission of group culture. Students are quick to see that these peculiarities may be used to great effect by choosing either an open or closed group according to which of the effects is required in a given situation.

USE OF RESIDENTIAL PLACEMENT

After residential placement each student is in a better position to identify the ways in which the environment can affect the creation of groups. Much more clearly than in fieldwork situations the constraints emerge, and also the useless nature of groups which are established with norms and standards at variance with those of the host institution. Groups in residential institutions highlight many other factors which are involved in non-residential groups but which can be overlooked. For instance, students can recognise the problem of withdrawal in a containing situation, the captive audience, and the pressures of larger groups and of the institutional culture.

At this stage role playing becomes very important as students take on the leadership of groups of their peers and endeavour to find out what kind of leadership style is compatible with their life style, and what kind of leadership practice is essential in different kinds of groups. Exercises here concentrate on single leadership with the emphasis on different places in the continuum of directive to non-directive styles–showing that responsibility for created social work groups is always the group worker's, whatever style of leadership he adopts. Other exercises are concerned to cover the problems of shared leadership and the level of co-ordination and co-operation this involves.

Emerging from these experiences comes the need to study recording methods. Students have practised recall of group activities since the early days of the course and have been encouraged to study the few examples of methods of recording which are available in the literature. They have tape-recorded their own groups and noted what the absence of non-verbal communication, apart from tone of voice, does to their perception of a complex group interaction. Also they have seen video-recordings of groups, seen the paraphernalia involved and experienced the anxiety of appearing on television. They know the freedom which having a recorder/observer in the group gives to the leader and have experienced this in action in the co-leader exercises. Now they usually feel that the only valid way of recording a group is to write their impressions of it immediately following the session and to refresh their memory from the notes immediately before starting the next session.

Material about groups from literary sources will have been fed into the course during the whole of its career. Particular interests shown by any student can be discussed and related to the core of the course structure. Thus individual tutorials are always available to students who have a problem about any part of the course or about a group they are working with in their placement. My own on-going experiences as a group leader in a variety of contexts are fed into the course as deemed appropriate, usually as illustrations of particular points which are emerging. The currency of this material goes a great deal of the way to ensuring that what is being discussed or experienced is not only practicable, but is seen as relevant and not just theoretical.

Occasionally, students become very much aware of the blocks to learning which exist in their own particular group and ask for help in overcoming them. This means using some kind of exercise which involves increasing personal awareness. I am aware that there is a controversy about whether a group work teacher, especially on an assessment-based course, can also operate as a group trainer. Having experienced the situation when a colleague was called in to perform this function and also having performed it myself, I would aver that a great deal depends upon the relationship the group of students has with the group work teacher, i.e. the level of trust which has been developed, the extent and intensity of their need, and above all upon the skill of the teacher as a group trainer. As none of these needs are unalterable constraints, it would appear that each situation must be assessed upon its individual merits. But clearly, as in the residential situation, if all members of the student group do not opt to take part, thus creating an elite, it tends to work against the trust and shared experience which the course has partly aimed at generating.

Finally, let it be said that I am aware that many people will say that a particular approach to group work is involved in the foregoing material. It would be tragic if this were not so. No one, even if aware of all that is involved in the group work process, can create learning situations for students which carry any conviction if they are in the form of a sterile exercise developed because someone else believes it to be good and effective. Clearly in this outline much is not accounted for, because it is to be found in the relationship between the group of students and the group work teacher. Equally, much that is known about groups is not found here because of the limits of time, personal preference and the need to create a basic understanding of the processes common to most groups and a skill founded upon that understanding. It is hoped that students will pursue their own areas of interest, but without some stable base upon which to found that pursuit they may either abandon it as fruitless or, worse, become involved in processes of which they have no ability to assess the value for achieving social work ends.

By the time students have completed the course they should have a reasonable base upon which they can build. They should be aware of the place group work occupies in current British social work practice and the band-wagon type pressures that are involved. They should also be quite capable of handling with a degree of competence and confidence group situations which come their way either in their work organisation or in their social work practice.

Chapter 7

FANTASY AND REALITY IN GROUP LIFE: A MODEL FOR LEARNING BY EXPERIENCE

Barry Palmer

I was taking part in a T-group within a group relations laboratory led by a team of Americans. It was in the early 1960s, at a residential centre in Sussex. Somewhere in the middle of the life of the group, I thought of a line of action which we might pursue; I forget now what it was. I explained the idea to the dozen or so men and women in the group and, glancing round the circle, obtained by nods, mumbled assent and other signals what I took to be an adequate measure of support for my proposal. I set about implementing the scheme.

The American trainer interrupted the proceedings to invite us to examine the process of decision making which had taken place. The event was only a few moments past, and clearly remembered. It was possible in retrospect to ask what measure of assent had in fact been obtained; to what extent individuals had been forced to agree or appear very ungracious by the method I had adopted; and whether the swiftness with which the operation had been completed indicated a fear on my part, never put to the test, that if the question were given a longer airing, serious objections might be raised. We went on to identify the variety of conditions which are taken to provide sanction for group action, such as a majority vote, unanimous approval and consensus.

For me, however, the importance of the incident lay not in these later elaborations, but in the recognition that an action, which I had taken unreflectingly and in pursuit of a future goal, had *happened.* Not that I would ever have denied that it had happened, if the question had been raised, but I would not normally have noticed it. Like the actions by which we keep a bicycle in balance as we ride towards the destination on which our attention is fixed, it was automatic and unnoticed. I now saw that the action was significant, and that its effects when explored might prove to be important and unforeseen. While I lived in my imagined future, my colleagues were encountering someone who was using a skilled technique of which he was unaware to disarm them into compliance with his plans. Their subsequent feelings about, and commitment to, the scheme, and to myself, might be significantly coloured by this experience.

The incident I remember now was no doubt not an isolated experience, but stands for a series of less vivid occasions in which the same shift of focus took place. Without knowing exactly what importance the discovery would have, I had recognised that, as someone who worked with other people in training courses, project groups and committees, I might learn something by examining the intuitive actions through which I sought to inform and influence those present. I was like someone who has learned to play the piano by ear, and finds that he must go back to first principles, even at the expense of playing less well for a while, if he hopes to attain the concert platform. (My account of this incident has been influenced by Michael Polanyi's analysis of the nature of skills (1973, pp. 49*ff*.).)

This was the first of two occasions on which my understanding of what might be happening in the groups of which I was a member went through a major transformation. At the second, a weekend conference two years after the event I have described, I assisted a colleague in running a series of sessions for a dozen men and women who had formed a Christian group in an electronics factory. The purpose of the conference was to assist them in taking stock of what they were doing in the factory, and how this measured up to their aspirations. In these particular sessions we were examining their aims and problems as a group, as these manifested themselves in their behaviour and discussion during the sessions. By this time I had had some practice in distinguishing between the content of the discussion in a group, and the total happening in which I was involved, of which the exchange of these ideas was only a part. I had also heard about Bion's description of the unconscious shared assumptions which influence group behaviour (1961), but could not at that time point to any incidents in my experience which were illuminated by these ideas.

During a period of desultory conversation, when the group seemed to have lost their sense of direction and my colleague and I found little that we could contribute, the subject shifted to the character and activities of an industrial chaplain back in the factory. Once again the precise details are now gone, but it was clear that in the eyes of the group the chaplain was unreliable, unhelpful and no credit to his cloth. Whatever the failures of the group in the factory, it appeared that things might have been very different if this chaplain had given his fellow Christians the support and guidance they deserved.

As I listened to this conversation it dawned on me that they were talking about my colleague. Once this supposition was made, the picture they were building up fitted my colleague, as he might be seen by them at that moment, very precisely–particularly regarding his supposed attitude to them, and theirs to him. The effect was eerie. It was clear that their conscious attention was upon the chaplain in the factory; yet the image and emotional colouring of the figure they were depicting were those of the apparently unreliable and unhelpful person in the room (who was also a clergyman). I do not remember whether we suggested to them that they were talking about my colleague; on similar occasions such suggestions have been greeted with incredulity, mockery or anger.

This incident stands out from what must have been a whole series, which bore in upon me that, when people meet, their interaction is influenced by their awareness of the 'here and now' circumstances in which they meet, and by the way they perceive these circumstances. In an established group working at an agreed, feasible task, these influences require no attention (unless there is a wish to study them). In a group which is for some reason unstable, they may distort or swamp any attempt to pursue the objectives for which the group has come together. Such incidents have also alerted me to the fact that people in groups build up a shared mental picture of the internal and external worlds of the group, the roots of which are unconscious, so that the actions of any individual express not only his own personality and intentions, but also the 'personality' and intentions of a group.

These autobiographical illustrations, interpreted in the light of later reflection, may provide a glimpse of the opportunities for increased understanding provided by participating in workshops, working conferences and laboratories on group relations. The account which follows is concerned specifically with the courses and conferences based on the model developed initially by Rice and his colleagues at the Tavistock Institute (Trist and Sofer, 1959; Rice, 1965), and subsequently by the Grubb Institute, at Bristol and Leicester Universities, and by a number of other bodies in the UK and overseas. Under the umbrella of the label 'group relations' many different goals are pursued, some concerned with developing the self-awareness of the individual, some with sensitivity to the communications of others, and some with the influence of the organisation upon the individual, and of the individual upon the organisation. In writing about the Tavistock/Grubb approach, which comes in the third category, I am not meaning to imply that it is the only valid or effective one, though I believe it has particular relevance to social group work. I have supposed that an account of one approach, written from the inside, may be of more use than a general survey.

THE INSTITUTIONAL SETTING

Although this approach has its origins in the small therapeutic groups conducted by Bion at the Tavistock Clinic (1961), the basic unit out of which educational events are constructed must now be seen as the course, conference or workshop as an *institution*, and not as a small group. There is a continuing tendency to regard the T-group (as described, for example, in Bradford and Gibb, 1964), or Small Group (as described by Rice, 1965; also called the Study Group), consisting of eight to fourteen participants, as the core event in the course, to which other events are tacked on, but this is no longer consistent with the theoretical basis of the Tavistock/Grubb courses. These are designed to further the understanding of institutions and organisations, and of the complex patterns of intra- and inter-group relationships which evolve within them. The Small Group in such a course, like any client group set up in a social work setting, maintains itself in an environment, and can only be understood if the dynamic relationship between the group and this environment is kept in view. Even in an isolated Small Group, meeting once a week, it is evident that the behaviour of the participants reflects their beliefs about the organisation sponsoring the course, and the fantasies aroused in them by the nature of the premises in which they meet.

A course may be residential or non-residential. If full-time, it may extend over any period from two days to a fortnight. Various programmes of intermittent sessions have also been employed. The purpose of the course is described as that of learning about the dynamics of group behaviour within institutions, with special attention to certain factors, such as authority, power, freedom, control, leadership and organisation; and to do so by studying an institution, and groups within it, in which one is a participant.

The programme consists of a number of events – Small Group, Large Group, Inter-Group, and others – each comprising a series of sessions interwoven with those of other events. The task of the Small and Large Group events is to provide opportunities to learn about the dynamics of group behaviour, by studying the behaviour of those who constitute the group, as it happens. The emphasis is upon each participant's experience of what is happening in the 'here and now'. The task of the Inter-Group event is similarly to provide opportunities to learn about the dynamics of inter-group relations, by studying the behaviour of those who make up a constellation of groups, in the 'here and now', in particular that of those who represent one group to another. The task of each event is clearly defined, and is commonly taken even by staff to be a task assigned to the members, which it is not. It represents an undertaking on the part of the management of the course, that each event will provide opportunities to learn about group behaviour, whether or not they are taken.

Most courses also include a number of sessions in which the participants' experience in the course can be related to theories of group and organisational behaviour, and to the participants' own work.

The staff of the course constitute its management, and as such are collectively responsible for it. They also take the role of consultant within the course, providing leadership to member groups by seeking to identify and put into words what they feel to be happening at any given moment. They seek not merely to label occurrences, but to give their evidence for their assertion, and to say *why* the group is behaving in the way they have suggested. In a session to which several members had come late, the consultant might feel, and say, that he had become a dangerous person to the group, who might take them to task for being late. Such a statement is of limited use by itself, since members can only confirm or deny it. A more developed statement would provide more scope for working at the evidence for the observation and the reasons for the group's attitude: 'I feel at the moment as though I have become a dangerous person who is expected to take members to task for being late. When John A arrived he said he had imagined himself being told to go away. Sarah B said she had been glad to meet another member of the course on the stairs, presumably to give her an alibi. Joan C avoided taking the nearest chair, which was next to me, and said on reflection that this was not just to get an ashtray: she did not want to sit next to me. Since the idea of lateness was not introduced by me, I suspect that the group is making me into an angry, reprimanding person, so that they can preserve the idea of a friendly, welcoming group which it is good to come back to. Otherwise they would have to accept some of the painful feelings, of letting each other down, for example, which go with the pleasant feelings of beginning to value the group.'

The consultant makes many comments which are not as put-together as this, but he is continuously working towards contributions which identify behaviour stemming from fantasies and assumptions, held in common by group members, of which they are unaware. He does not take up the role of chairman, or initiate exercises, on the grounds that part of his job is to assist in the examination of the group's fantasies about his own power and authority. He does not short-circuit this learning process by taking the power attributed to him for granted.

Faced with a consultant who does not fulfil many of the group's expectations of a leader or teacher, and with an object of study, the group, which is elusive, the participants become intermittently caught up in proliferating 'survival strategies' (Palmer and Reed, 1972), in the attempt to maintain for themselves a coherent, secure social structure which will protect them from feelings of chaos, insecurity and absurdity. In Bion's terms (1961, pp. 143*ff.*), the basic assumption group becomes dissociated from, and tends to overwhelm, the work group. This may not sound very useful; but it is the opportunity to experience being overwhelmed by the feelings and fantasies of the basic assumption group, to recover, and to recognise the experience, which the courses seek above all to provide. (I am indebted to Eric Miller of the Tavistock Institute, in papers prepared for the staff of a conference, for making this objective explicit.)

EVENTS

The form and typical content of the events most frequently included in these courses have also been described, at different stages in their evolution, by Trist and Sofer (1959), Rice (1965), and contributors to Colman and Bexton (1975) and Miller (1976).

Groups comprising up to about fifteen members
It has been found that groups comprising between ten and thirteen participants, including one consultant, provide optimum conditions for learning about group processes in a simple social setting. These are generally referred to as Small Groups or Study Groups. The Small Group provides the most favourable opportunity to recognise the influence of unconscious shared fantasies upon group life, including the fantasies which influence behaviour within a dependent relationship such as that between leaders and followers.

Some recent courses have included a 'Mini-Group' or 'Very Small Group', consisting of five or six members and a consultant. Comparison between behaviour in groups of the two sizes suggests that people in the smaller group establish a relationship with the group by asserting their individuality, so that the character of the group for its members is mainly determined by the individuals of which it is comprised. In the larger group there is a greater tendency for members to lose their distinctiveness, so that an idea of a group is built up which is less dependent upon the prominence or withdrawal of individual members. (As group size is increased beyond about a dozen, the tendency to form subgroups increasingly complicates the picture. Groups of over about fifteen are therefore unsuitable for pursuing the aims of the Small Group event, though they are of course no less valid or interesting for study.)

The Small Group event thus provides the most favourable setting for coming to recognise the influence of the shared idea of a group upon the behaviour of individuals. This may be a particularly difficult shift of attention for social workers who are more at home working with individual clients, and whose habitual focus of attention is the client as an individual rather than the group of two which comprises social worker and client. The Small Group provides opportunities for discovering and exploring the fantasies which arise between leaders and followers, and how both react to the anxieties aroused in them by their part in a dependent relationship. Many social workers have recognised in themselves, in their feelings about consultants, some of the feelings their clients may have about them. They have also been able to use the consultant to examine vicariously how the social worker responds to the pressures placed upon him by a client or client group.

Because of this identification with the consultant, the Small Group event can also be a misleading experience in isolation from other events. In the absence of other models, those who work professionally with groups may begin to imitate elements in the consultant role which are not consonant with the different task in which they are engaged in their own work. Alternatively, they may violently resist the imagined suggestion that the consultant is demonstrating universal principles for conducting groups, to the extent that he rejects elements in the role which have significance for his own role.

Groups comprising more than fifteen members

Many courses include the study of groups which are too large for the individual in them to hold in his mind, consistently, an idea of the group in which every member is distinctly identified. He tends to be preoccupied with a few larger-than-life individuals, and with the group as an entity which, to a greater extent than in smaller groups, takes on a life of its own. Often this group is felt to be powerful, menacing and prone to violence; at other times it is a warm sea of emotion in which one can sink into blissful oblivion.

The most usual Large Group size is thirty-five to seventy members (see Kreeger (1975) for a valuable collection of papers on training and therapy in large groups). Recently there has been increased interest in what has been called the Median Group, which consists of eighteen to twenty-eight members and is the size of many committees, classes and small residential establishments. The Median Group appears to be inherently unstable, in that it holds out to the individual a promise of the kind of interpersonal relationships which can be established in smaller groups, which cannot be fulfilled. The group tends to take on the configuration of a smaller, 'in' group and a remnant of 'out' individuals. The membership of the in-group and the remnant may fluctuate or, as in many committees, become institutionalised.

Those who work professionally with Large Groups, whether within the size ranges employed in these events or larger still, and whether gathered together or dispersed within an organisation, can gain valuable insight from this event into the pressures of such groups upon the individual. Others who work only in pairs and small groups may discover how they react to larger social systems, such as their department. If they tend to avoid the anxieties aroused in them by larger groups, they may consider the effect of this upon the integration of their own work into that of their agency.

Inter-group and institutional relations

There are several designs for events in which the participants experience and try to understand the way groups behave in relations with other groups. According to one model the participants form groups amongst themselves and, with the help of consultants, study the relations which evolve between them, using representatives to carry messages, negotiate meetings, and exchange views of the feelings and fantasies which groups have about each other. Another model focuses attention upon the relationship between the members (i.e. students) and staff of the course, and thus brings authority relationships within an institution sharply into focus.

Whilst inter-group theory is less developed than small group theory, so that the staff contribution in such events is less consistent, the incidents which arise are frequently so rich in relevance to professional, social and political relationships outside that the implications cannot be fully explored within the course. It also has the advantage that, since it entails action as well as sitting and talking, it invites the participants to reveal, through behaviour, the beliefs and fantasies which inform their work – to reveal them, not only to others but to themselves. This is important with people like social workers whose knowledgeability about human behaviour may limit their spontaneity in the Small and Large Group events.

Learning about inter-group relations has relevance to the group worker whose work entails obtaining permission, resources and goodwill from his agency, other agencies, courts, caretakers of premises, schools, the police and other bodies. It highlights the distinct skills which are required in creating and sustaining the project as a facilitating environment within which the client group can pursue its aims. It also demonstrates the proneness of all groups which have value to their members to idealise themselves and project hostility, meanness, stupidity, corruption and malign power upon external bodies. The group worker may therefore be alerted to the dangers of confirming his clients' beliefs that they live in a hostile environment, when he is seeking to help them form a more realistic appraisal of it.

Since coherent action on the part of a group entails speaking and acting through representatives, the event provides a stimulus for the group worker to consider on whose behalf he acts – the agency, the client group, the social work profession, the taxpayer – and the authority he has from these groupings.

AREAS OF EXPLORATION

The approach to learning about group behaviour described here brings some themes into prominence and leaves others relatively unexamined. The illumination of these themes may be more significant to the participant than the understanding gained of the behaviour of groups of different sizes, or of inter-group processes as such. I wish therefore to discuss some of the elements of group and organisational life which are most frequently highlighted.

Unconscious processes

As has been said, the staff aim to increase the participants' awareness of the unconscious processes which influence relations within and between groups. It sometimes appears to participants that consultants are putting forward assertions about bizarre and primitive motivations which, even if present, cannot be taken into account in normal social work practice. Insofar as assertions are unsubstantiated they are rightly treated with scepticism; I have already discussed (pp. 85–6, above) the importance of providing evidence for interpretations, and explanations of *why* the group is behaving in the way suggested.

The justification for going beyond the common sense, taken-for-granted view of what is happening in the group is that, if one reflects upon the assumptions implied by people's behaviour, these frequently appear to have arisen from thought-processes other than common sense. Often we accept a shared common sense view of what is happening in a group or institution, the power of which is such that we never notice the discrepancies between this view and actual events. Thus, for example, a group of social workers may believe, and assert, that they are helping and caring for one of their number who is in distress, and the belief may be so powerful that no one notices that the continuing attention of the group is increasing the member's distress. The suggestion that the group is demonstrating a shared wish to create a client to look after is often strongly resisted, because it conflicts with group members' images of themselves as caring people.

In the group work setting destructive projection and scapegoating may be averted if the group worker is alive to the possibility that the behaviour of group members may reflect the state of the group as a social system, as well as the history and external circumstances of individuals. In a hostel for offenders, for example, it is only too easy to regard a resident's stealing as a manifestation of a propensity to offend, and overlook the possibility that it is a response to shared fantasies in the hostel that, for example, some residents are getting preferential treatment from the staff. The former view leads to preoccupation with the offending resident, the latter to consideration of the origins of the shared fantasies.

The client relationship

The relationship between staff and members in a course is represented by various mental images, at different times and with different constituencies. It may be seen as one between management and shopfloor, teachers and pupils, parents and children, prison officers and inmates, or social workers and clients. These images may be put into words by members or, more significantly, made manifest in their actions. In the early stages of a course members can often only 'behave' their expectations; in the later stages it is possible to identify in words the expectations they have been manifesting in behaviour, and so enable them to assess the adequacy of their view of, say, the worker–client relationship, which they have used as a model for the staff–member relationship.

In one non-residential course for social workers, an opening plenary introduction was followed immediately by the first session of the Small

Group event. In one of the Small Groups, after a few mutual introductions, the group lapsed into a long and painful silence. The members' behaviour seemed to imply the belief that they could do nothing until the consultants had told them how to proceed, and aroused in the consultants fears that the group would break up before the end of the course. At this moment members were apparently prepared to abort the course and learn nothing, rather than act as though they had any views or feelings to contribute. A consultant eventually broke the silence, saying that he felt like one of the prison staff who were at that time being faced with the decision whether to force-feed IRA prisoners or to let them die. This imagery appeared to catch hold of some of the feelings in which the members were immersed – feelings perhaps of being imprisoned, of hunger, of dying – because the group was temporarily released to begin to discuss what was taking place. Most of the course continued in this uncomfortable vein, yet comments subsequently indicated that many had learned a lot from the experience. Towards the end it was possible to discuss the fix in which consultants and members had found themselves at the beginning, arising from their differing expectations of the nature of their relationship. Members were able to re-examine their own relationships with clients, both from their experience of the 'client' position, and from their identification with the plight of the consultants.

Role and authority

The stated aims of most courses based on the Tavistock/Grubb model include that of examining the nature of authority. This is one of the features which distinguish them most clearly from most other approaches to group relations training. Klein and Astrachan have pointed out that the T-group approach also recognises the importance of relations with authority figures, but that the typical roles of T-group trainer and Small Group consultant are very different. The T-group trainer 'deliberately uses his authority in order to get the members to relate to one another in ways which modify the hierarchy and allow collaboration. The trainer thus truly leads . . .' (Klein and Astrachan, 1971, p. 672). The Small Group consultant is described as one who 'performs his task by staying in role. He does not define the activities of others, plan for the group or organise resources. He does not motivate others to attend to the group task' (p. 668). The contrast between the two roles is frequently presented as one between a trainer who is involved with the members of the group, and a consultant who is detached (see, for example, the review of the results of group training by Smith, 1975).

The fundamental issues raised by this contrast are sufficiently fascinating to tempt the writer to go out of role and pursue them without consideration for the purpose of this paper. If he does not do so, it will not be for lack of human feeling, but out of a belief that he has no authority from the editor of this book to do so.

The contrast is not, as is sometimes suggested, merely one of personal or institutional style, but of aim and task. The trainer aims to provide experience of leadership which is participative and open rather than hierarchical, authoritarian and self-concealing. The task of the T-group which his behaviour implies is that of returning people to their organisations with a different model of leadership inside them. There is an implied judgement that the participative, open style of leadership is possible, and would be beneficial, in all the organisations from which the participants come. The consultant aims to provide experience of leadership which is reflective about the leader's experience; which regards the leader's feelings and fantasies as valuable evidence of the state of the working group of which he is a part, which must be understood before it is acted upon. The task implied by his behaviour is that of returning people to their organisations with this attitude to their own on-going experience as leaders. It is judged that this attitude is possible, and would be beneficial, in all the organisations from which the participants come. In both cases there is a value-judgement which needs to be scrutinised; it should, however, be noted that the nature of the judgement is very different in the two cases.

The consultant's role, as thus described, demands that he seeks continually to distinguish between his own feelings, about the group and his position in it, and those induced in him by the group. Bion (1961, p. 149) has described the experience of the consultant who 'feels he is being manipulated so as to be playing a part, no matter how difficult to recognise, in somebody else's fantasy'. The fact that he does not buy all the parts which are offered him – mother, father, god, computer, puppet, slave, devil, hero, brother – gives rise to an impression of detachment. There is no doubt that consultants sometimes use a dead-pan approach as a defence against exposure and intimacy. Insofar as we do this we are unable to fulfil our role, since we are then unable to recognise the shared fantasies which are moulding the group's behaviour. There is, however, another kind of detachment which is a rejection of a defence. In order to do his job the consultant has to tolerate anxieties about rejection and isolation, as well as about intimacy and exposure. If he cannot tolerate separation and hostility, he abandons his working role and accepts a role in the group's shared dream. The social group worker, like the consultant, is faced with steering the same hazardous course, between using his role as a defensive barrier and abandoning his role altogether.

In courses for social workers, as we have seen, the consultant is readily seen as a candidate for the role of caseworker or therapist, with group members either competing to be his client or putting forward one member to represent the needs of them all. If this role is refused, the consultant is frequently seen as an agent of an external management, pressing the task of studying group behaviour upon an unwilling group, and committed to administrative ideals far removed from those of professional social work.

In the Inter-Group event this tendency becomes more prominent. In a course for recently qualified probation officers the staff group found themselves being treated as officials, who were approached over administrative matters like the availability of rooms or the legitimacy of a proposed course of action, but who were not expected, or sometimes even allowed, to give professional advice based on understanding of inter-group relations. It appeared that the officers were demonstrating within the course their view of the job of those in senior grades in their areas.

In interpreting episodes of this kind, the consultant endeavours to distinguish between the varying degrees of power and impotence attributed to him as a person, and the authority he has by virtue of his role. What is the authority delegated to the staff group by the institution or institutions sponsoring the course, and what is the authority delegated to him by the staff group, to take the role of consultant in this event? What authority was the staff group seen to have by the participants or their employing organisations when they applied for the course and so endorsed that authority? He endeavours to make clear that his authority stems from his role, which is the bundle of activities which he contributes to a particular working unit, such as the course as a whole or an event within it. His behaviour is therefore open to assessment and criticism according to its effectiveness in promoting the primary task of the unit in which he is working.

The elucidation of this dimension of organisational behaviour is important for the social group worker, since he also works within an organisational setting, not in a vacuum which he can fill with his own ideals and aspirations. He needs therefore to be alive to the extent and limits of the authority delegated to him in his various activities on behalf of the agency, and to the extent and limits of the authority endorsed by those who accept the role of client.

The effectiveness of the consultant or social group worker is determined by the fit between the role authorised by the organisation and the skill, creativity, courage and imagination which he brings to the role. If his authority is inadequately defined, or the role is incoherent, he may find himself unable to use the personal resources he has. If he lacks the necessary competence, or is unable to use his gifts because of internal conflicts, he will be unable to use the authority delegated to him.

Caring

Many group relations courses for social workers turn out to be collision courses, in which members pursuing one set of goals run into a staff group pursuing another. The conflict is often seen as one between a belief in the priority of the needs of the individual and a belief in the priority of the needs of the group. Faced with a staff who are prepared to allow people to be uncomfortable, frightened and bewildered, course members reject them as the embodiment of all that is bad in management, and seek to establish a counter-culture in which every individual gets the attention and care he wants. The issues raised have special significance for those engaged in social group work, where the same question of priorities arises, and can best be demonstrated through an illustration.

It is the first session of a Small Group. This follows an introductory plenary session, in which the staff have been introduced and the details of the programme explained, and one 'Orientation Group', in which groups of half-a-dozen members have talked about their work and their expectations from the course. A man arrives slightly late, having as we learn later been out to move his car. He finds the chair on which he had placed some papers taken by another member, and takes the one remaining, less comfortable, chair. He demands, belligerently, for someone to introduce him to the two consultants, one of whom is me. There is a heavy pause, in which no one responds to his request.

It is easy, months later, to map out the possible alternative responses for the consultant, as though one were Bobbie Fischer working out alternative lines of approach to a chess position. In the heat of the moment it is less clear whether we responded rationally or defensively. I doubted, fleetingly, whether anyone knew who we were – in which case it would have been reasonable to take the heat off other people and introduce ourselves. I then decided that some members must have picked us out in the opening plenary. In fact each of us had spent the last session with group members who were also in our Orientation Groups. I therefore made no move to solve the group's problem, and neither did my colleague. At a later stage I referred to the unwillingness of group members to assist the latecomer, and tried to promote examination of what this implied.

I have little doubt that group members saw it as the consultants' job to introduce themselves. We were the leaders, we presumably had no doubt who we were, and it was in our power to put a member out of his misery by a simple act. By not doing this we allowed ourselves to become objects of anger and suspicion, without normal human concern, wedded to some undeclared manipulative technique. At this moment care was understood in simple terms as an immediate response to an expressed need, and according to this definition we showed no care.

The justification for our lack of response was our concern that members should learn about the behaviour of groups and, at this stage in the proceedings, about the stresses of joining and forming a group. Why does no member help the latecomer out? What are the grounds for the assumption that the consultants should introduce themselves? Does the latecomer's belligerence conceal fear and confusion, with which no one can empathise because they are having too much trouble overcoming their own?

Almost invariably the consultant is invited, by some such manoeuvre, to show his goodwill and kindness by meeting a simple need. If he succumbs, the group are deprived of an opportunity to grasp the nature of his role, and of the course as a whole. The course is not intended to provide reassurance that somewhere there are authority figures who respond unstintingly to human need, but to allow people to experience some of the dilemmas of working in organisations, in conditions where they can be more fully understood. Insofar as the staff stay in role, they manifest their care for the members' wish to learn.

Having chosen a strategy which opens up some of the anxieties as well as the potentialities of group life, the consultant has the technical problem of assisting in their elucidation. In the example I have given we did not in that session get very far in elucidating the incident of the latecomer. Our prudent backwardness in submitting to the pressure of the group was not matched by a sufficient forwardness in articulating the dilemmas of consultants, latecomer and members in such a way that the incident was comprehended as an emotional experience. The reverberations hung around until the final session, when their influence upon continuing and current relationships became apparent and was discussed. There was thus the opportunity to learn from the whole sequence of events; but other learning possibilities were inevitably lost.

Many people who work professionally with groups are faced with similar problems. Is their task to meet short-term needs or open up longer-term developmental opportunities? In what ways is it necessary for them to show their concern for their clients by satisfying short-term survival needs, so that they are seen as trustworthy when the group enters the turmoil which is integral to any developmental process? And, if their task is developmental, have they the skill and ego-strength to assist people in using crises for learning, or do they bite off more than they can chew?

Purpose of education in group relations

The thesis of this paper is that courses of the type described provide the social group worker with an opportunity to walk around inside various group situations, and identify some of the processes that are going on, and the part they themselves habitually play in these processes. This is education, not training: the precise bearing of what is learned upon the participant's work remains to be determined. It may be major or peripheral, and may be apparent immediately or only after months or years. Nor can the staff of any conference or workshop guarantee the issues which will be illuminated, even for the most committed participant. Although useful theories of group behaviour have been developed, every event is unique and evolves out of the process by which it is set up and the character and concerns of those taking part.

Every individual brings to social relations a repertoire of habitual responses which are unique to himself or herself, and which serve the function of bringing a potentially unpredictable encounter within a framework of conventions and role relationships. This sets a limit to what he has to worry about, and enables him to direct his attention and energy to achieving the outcome he wants. We normally learn how to do this, by apprenticeship and by experience, without knowing what we know, and most people get by with what they learn informally and unreflectingly. Social work is one of a cluster of activities in which more than ordinary weight is placed upon the individual's capacity to be aware of these responses and when necessary modify them. The expression 'interpersonal skills' sounds mechanistic and manipulative, but the fact remains that in social group work the primary skill required is frequently that of finding the best response available to what client groups say and do. Peter Lomas (1973) has suggested that the essence of this skill lies not in any sophisticated technique, but in a resilient ability to continue to respond as an ordinary human being meeting other ordinary human beings, in spite of pressure to become caught up in the shared fantasy of, for example, an extraordinarily powerful or loving social worker meeting an extra-ordinarily weak or needy group of clients. The study of group behaviour is a means of bringing our habitual ways of reading social situations, and our habitual responses to the situations so interpreted, out of the shadows of our tacit knowledge, the knowledge that is in our bones, so that we can examine these responses and assess their adequacy. Once identified in experience (and not merely intellectually) they may be progressively open to modification.

The social group worker needs to be able to think about his experience, and so extricate himself from the ever-present tendency either to be engulfed by his group, or to be compulsively detached from it. Theories of individual, group and inter-group behaviour, if they are grounded in experience, provide him with tools with which to think. They enable him to survive, to make sense of what is happening, and hence to arrive at policies and decisions about how to proceed. Even if these are mistaken he knows why he is doing what he is doing, and hence can learn from his mistakes. If he is merely responding automatically to stimuli he is stuck and unable to learn (compare Bion's theory of the nature of thinking (1962) summarised in Grinberg *et al.*, 1975 and Palmer, 1973).

This is not to say that the existing theories of group behaviour are all that solid. The choice is not, however, whether to work with a theory or not, but whether or not to be aware of the theories with which one is already working.

The specially constructed course or workshop, away from the work situation, is only one of a number of ways of learning about group behaviour. The results are unpredictable. Such research findings as are available indicate that changes in attitudes and behaviour resulting from group relations training can seldom be demonstrated to persist, for a total course membership, long after the course is over. This confirms the impression of many who run courses, that not everyone is able to take the opportunity provided by a course; and that the chances of a course member being able to retain and develop the insight he has gained are greater if he returns to an organisation in which his interest in continuing to learn is reinforced by that of others.

It is possible to learn about group behaviour through examination of one's past experience of working with groups, provided the emotional quality of the experience is still vividly recalled. This may take place in individual or group supervision, which has the further advantage that the problem of transferring insights from the setting in which they arise to the setting in which they are applied is reduced to a minimum. The advantage of the course away from the work setting is that the participants have greater freedom to reflect on their experience without the pressure of responsibility for clients. Furthermore, while there is reluctance to expose one's competence in front of other social workers, most people are more prepared to make fools of themselves in front of other course members than they are in their own agency. In other words, there is more space in which to regress, to lose control, and then to recover and examine where one has been. For many people, therefore, it appears that the group relations course provides the best opportunity for the breakthrough in understanding group processes which may be necessary before they can continue to learn from their on-going working experience.

Chapter 8

GROUP SUPERVISION IN FIELDWORK PLACEMENTS

Hilary Davies

INTRODUCTION

In recent years frequent reference has been made to group supervision by people involved in social work education, and particularly by those who are interested in the development of the teaching of fieldwork practice. There has also been some interest in the planned supervision of groups of field social workers. But there is comparatively little evidence of the use of small groups produced by those involved in the supervision of fieldwork. There have been very occasional papers describing the use of small groups in student or worker supervision – Harper (1969), Central Training Council in Child Care (1971), Smith (1972), Davies and Taylor (1973) – but generally documentation of experience from this side of the Atlantic is very sparse.

This paper proposes that group supervision of the field practice of social work students has a potential for enabling learning to take place which is sufficient to interest fieldwork teachers in this method of teaching. Although the main focus is on the supervision of students, much of what is written is equally relevant to the supervision of fieldworkers.

DEFINITIONS

As group supervision is explored as a way of fulfilling supervisory tasks, it may be helpful to have in mind Charlotte Towle's (1963) definition of the supervision process as being made up of three functions. Towle identifies the supervisory functions of administering the agency's service, teaching the supervisee and helping the supervisee. The new supervisor will perhaps move most easily into the role of helper, as that is nearest to the central function of his former full-time role of social worker. But hopefully he will develop growing competence in the roles of administrator and teacher. At various times, different functions assume more importance in the supervisory process. Obviously with students on fieldwork placements, the teaching function is of central importance and the fieldwork teacher will have the other two aspects of the role firmly in mind throughout work with each student.

For the purposes of this paper, group supervision is defined as 'a regular pattern of focused discussion, shared between supervisor(s) and two or more supervisees, which has a primary focus on pieces of work being carried by the supervisees'. All members of the group see themselves as sharing responsibility in a variety of ways for the work being done. Within that definition a number of different models are possible:

(1) a group of students and a supervisor who conducts all supervision in group meetings ('pure' group supervision);
(2) a group of students being supervised individually by their supervisor but also meeting as a group for some supervision with the *same* supervisor;
(3) a group of students having individual supervision with one supervisor and sharing group supervision with another supervisor on the same placement.

There are different permutations of these models and each will have advantages and disadvantages in the context of different agencies, ieldwork teachers and student groups. Field teachers will ultimately develop a preference for one or other model, which seems to fit most closely with the needs of his agency and his students, and with his own skills and interests. Harper (1969) chooses the second model, but other experiences indicate that some confusion occurs about the function and purpose of ach type of supervision when more than one sort of supervision is xperienced at the same time during a placement. Unless purpose and focus an be defined and understood clearly by those involved, some important ssues may not get raised and frustration will grow out of the uncertainty.

For this reason, and for others to do with experience and personal reference, the first model of 'pure' group supervision is the one primarily eferred to in this paper. As part of this model, urgent individual onsultation would be available with the same supervisor, with the agreed xpectation that the discussion will be shared, formally or informally, in ue course with the other members of the group.

Kathleen Curnock's recent study of *Student Units in Social Work 'ducation* (1975) identified a wide range of ways in which learning groups ere being used in fieldwork teaching, all of which were described by eldwork teachers as 'group supervision'. It is important for fieldwork achers to be clear about their own definition of group supervision and to ommunicate this to relevant people – agency colleagues, students and ourse tutors – who may be involved directly or indirectly in it as a method f learning.

APPROACHING THE USE OF GROUPS IN FIELDWORK TEACHING

A fieldwork teacher's initial interest in group supervision may be motivated by awareness of an untapped resource for learning – the student group in a training unit; by students' own expressed wish to be involved in group learning; by the interest of course tutors in encouraging this method of placement teaching; by the group work 'band-wagon' which indicates that all groups are 'a good thing'. If these, and many other reasons are developed further, very quickly questions begin to emerge about the special skills and knowledge required by a fieldwork teacher who decides to work with groups. How different are they from those needed for work with individual students? What implications does group supervision have for agency accountability for work being carried by students? What about individual students' learning needs which may be overlooked? What about placement assessment reports – how will they be written and by whom? The objective of the rest of this paper is to suggest some ways of thinking about these questions.

PREREQUISITE SKILLS OF THE FIELDWORK TEACHER

First, it is important to emphasise the relevance of the knowledge and skill already possessed by the fieldwork teacher who has been working with students individually. It is probably important for fieldwork teachers to have achieved a level of competence and personal comfort in the role of supervisor fulfilling the administrative, teaching and helping functions of supervision, before moving on to the more complex area of supervising in groups.

Ideally it will also be helpful if the fieldwork teacher has had an experience of functioning in a group where there has been opportunity to observe and understand some of the processes of the group and to develop a degree of comfort in the group situation (see, for example, Palmer Douglas in this Reader). There are different ways of acquiring this experience and it should enable the fieldwork teacher to be able to view the supervision group more objectively and so interact with the group and its members in a more informed way. It may also enable him to survive without paralysing anxiety those periods in the life of any group when it is difficult to make sense of what is happening.

In identifying more specific areas of understanding needed by people working with learning groups, the following themes form a very partial list of those areas requiring consideration. First, it seems essential for the fieldwork teacher to have some understanding of how people learn (and specifically how adults learn) and to be developing his own stance in relation to sometimes contradictory education theories. Similarly, it will also be important to become aware of theories about small groups from psychology and sociology which can provide useful frameworks for the thinking of the group supervisor. Examples to be considered here will be the composition of effective groups and group leadership. (Communication patterns in groups and stages of group development are also useful areas of knowledge which group supervisors might consider – see Bavelas (1968), Douglas (1970).)

ADULTS' LEARNING

Of course, it is equally important for fieldwork teachers working with ndividual students to have an understanding of adult learning. For the erson working with groups, it is of value to have this knowledge available vhen planning and setting up the group and during the life of the group vhen one of his central tasks is to monitor the progress of each member. Most people have their own philosophy about how human beings learn and t will be very much influenced, positively or negatively, by their own earning experiences as adults and children.

In thinking about learners in social work, it may be useful to have in nind a continuum stretching from the 'apprenticeship' model of learning, vhen an experienced teacher is responsible for transmitting his skills and nowledge to a learner – what Paulo Freire (1972) has described as a banking' model of education. At the other end of the continuum the earner is plunged into situations with little structured learning pportunity and is required to learn from his own experience. Hopefully ery little social work learning now resembles either of these two extremes.

Knowles (1972), in his discussion of pedagogic and andragogic models of earning (pedagogy being the art and science of teaching children, and ndragogy the art and science of helping adults to learn), emphasises the eed of the adult for increasing self-directiveness as a learner. The adult rings with him to his learning the rich resources of his past life as an aid to earning, and he is motivated to achieve in order to perform specific tasks nore effectively. Therefore he will want to learn in a way which enables him o apply his knowledge to problems immediately in his own life.

From these assumptions about adult learners, Knowles builds a model or adult learning which involves the learner very fully in planning his own earning. This shared learning takes place in an atmosphere of informality nd mutual collaboration. Emphasis is put on experimental learning and elf-directed inquiry, with the teacher being a facilitator rather than the ansmitter of knowledge. There is much that is attractive about the ndragogic model but it is necessary to be aware of the potential isadvantages of this model too, and to adapt it for use by individual eachers in particular situations. For example, accountability for service to ients may sometimes require a fieldwork teacher to occupy a much more authoritarian role than a totally andragogic model would allow.

A fieldwork teacher who adopts a relatively andragogic model will wish to include students in his thinking about the objectives of group supervision, what its advantages and disadvantages might be, and what it will involve for each student. This should be done at a stage when students still have a choice about whether to be involved in it. This will be either before a final allocation of placements is made, or as soon as students arrive in an agency when the decision can be made in the first few days. Ideally the former is preferable, as individuals will feel less pressure to join in group supervision when they still have time to choose another agency and thus le[t] a more motivated student be involved in the group learning. Once the placement has begun, then there may be pressure to join in to make up a viable group, or in order not to feel left out of a shared experience. Course tutors will need to be fully involved in the fieldwork teacher's thinking before placements are offered in this way.

Once a group is identified, then a structure for learning can be agreed and a contract established between members of the group. This includes plan[s] for evaluating the progress of the group and modifying its structure; for th[e] writing of placement reports and sharing of records. In order for th[e] fieldwork teacher to contribute effectively at this stage and as the group proceeds, it is necessary to have some knowledge about theories of learnin[g] (see Hilgard and Bower, 1966; Bigge, 1964; Somers, 1969).

As the fieldwork teacher monitors and evaluates the progress o[f] individual students in a group, it will also be necessary for him to have som[e] understanding of individual learning patterns and the stages by which learning progresses. The complexity of communication and interaction i[n] groups can sometimes make it more difficult to chart the progress of a[n] individual, so it is even more important for a fieldwork teacher to hav[e] some guidelines.

Having made that comment, it is necessary to add that there ar[e] occasions when the learning opportunities provided by the group enable a[n] obvious step forward to be taken by a student member. A student who, i[n] individual supervision, would allow only one perspective to influence h[is] understanding of various clients' refusal to open the front door, is a goo[d] example of this. The closed front doors were seen as evidence of the client[s'] thought-out decision to withdraw from work with a social worker, and s[o] for the social worker to do anything other than disappear was interprete[d] as an infringement of the clients' rights and freedoms. No other possib[le] interpretations were accepted as relevant and so supervision discussio[n] rapidly became deadlocked. Then the student moved into grou[p] supervision for the final part of a long placement. In the second session h[e] became enthusiastically and seriously involved in requiring anoth[er] student to consider other interpretations of a similar incident, when th[e] other student was seeing it exclusively in terms of rights and freedom.

Everyone had a characteristic way of approaching and assimilating new experiences, related to the ways which have been learned for handling the discomfort, and sometimes distress, imposed by change. Change is a central aspect of learning, and some students may handle the stress of new learning experiences in ways which prevent a free approach to new experiences and inhibit change of feeling and thinking. These may be described as learning blocks and one of the reasons they arise may be the unacceptable dependence the student feels in a new situation (Selby, 1968). This uncertainty about dependence on the fieldwork teacher was probably the reason for the block experienced by the student described above. It is also important to bear in mind that there are other possible reasons for this sort of difficulty which are intellectual rather than emotional. For example, the student may be failing to understand the fieldwork teacher's method and level of conceptualisation.

It is inevitable that the learner will experience periods when he feels very incompetent, and at these points he may express anger at the learning situation and those responsible for it. If a supervision group includes a number of members who are experiencing this stage at the same time, the leadership task of the fieldwork teacher becomes difficult temporarily. As in many other things, understanding what may be happening is halfway towards dealing with it. Fieldwork teachers could profitably spend time looking at the work of educationalists who have identified general stages in learning patterns and have described them in different ways (for example, see Reynolds, 1965 and Whitehead, 1962).

The fieldwork teacher needs to remember that, as in the stages of human development, so in the development of learning there are no distinct boundaries and overlaps and regressions occur frequently. There is no clear point at which a child becomes an adolescent, and there is no clear point when the learner moves from the stage of understanding new information to the stage at which he can make use of this understanding in his practice.

THE COMPOSITION OF SUPERVISION GROUPS

So far, little has been done in the social sciences to bring together relevant theory about small groups from sociology and psychology. Sociologists have explored small groups mainly from an external perspective, seeing them as parts of larger social structures. Psychologists have tended to focus on the internal life of the group itself. In considering the composition of supervision groups, it is necessary to consider both perspectives.

The supervision group will interact with, and be affected by, parts of the larger social structures within which it operates; for example, the courses from which students come, and the agency where the placement takes place. The decision about the size of the supervision group will be affected by administrative issues of accountability.

It may be that the often quoted number of eight members for the optimum sized small group is considerably larger than is feasible administratively. It may also be too large to meet each student's need for detailed focus on the work he is doing, and for the fieldwork teacher to manage issues of accountability. So a maximum of five members may be more appropriate if all supervision is to take place in the group. In Curnock's (1975) study complaints were registered by students who had experienced group supervision 'where student groups were too large and it was felt that the supervisor could not be sufficiently in touch with the work being carried out by all of them'.

In selecting members of supervision groups, and recalling the previous discussion of the need for students to 'select themselves in' to this experience, the fieldwork teacher will have in mind questions about the need for all members to be at the same stage and from the same course, and whether students with marked difficulties should be included. Provisional answers to these questions must be arrived at before any student is in the position to opt in to a group.

If all the members of a group come from the same course, they will bring with them into the group some of the feelings and patterns of behaviour from the course. This can be an enabling or disabling factor, depending on what is happening on the course and whether the students react positively or negatively to it in the group. A group of students all from a course year which was characterised by some depression and alienation, carried the depression into the supervision group, which showed low energy and productivity. But one member was left to carry most of the depression while the others struggled to find more commitment to their practice than they had been able to find for their course learning. For quite long periods the obvious, withdrawn silence of the other member appeared to go completely unnoticed by the others.

But if learning in the field and course is proceeding moderately well, then both areas will be enhanced by students from the same course sharing a supervision group. Learning can also be enhanced by the variety provided by students from different courses in a group, but to achieve this effectively the fieldwork teacher will need the extra time it takes to communicate fully with more than one course tutor's group. The feasibility of mixed groups will be influenced by practical factors like placements beginning and ending at the same time. This is important if the group is to develop an identity and move forward without having to retrace its steps to incorporate new members, or go through the process of ending with some members while others are continuing.

When a supervision group is being composed, it needs to be seen in relation to any other students who may be in the agency at that time but not in the group. Whether or not they are being supervised by the same fieldwork teacher, it is likely that there may be feelings of rivalry and exclusion. So the fieldwork teacher needs to be clear about the reasons for not including certain students, able to share these reasons with the students and to continue to work with feelings which may arise. In fact students are not the only members of the group's external world who may feel they are missing something. In one small agency, a staff member found frequent 'good' reasons for interrupting group sessions with brief messages – quizzically demonstrating that he was more than half aware of what he was doing. By thoughtful communication with others, the fieldwork teacher can go some way towards de-mystifying feelings about the 'group within a group' and so help maintain sharing between students in the group and other agency members, from which much important informal learning is derived.

If group effectiveness is partly determined by the attributes each member brings to the group, the fieldwork teacher should look for certain qualities in the students being selected. Bertcher and Maple (1974) suggest that a mixture of homogeneity and heterogeneity works best in a group – a combination of people whose *behavioural* qualities are dissimilar, but whose *descriptive* qualities are similar.

The fieldwork teacher who uses this theoretical guideline may choose to set up a group for students who are descriptively similar (e.g. at the same stage in training, or with similar lengths of work experience) but behaviourally different (e.g. in assertiveness, conscientiousness). On any continuum describing behavioural or descriptive attributes of individuals, it is also important, in composing groups, that no one member is at a point which is far away from where other members are on the continuum. If one student is at a point where he is experiencing much greater difficulty with his work than the others, a disproportionate amount of time may be spent by the other members in helping him to catch up at the expense of their own learning. The difference between him and them may be reinforced and so the chances of his moving on will be diminished.

At this stage of understanding of small groups and of group supervision, it is misleading to suggest that there are any very exact criteria to use in composing groups, but there are guidelines which can be tested for their usefulness in practice. Testing them requires co-operation and good communication between course and field in planning placements.

GROUP LEADERSHIP AND THE ROLE OF THE FIELDWORK TEACHER

Social psychologists have explored different styles of leadership and their effect on the behaviour of groups. White and Lippitt (1968) in the 1930s studied the effects of authoritarian, democratic and laissez-faire leadership in small groups in children's clubs and produced the following findings.

Members of groups with authoritarian leadership reacted in two different ways, one aggressive, the other apathetic, with both types of behaviour existing alongside relative dependence on the leaders. The aggressive members were rebellious to the leader and friendly with each other, the apathetic were generally submissive and showed evidence of destructive frustration. Some of the discontent did not appear on the surface. In achieving certain specific practical tasks, this style of leadership enabled the group to be most effective, when efficiency was more important than creativity.

Members of democratically led groups had friendly, personal relationships with each other. Individual differences were shown and members looked to each other for mutual support. Members were able to continue to work in the absence of the leader and both work and play showed a higher level of originality or creative thinking than that under the other styles of leadership. There was more creative thinking about the work in progress than in autocracy and it was more sustained and practical than under laissez-faire leadership.

The laissez-faire group was notable for its lack of achievement. The presence of a relatively passive adult operated against any co-ordinated group activity.

Applying these findings to small groups of adults where the objective is to enable learning to take place, the democratic style of leadership would appear to have most to offer in group supervision, if a specific objective of the fieldwork teacher is to develop a mainly andragogic model of learning.

Analysing the function of leadership in small groups is a complex task, still not fully understood. It may be helpful to explore examples of the functions which have to be performed in supervision groups and to see how these relate to the role of the fieldwork teacher as leader.

Various writers have identified two different levels of activity in small groups which go on simultaneously. These levels have been described using different words or phrases but substantially they are referring to the same processes. Words used include instrumental and expressive levels, goal achievement and group maintenance levels, task and socio-emotional and finally, work group and basic assumption activities. As Somers (1968) says, '*every small group works on tasks and works on relationships* – the teacher must also relate to and deal effectively with the group in both of these major dimensions of group life and functioning'. The fieldwork teacher must enable the group to work at both levels so, in the supervision group where one member was being allowed, or perhaps required, to carry the depression for the others, it was the function of the fieldwork teacher to draw the attention of the group to this. The aim would be to help the group members to work towards allowing more flexibility of role to the 'depressed' member by taking back bits of the depression themselves, so freeing him to achieve more of his learning goals in the group.

But this is not solely the role of the fieldwork teacher. Other group members can be encouraged formally and informally to take over aspects of the leadership function once they have become aware of what these functions are. For example, awareness of the instrumental leadership function of structuring individual group sessions, and encouragement to all group members to share this function, may enable a structure of rotating 'chairmen', responsible for starting and ending meetings, etc., to be an effective part of the group's work and also an additional learning experience for students.

The fieldwork teacher's awareness of students' need, at times, to have access to an oracle with all the answers, may help him to resist the temptation and pressure to take on and remain in this sort of leadership role. Not only the fieldwork teacher may be viewed as the potential oracle. A supervision group had decided to allocate regular sessions to discussing basic principles of practice related to the work they were doing. For the first of these sessions, the chairs were mysteriously arranged in a line (as opposed to the usual circle) with one chair in front, allocated to and taken by the student leading the session. Discussion limped off to a disjointed, uneasy start. Only after attention was eventually drawn to the new seating arrangement and what that might mean, could the 'designated oracle' express relief, chairs were moved back into a circle and the group's usual relaxed, thoughtful interchange began.

People are a rich resource for each other's learning and the fieldwork teacher will probably want to exploit this in the supervision group. If the learning theory concept of modelling as an effective means of changing behaviour is accepted (modelling being the process by which an individual learns new behaviour by imitating the behaviour of another person and then adapting it to his own style), then group supervision provides a range of peer group models as well as the model provided by the fieldwork teacher. Peer group models may be easier to identify with because people may feel daunted by the superior skill and knowledge of non-peers and therefore unable to believe that they could function in the same way themselves. Peers can also sometimes understand and respond to each other's difficulties more accurately because of their nearness to the experience. So if the fieldwork teacher is influenced by this, he will want to enable group members to take on aspects of the teaching function as often as possible.

This does not mean that the fieldwork teacher abdicates his teaching role. He is ultimately responsible for assessing the learning needs of each student and evaluating the progress made, how each member is using the group and how the group facilitates each member's learning. Experience and understanding will gradually enable him to move in and out of the teaching role in a way which is appropriate in each student group.

The following extract from the transcript of a supervision group evaluating its experience at the halfway point, gives some clues of how the fieldwork teacher's role worked for its members:

Student A: If you [hesitation] . . . by the way you are in the group you show that you have a different role, but you are not the same as us in that you have got superior skills. Do you agree? [to students B and C]

Student B: I was thinking that if we didn't have a supervisor we would probably be more frightened at discussing things the way we do. I feel in a way that [the supervisor] is there and if we are way off track you will ask us to look at it in a different way. If there was just the three of us discussing, we would do it to one another to a certain extent but it would be more of a worry that we would go on and on discussing something that in the end was perhaps totally irrelevant. Well that's how I feel.

Student C: You need someone to draw things together at the end and whether one of us would be prepared to do it – you've got to have someone in the group who is going to take the leadership role.

Student B: On the whole when we have had particular problems – anyway it seems from listening to the tape – it seems we have been fairly satisfied at the end of a discussion and if you [to fieldwork teacher] didn't draw the bits out of it, it would . . . it would still be very woolly and we would be left with all these things thrown at us but not knowing really where to start next.

WHY GROUP SUPERVISION? – ITS ADVANTAGES AND DISADVANTAGES

Students in social work training learn a body of relevant knowledge, develop understanding of their own and other people's attitudes and values, and apply this learning to practice intervention in social situations through the development of skill in action. Acquiring new knowledge can be described as a primarily individual activity which is aided by a whole range of teaching/learning experiences. Ultimately it is the learner who must learn – no one can do that for him. But other people can help him to practise using the knowledge and open up different ways of developing it, and it is in this area that group supervision can establish its objectives.

More specifically, the social worker needs to appreciate and be sensitive to different points of view and ways of thinking and to be clear about his own and other people's value assumptions. He needs to become aware of his own inhibitions and defences and to develop a growing independence in his practice. These objectives will be pursued in individual placements but clearly group supervision can offer a wider range of points of view and value systems with which students can engage, and learning at some stages is likely to take place more effectively in groups. For example, when students are ready to learn to become more independent in their work, it will be easier to practise this in a group than in the relatively protected environment of individual supervision. Groups may also enable people to work at objectives like the development of verbal and relationship skills with a number of people and the ability to think critically through the challenge of a range of ideas. They also make it possible to create a range of experiential learning opportunities (e.g. role play).

It is important to remember that students have committed themselves to these groups to learn and not to be involved in therapy. So, as in individual supervision, the fieldwork teacher needs to have clear guidelines in mind about what is and is not appropriate for work in supervision groups and to be able to share this with the members. This defining of boundary is not a simple task because, if one of the objectives of the group is to encourage the student's self-awareness and to enable him to relate more effectively, then this can at times be very near to therapy. But living creatively with this sort of uncertainty is not a new experience for fieldwork teachers and ultimately each person must develop his own guidelines for proceeding.

A group of final placement students began a discussion of the advantages and disadvantages of group supervision in the following way in the transcript of a review session:

Student B: Well the first thing that comes to mind is how valuable it's been . . . [hesitation] . . . discussing other people's cases. You know we complained a lot on the Course about not doing enough case discussions and how we thought that would have been a lot more valuable. But if everyone's practical placements were set up like this we wouldn't need the case discussions.

Student A: Particularly in a group this size where you really do feel you know other people's families . . .

Student B: [breaking in] it's nearly as good as having all the cases yourself.

Student A: I mean, on the Course where everyone has a case discussion it was very unsatisfactory really; you only got to know all the things you needed when it was time to stop discussions.

Student B: And you didn't follow it week by week anyway.

Student C: And also with other people having difficulties you are also having similar difficulties too and you can be more objective about other people can't you?

Fieldwork teacher: In groups on the whole the edges became much more blurred so that at one point a person who is normally finding it difficult may be the support of someone else having difficulties, so roles can be reversed quite quickly.

When these students were asked to make written comments on their placement generally, after about six months of being back in their work agencies, they produced the following comments on group supervision:

> I would like to do it again as I feel I could use the experience and get more out of it a second time – particularly in the area of handling and showing aggression and negative feelings. I've been quite conscious of this in groups since the placement and have been able to voice negative feelings – but found that other people often can't. Now they are probably having the difficulty we had in the group.

And from a second student:

> Group supervision helped me to begin to move from the one who always received support to a position where one could also give it . . . It was good learning to see how the group dynamics progressed and how, at the end we were secure enough to be able to look at some of the group's weaknesses.

But now some of the disadvantages are described retrospectively by a student who was at the opposite point in training, i.e. on a first placement on a pre-professional course.

> On looking back, I do not think it was able to provide sufficient individual help. Each problem had to become a generalised principle in order to make it a general learning experience. However I do think it was more stimulating than one to one supervision and that it tended to minimise the focus of attention on the supervisor. This I think can be helpful if one does not get on too well with one's supervisor, as some of my later experiences showed me. I still feel glad I was able to participate in group supervision but I do think it needs to be combined with one to one.

These comments provide evidence of students' need to experience group supervision late in their training, not at a point when preoccupation with their own needs and uncertainties about establishing an identity as a professional helper may prevent them from being able to share their experiences with other people. When early uncertainties have been resolved, then sharing is more possible.

Finally, comments from two students who were in the same group, reflecting on the different effects group supervision had on their experiences when they returned to the field. At the end of the placement Student A wrote:

> I moved into group supervision with some reservations [about being vulnerable, losing the support of individual supervision, etc.] but now feel confident that this experience was worthwhile. It offered me an opportunity to work indirectly with a greater variety of cases, to learn a little more about group dynamics and to be more selective about what is necessary to bring to supervision, and what one can take responsibility for oneself. One main disadvantage was that positive work with clients can get obscured by the inevitable concentration on crises and on the negative aspects of each other's work.

Student B wrote:

> Group supervision helped us all, I feel, to be less demanding and more self sufficient, and certainly encouraged me to make more decisions. This I feel has something to do with the time element, but is also involved with the recognition of colleagues' needs. This at first can be quite a difficult and anxiety provoking situation but certainly a valuable learning experience.

The two students included these further comments eight months after they were back at work. First, Student A:

> In a busy Social Services Department one is inevitably under pressure in relation to maintaining regular supervision with a senior. Because of the nature of the work one is inevitably reliant on one's peers for immediate support in crises. Group supervision is a very useful way of learning how to give and take in a peer group.

Student B was in a less busy Social Services Department and wrote:

> I have received individual supervision–$1\frac{1}{2}$ hours a week. However my senior has felt that I am too self reliant because I have not raised problems with her except in supervision. This is something which I feel group supervision contributed to enormously, but in my particular case it has caused problems because I am relatively independent. Despite this I feel that the use of group supervision and the encouragement of peer group support is useful as social workers in other authorities are required to make more decisions and usually receive less supervision.

So what appeared as an advantage in one situation, appeared as a disadvantage (at least temporarily) in another. Perhaps this reflects basic uncertainty about what social work expects from social work education.

Areas of difficulty which will need considerable study as fieldwork teachers become more experienced in group supervision, include the writing of placement assessments on individual students and the involvement of course tutors in the shared discussion of the placement. Initial experience has shown that it is feasible for reports on students to be written in the group with the fieldwork teacher taking the primary responsibility for producing the document (much as he normally would in individual placement assessments). Questions remain about the most appropriate outline for such an assessment to follow – does evaluation of group supervision learning require a different format? These reports are also being written at a point which coincides with the ending stage of a group's life, when members are disengaging and are preoccupied with their own lives after the group has ended. So it is often difficult for them to focus in detail then, on each other's learning.

Thought has to be given to planning tutors' visits to the agency, particularly if, as often happens, the students in the group do not share the same tutor. Should tutors come separately and focus just on their own student in the group? Or should they come together, which may mean that for a group of four students there can be up to nine people in the discussion? This may make detailed focus on an individual student difficult to maintain. It becomes less of a problem if there are fewer tutors and if tutors have a detailed awareness of the placement learning of their student from tutorial discussion, if the student is on concurrent placement.

COMMENTS IN CONCLUSION

The work of Sales and Navarre (1970) has provided the only known evaluative study of the effectiveness of individual and group supervision. They studied the field experience of students at the University of Michigan School of Social Work, focusing on the acquisition of practice skills as the primary objective of field instruction. Their findings revealed that both modes of supervision result in equivalent overall student performance, although there were some minor, interesting differences within this overall pattern. For example, group supervised students tended to be more interested in agency practices, to consider innovation and to comply with recording requirements, and to be more able to identify areas of competence in their own practice. Individually supervised students tended to be better at detailed assessments of their cases.

So, rather than viewing student fieldwork supervision as being either group supervision or individual supervision, perhaps it is necessary to be aware of the range of complementary experiences from which students can learn. Learning can be facilitated by the shared relationship between one student and one supervisor and through informal learning with other agency workers who are prepared to talk about their work. It is also true that some learning about one's own and other people's feelings and behaviour can only take place when the learning opportunities of a group are fully utilised. Fieldwork practice offers one interesting opportunity for this to happen. Ideally, then, students should have the chance to learn from all these experiences during the course of their social work training.

SUMMARY

Initially, this paper provides an operational definition of 'group supervision' for the purposes of its study and looks briefly at other types of groups used in fieldwork teaching. There follows a discussion of the interests and reservations of fieldwork teachers as they first consider group supervision. The main body of the paper explores some themes which might usefully be considered by those who are interested in developing skill and understanding in the use of small learning groups in fieldwork teaching. The paper concludes with a discussion of the advantages and disadvantages of group supervision, and includes the comments of students who have been involved in placements where it has been used.

I would like to acknowledge the help of students, colleagues, teachers and course tutors who have shared in this exploration of group supervision.

Chapter 9

THE DEVELOPMENT OF GROUP WORK IN A SOCIAL SERVICE DEPARTMENT

Herbert Laming and Sheila Sturton

INTRODUCTION

For most social service departments, group work is a peripheral activity. If social workers have time, enthusiasm and a certain pioneering hardiness they may be able to undertake an occasional piece of group work practice; but rarely is group work seen as an essential part of an area team's work, or the development of group work skills accepted as a priority in a department's training plan. Casework remains the 'core' method, both in the field and on professional courses; and the build-up of group work expertise is painfully tentative and slow.

Many practitioners and managers would maintain that this situation is inevitable, given present scarcities of time and money: the growth of group work must await the day of greater resources and a settled staff population. However, we feel that this is an unduly conservative policy. Alternative helping methods such as group work have a contribution to make right now to the quality and diversity of care provided by social service departments; and if existing social work staff with an interest in group work could be properly supported and guided in their efforts to work with groups, the service offered to clients would undoubtedly be enriched.

In this paper we describe an attempt by one social service department to promote the use of group work on this basis, by combining the energy and interest of existing staff with the additional resource of a group work consultant. The department set up its 'group work programme' in July 1971, in a period of great change and upheaval, so the feasibility of the programme was vigorously tested from the outset. The results have been most heartening and exciting, and we would like to share them with a wider audience, in the hope that other departments may be encouraged to try something similar. In the account that follows we explain our reasons for starting the programme, describe the early planning stages, and attempt to assess the progress made after three years in terms both of staff development and improved service to clients.

WHY GROUP WORK?

In a general sense, group work requires no justification. As a method it is well established in most social work agencies in the United States, and has been used productively for some time in certain settings in Britain as well. If social work has value, then group work has value as a legitimate branch of social work. Moreover, in our society it is unusual for people to limit themselves to one or two exclusive relationships – most people need and use membership of a number of formal or informal groups during their lives. This being so, it is understandable that some people will prefer to receive social work help through the medium of a group; and it is quite clear that group work is the most logical and appropriate form of help in situations where clients need to meet together to achieve shared goals or carry out common tasks.

Senior staff in the department certainly recognised the value of group work in this broad sense; but they also shared a more specific understanding of its function within a social service setting. They were agreed that social service departments should aim to develop an imaginative range of services, with as much opportunity for client choice as possible – which, of course, meant an appropriate and skilful use of all available social work methods. This was not to deny the importance of casework, or to make invidious comparisons between the various methods. Rather we were advocating a service which would be flexible, meeting need in a variety of ways, and offering help along a number of dimensions. It seemed probable that casework would continue to provide the backbone of local authority social work; but we felt that to offer casework alone – however effectively and purposefully – was surely to exclude some potential clients who could not use individual help, to reduce the effectiveness of help given because it left out the valuable dimensions of group membership and community support.

For example, consider a client coming to an area office who is suffering depression, isolation and a general lack of stimulation. In the kind of department which should be our goal, a range of options would be open to this client: individual or family help; membership of a small therapeutic group in the community; participation in a social club; possibly attendance at an occupational day centre; conceivably sharing in some voluntary project; or any sensible combination of these. The social worker and client would examine together the various possibilities in the light of the client's situation and preferences, and the client would be helped to make a choice, with of course opportunities for reviewing that choice from time to time. Needless to say, this presents an idealised picture – but the use of group work within an area team would be an important step towards achieving this 'ideal'.

On the residential side, group work needed even less of a justification. Social service departments are heavily committed to the provision of residential care – and residential life inevitably involves group living in some form. To maximise the beneficial and collaborative aspects of residential living, skilful use of group work is essential. So, if our social service department were adequately to fulfil its commitment to residential care, the residential staff would need help with group work of every kind – from informal groups to the structured 'community' meetings appropriate to some settings.

Given that the use of group work in field and residential settings was desirable, who was to carry it out? Probably the major obstacle to developing such a flexible and sensitive pattern of care is the lack of staff trained in methods other than casework. Yet we did not regard this as an insuperable difficulty. Underpinning the three social work specialisms is a fundamental generic method; if we could make use of this, seeing work with individuals, groups and communities as springing from the same knowledge and practice base, then social workers trained in one method might fairly easily transfer to another. In particular, caseworkers could undertake excellent group work, if helped to grasp what is common to both methods, while remaining sensitive to, but not alarmed by, what is different. For residential staff, who were already working in a 'group' dimension, we thought there should be even less hesitation in practising group work – if given help to make conscious their appreciation of group dynamics, and guidance to tackle the more formal aspects of residential group work.

It was on this basis of a firm belief in the generic nature of social work practice; in the need for group services in situations hitherto served by casework only, or not at all; and in the viability of training and supporting field and residential staff to do group work, that the department set up its group work programme in 1971.

PLANNING THE GROUP WORK PROGRAMME

Before the programme began, a limited amount of group work was being carried out in one or two areas in the county. The former health and welfare department had employed a group worker to develop group services alongside a casework team, and this experiment had worked well. The children's department had not shown so much enthusiasm for group methods, but a few foster-parent groups had been run, and a flourishing group for mothers of 'at risk' families was in one area.

In July 1971, shortly after the inception of the social service department, a new post of 'Group Work Adviser' was created, with responsibility for promoting the use of group work in field and residential work. The deputy director assumed overall control of the group work programme, and provided regular supervision for the Group Work Adviser. Policy for developing group work was initially agreed upon by the director, deputy director, and the field, residential and training assistant directors; and their support and encouragement has been consistent throughout, and of crucial importance in establishing and maintaining the programme. The following points formed part of the initial policy proposals:

(1) Group work services were to be developed in four main areas. First, with clients who were usually only offered casework but might in fact benefit from the support and understanding available within a small group. Secondly, in areas beyond the problem solving or treatment context of casework, where group services might 'enrich life' for vulnerable people within the community – such as those in need of day care or social clubs. Thirdly, for semi-skilled or ill-supported people in the front line of service to clients, who might be helped through group meetings to share anxieties and develop a sense of job identity (e.g. foster-parents or voluntary workers). Finally, for residents and staff in residential settings, who would benefit from formal opportunities to sort out the ongoing problems of living together.
(2) Except in extraordinary circumstances, each group run in the field would have only one social worker involved in it. In residential settings, group work would be done by the head of the establishment, though outside social workers might help.
(3) The Group Work Adviser was to have no power to instruct people to develop group work, and would have no special resources to call upon. The programme was to grow through persuasion, and by advertising the successes of early group experiments. Group work would thus be competing – healthily – with all the other usual work pressures and demands on staff time.
(4) Support for staff practising group work would be provided in a number of ways. All field staff in the department were encouraged to spend an hour-and-a-half a fortnight in some form of in-service training, and the department provided a wide range of seminars and courses. Group work was to be offered as one in-service training option, with additional expectations: the classes would take place weekly; all participants would be expected to develop and work with a client group during the period of training; and all group meetings were to be recorded. As an alternative form of support, particularly on the residential side, the Adviser would provide individual consultation separate from in-service training; this might, for example, consist of visits to a home to discuss the progress of the residents' group with the staff.

Once these proposals had been discussed and accepted by the

management, a paper on the possible uses of group work was circulated within the department, to open the campaign. During the following weeks the Group Work Adviser was busy with the promotional aspects of her job–attending staff meetings to talk about group work, alerting headquarters staff to the value of the method, building up a group work library and preparing sample records for use as teaching material. As staff from various field and residential settings began to express an interest in acquiring group work skills, the emphasis shifted from advertising the method to providing support and training. The programme rapidly became self-promoting anyway, since the participants' enthusiasm and conviction was catching, and the Adviser soon had to deal with a steady flow of inquiries and requests for help.

The kind of consultation and training which was developed for field and residential staff is described in the sections that follow. Once the programme was established, the Adviser spent roughly two days a week running the in-service training classes for field staff, and a further two days visiting homes and hostels involved in group work; maintaining necessary links with the management, and writing records and reports, took up the remaining time. This work pattern evolved naturally as the programme itself took shape, since there did not seem to be any obvious precedent for the Adviser's combined role of method missionary cum consultant.

DEVELOPMENT IN THE FIELD

There were approximately twenty-five recruits to group work in-service training each academic year from 1971 to 1974. Some of the participants came from other agencies–such as Child and Family Psychiatric Clinics, the education department, Young Volunteer Force–but the majority were fieldworkers from our own department. The training was broken up into three terms each year, with roughly twelve sessions per term, and was provided in small 'classes' of six or seven social workers. At the end of each term those who wished could leave, and new entrants could join; but most participants stayed the whole year. All who took part did so on the basis of the expectations outlined in the policy document quoted earlier–i.e. as well as attending the weekly training sessions they were committed to setting up a client group during the course of training, and to recording the group meetings. Before anyone was accepted for the course, the Adviser would contact the relevant Senior to discuss the candidate's suitability for training and assess the feasibility of adding group work to the area team's workload. It was, of course, vital to maintain this sort of liaison with middle management in order to ensure that group work developed harmoniously and sensibly alongside other forms of community care.

Since in-service training was the prime medium for supporting group work in the field, it is worth describing the functioning of a training 'class' in some detail. A typical class might have six participants, four from the department and two from other agencies. One or two people might be already committed to setting up a particular group on behalf of their area team; others would be choosing between a number of possible groups, any one of which might be a valuable piece of practice. Early training sessions would have a substantial input of theory from the Group Work Adviser, who would help the participants clarify the need for suggested groups, decide which group to start, set down a purpose and contract for the proposed group, select members, choose premises, etc. Anxieties about working with a group for the first time would be shared, and records of initial interviews with prospective group members would also be brought to the training sessions. As the various client groups got going, the training class would focus more and more on reading and discussing each other's records of group meetings.

Obviously, clear consistent recording was vital for the effectiveness of this pattern of training. Many social workers balked at the prospect of committing group process – and especially their part in it! – to paper each week, but with encouragement and guidance a sound standard of recording was attained. To help the most hesitant, a very simple hand-out was prepared suggesting the basic ingredients of a group record. These included:

members present
absences and reasons for them, if known
who sat where
a full description of the start of the meeting
how the group's work progressed – topics raised, the group's responses, difficulties encountered, feelings expressed, the worker's activities, etc.
a general indication of how each work theme was concluded
whether the worker felt help was given
the meeting's ending in some detail.

Throughout, social workers were asked to be aware of two complementary aspects: how the group was working, and what it was working on. Naturally, staff developed their individual styles of recording, and these varied widely; yet usually enough material was provided to enable the training classes to get to grips with the progress of the group described.

This form of training group supervision based on the sharing of records proved popular and successful. Despite a very small number of 'drop-outs' from training (people who found they lacked the time or inclination to develop a group), 95 per cent of the participants set up and worked with a client group during the course of training. The Group Work Adviser tried to ensure that social workers only developed groups which were seen as necessary by their team colleagues, so that group work was properly integrated into the range of social work services within a particular area. As a result, the groups were widely used as a helping resource by the casework staff, who often made appropriate referrals for group membership. And there is no doubt that the clients themselves usually greatly valued the opportunity to experience group membership, and made constructive use of the help available through group work.

Attendance at in-service training was excellent, despite the pressure of work; and recording, as indicated earlier, was done promptly and adequately. Social workers were stimulated by the chance to learn about each other's group work, and became very supportive to those struggling to start to maintain difficult groups. Where possible the Adviser tried to draw on analogies from casework when helping people cope with the problems they were experiencing in their group work, so that there was a growing appreciation of the practice base underlying both methods. One of the 'spin-offs' from group work training was an improvement on some social workers' casework practice, as they appreciated afresh the value of concepts such as the structured use of time, contract setting, etc.

A very wide variety of groups was developed during the first three years of the programme. The following examples may give some indication of the spread of group work, and its versatility:

Groups in unstaffed mental health hostels: weekly meetings for the residents to help them talk through their shared living problems.

Groups for foster-parents: we found that a few weekly sessions with a clear focus were more effective than infrequent meetings spread over months.

Group for married couples where one partner was severely physically handicapped: fortnightly meetings for over a year.

Activity groups for children at risk, run both by our department and Child and Family Psychiatric Clinics: weekly for at least six months.

Groups for mothers of 'at risk' families: weekly for long periods – up to three years.

Groups for young mothers experiencing difficulties with pre-school age children, especially run by Child and Family Psychiatric Clinics: weekly for at least six months.

Group for elderly blind clients: weekly for a number of years.

Support/training groups for volunteers: fortnightly or monthly for six months to a year.

Discussion groups in day centres: weekly or fortnightly, as part of the regular day centre programme.

Various groups for deaf clients: weekly or fortnightly, usually with manual communication.

Groups for psychiatric patients in the community: weekly for at least a year – membership open-ended, with clients leaving as they felt in less need of support.

Groups for parents of mentally handicapped children, possibly linked to use of a play group facility: weekly for about ten sessions seemed the most effective pattern.

Group for teenage foster girls: weekly for four months.

We found that it was important to adjust the frequency and duration of the group meetings to suit the needs of the members, the nature of the group task, and the availability of staff to work with each particular group. These considerations led to the differences indicated above between the life span of the various groups. Every group was set up with a clear 'contract' about its purpose and function, established through discussion with the group members and enlarged or altered to match the development of the group. Clients were always encouraged to comment on the way their group was functioning, and participate fully in its evaluation and improvement.

It is clear from three years' experience of the group work programme that our original policy proposals were sensible, and did not need any major modification. The areas where we had suggested that group work might be developed were found to be appropriate, and teams threw up continual and varied demands for new forms of group services. Many clients responded enthusiastically to the opportunity to join a group, and sometimes made progress as group members which they had not been able to achieve as casework clients. They particularly valued the consistency and regularity of group work, the chance to give as well as receive help, and the additional perspectives gained from sharing difficulties with others.

Despite competing demands on staff time there was a roughly equal number of recruits to the group work programme each year, and the standard of participation and recording remained high throughout. We found that social workers were well able to undertake group work on their own, and that early requests for 'co-workers' were nearly always linked to the need for support. Once staff trusted the help available from in-service training, the wish for co-workers died away – with the exception of work with the younger children's groups, where two adults did seem helpful. Our decision to make group work 'fight for survival' among all the other demands on staff time had been perhaps the most controversial part of the original policy proposal, yet this too was soundly vindicated by experience. Social workers had continually to justify their involvement in group work, and this led to a most professional standard of group work practice, which had nothing to fear from the scrutiny or criticism of caseworkers!

DEVELOPMENTS IN STUDENT TRAINING

As group work became established in the field through the spread of in-service training, it was possible to develop student placements which offered experience in this method. We received requests from various courses to provide short placements (usually about three months) specialising in group work, but felt that such placements were too brief to enable students to go through all the stages of setting up and working with a client group. Moreover, group work as a specialism in a social service setting is a doubtful proposition; whereas if included as part of a team member's usual workload it can provide a stimulating work experience which complements the peculiar stresses of casework and emergency duties. So we preferred to offer students longer placements which involved work with individuals and groups, on the basis that this would best equip them for general social work practice in its present form, and would underline the generic base to the two methods.

To provide such placements we were able to use experienced student supervisors who had taken part in group work in-service training. Each student was expected to set up, work with, and close or transfer one client group; and also undertake a limited, balanced amount of casework. To ensure that the group work side of the placement was adequately supported, fortnightly meetings were held for supervisors, students and the Group Work Adviser, where group records were discussed and general group work issues examined. These placements were most successful, and resulted in a great deal of useful learning about both casework and group work.

DEVELOPMENTS IN RESIDENTIAL CARE

Progress on the residential side has been exciting and encouraging. With the support of the principal officers at County Hall who managed residential services, a number of heads of establishments decided to 'try out' some form of residents' meetings in their particular setting. Once an officer-in-charge had expressed interest in starting such a group, the Group Work Adviser would visit the home or hostel to discuss the possibilities, ensure that all the staff were involved in the early planning stages, and offer some form of on-going help if this was felt to be necessary. Invariably, residential staff did want support over setting up a group – and would often have preferred the Adviser to 'take over' responsibility for the group altogether. However, we were clear that this responsibility was part of an officer-in-charge's general remit, since meetings for residents and staff could not sensibly or effectively be held without the full participation of those in charge of the establishment. We therefore encouraged heads of homes to convene the residents' meetings themselves, but offered full support in a variety of ways according to the preferences of the residential staff. Sometimes the Adviser joined the staff in running the group; a local social worker with experience of group work might participate instead; or the residential staff might proceed on their own, but with regular consultation sessions with the Adviser. A few heads of homes attended the in-service training programme, but on the whole we found that support in the actual home setting was most appropriate.

We had some excellent results with group work in old people's homes. Over the three years a dozen homes started regular meetings open to both staff and residents, at which the 'contract' covered any matters of shared concern – from planning outings to discussing the problems caused by senility. These meetings (which usually took place fortnightly) were often well attended, with up to thirty residents joining in; and many residents, despite difficulties due to impaired hearing or mental deterioration, participated with energy and enthusiasm. Staff as well as residents enjoyed the discussions and felt they got a fresh perspective on their work, and a unique opportunity for communication with the residents. Although these groups varied in programme and use from home to home, a general pattern seemed to emerge: initially practical complaints about facilities or rules were made, followed by a widening and deepening discussion about many topics, including such normally taboo subjects as depression and death. We hope that these meetings went a little way towards helping the residents feel part of a shared enterprise in communal living, and easing the isolation and loneliness that many people seem to experience once established in a residential home.

Other forms of residential group work which were developed included groups in mental health hostels, a mothers' group in a Family Rehabilitation Centre, and a most effective group in a hostel for mentally handicapped women. One children's home set up regular meetings for all the older children, which proved a useful way of involving them in the running of the home; but unfortunately many of the residential child care staff in other establishments were resistant to the idea of children participating in discussions of domestic matters.

The range of homes and hostels within which communal meetings for residents and staff proved helpful, confirmed the validity of this form of group work in residential care. As long as staff were willing to talk over domestic issues openly and honestly with the residents, and take their suggestions seriously, such meetings were of immediate benefit. Residents – whether mentally handicapped, elderly, or children in care – appreciated being consulted and involved, and showed great responsibility in their approach to discussion about affairs in their particular home or hostel. Once residents and staff had learned to trust each other in the group, and had become accustomed to group discussion, the topics raised often moved beyond domestic matters into areas of wider emotional concern – loneliness, feelings of rejection by family, or conflicts between residents. Nonetheless, the practical issues to do with day-to-day life in the home were recurring themes, and it was clear that regular opportunities for sharing domestic problems were a most necessary facility for residents and staff in any establishment.

EVALUATING THE PROGRAMME

Measuring the value of any piece of social work practice is a fraught exercise, since skilful criticism may discredit a lot of the material proffered as evidence of a method's success. Yet throughout this article we have indicated confidence in the effectiveness of the group work programme, and obviously this confidence was the outcome of a process of evaluation. It may, therefore, be helpful to conclude by listing what we regarded as valid indices of the programme's success.

Evidence from group members themselves seemed the most important factor in evaluating the groups. Attendance levels were one useful measure of client satisfaction, as were individual or collective expressions of greater well-being due to group membership. With some groups there was objective evidence of members' progress – for example, a reduced readmission rate to psychiatric hospital in a group for chronically depressed clients. In many instances caseworkers, doctors or allied professionals were involved with group members, and their views on the help provided by group work was obviously crucial. There was also, of course, 'internal' evidence of the progress of some groups: evidence of a growing capacity for planning, for caring, for sharing problems, for tackling increasingly demanding tasks, and so on. In the case of residential work, various desirable changes in the lives of some institutions could be attributed to the group meetings – a wider range of activities, relaxation in the rules, or perhaps a voluntary assumption of domestic tasks by the residents. And, needless to say, we also respected the group workers' own views on the value of their practice: scarcely an objective measure, but certainly significant, if one was to have faith in the professionalism of staff!

Factors such as these are far from original, and extremely basic; yet we felt they provided an adequate way of evaluating the various forms of group work undertaken. The effectiveness of the total group work programme could be measured through additional indices: the recurring popularity of the training courses; the enthusiasm and persistence shown by residential staff in sustaining group work; and the growing demand for student placements in the method.

CONCLUSIONS

We have described the growth of group work in the department over a three-year period from July 1971. The results achieved in the field and in residential care encourage us to believe that the wider use of group work in a social service setting is beneficial to many clients. Moreover, group work has been shown to be well within the capacity of caseworkers and residential staff, if they are given consistent support. There is every indication that the group work programme will expand as staff gain confidence in their group work skills and become more sensitive to areas of need which may respond particularly well to group methods. We hope that our experience will be of interest to social workers in other agencies, and may perhaps stimulate further developments in the use of group work in local authority settings.

We would like to thank the Editor of *Social Work Today* for permission to reprint this paper which orginally appeared in *Social Work Today*, 26 October 1976, vol. 8, no. 4.

PART III

ASPECTS OF PRACTICE

Traditionally, social work in this country is devoted to the concept of the primacy of the individual, belief in the value and uniqueness of every human being. How then can social group work enable the profession to achieve its objectives and accord with this value stance? The papers in this section describe various types of group work in field and residential settings. Implicit in all of these groups is the maturing or healing opportunities offered to individuals, who may have been deprived or damaged by other groups, including their families.

Lorna Walker describes her experiences of helping the members run a group for economically and emotionally depressed parents. In reading this account we have a rare opportunity to observe precisely how 'leadership' skills are devolved to disadvantaged people in groups. Implicit is the flexibility in role taking required by the group worker: sometimes giving advice, suggesting limits; other times standing back to allow the cultural norms of the members to assert themselves. Throughout the life of the group the care and concern for the individual is manifested by the continuing appraisal of the changes in the members, and the acceptance of the withdrawal of members not suited to the climate of work in the group at that time.

Lorna Walker lays emphasis on the value of activities as a means of enabling relatively inarticulate people re-enact and find alternative solutions to their problems. A critical event in the progress of the group was an 'inter-group' meeting over a meal with another similar group.

Catherine Briscoe's paper focuses on this aspect – the contribution activities can make to achieving group purposes, and the factors affecting their selection. She assumes that as groups move through different stages of development in their life cycle, the timing of activities can either help or hinder the progression of the group.

Another important differential that Briscoe discusses is the nature of the contract between group and worker. With some groups this is explicit – the members come expecting to work on problems they own and admit to. Other times the 'contract' is less voluntary; for example, working with probationers, or in 'situation centred' groups such as parents of handicapped children where members may disagree about the priorities of their various problems. A third category is described as work with 'outreach' groups, where there is no contract initially. With these three types of groups there would be quite a different need for decisions about the activities to be engaged in, and the appropriate person(s) to organise them. Briscoe concludes with some practical suggestions as to how social workers might develop their knowledge about activities useful in groups.

Alice Breslin and Sheila Sturton describe a successful innovation in a hostel for mentally handicapped women: the initiation of community meetings with staff and residents. The purpose was both to increase the participation of the residents in running the hostel (for many of them their permanent home), and to share and resolve the problems of living together. Breslin and Sturton describe how the 'activity' of verbal communication can be improved, increasing the self-esteem of the individual and enhancing their sensitivity to others.

The authors state that a residential group has value proportional to its effect on institutional life outside the meetings. They are able to point to sufficient evidence of an increased sense of well-being and development of social skills in the residents to warrant the use of formal group work methods with the severely mentally handicapped.

Group workers are aware that for most people in this society, the family is the primary model of group life. Rosemary Whiffen writing about the theory and practice of family therapy also emphasises the complex task of group workers, with artificial or natural groups, whose focus must be on both the individual and the group. Family therapy aims both to understand and alleviate the damaging pressures which families may exert on the individual, and to liberate and enhance its nurturing and creative forces.

She describes the use of a systems approach in several case examples. Encouraging the families to work on a particular current problem or conflict, coupled with the outside intervention, appears to have had the effect of creating a new balance of family alignments which were beneficial to both the whole, and the individual who was put forward as the 'problem'. This model includes the use of activities such as family sculpting, giving designated tasks and other methods which do not wholly rely on discussion.

David Thomas discusses the changes that may accrue to individuals through their involvement in a community group. He focuses on *process* outcomes (emotional and educational gains) rather than *product* (material gains). Community work can help individuals move from a socially marginal group, to becoming more active members of their community: in that process Thomas believes some individuals increase their capacity for reflection, vision planning and action. The individual begins to conceive of himself as part of a system acting with others for change, and to recognise new roles and responsibilities. Thomas concludes by suggesting the different areas of their lives, public and private, which can be changed by the community group experience.

Chapter 10

WORK WITH A PARENTS' GROUP: INDIVIDUAL AND SOCIAL LEARNING THROUGH PEER GROUP EXPERIENCE

Lorna Walker

INTRODUCTION

The following is an account of some attempts to help families break through the restraints of powerlessness and failure by means of group experience for both parents and children. The term 'socially deprived' is defined and its indications for group work treatment are considered. The group worker's task with relation to this type of adult client is also considered. Examples are given of how one such group was formed; the resources available; and how goals were decided and achieved. The Under Fives' Play Group is described, and its links and interaction with the Parents' Group discussed. Other aspects considered are Conflict, Termination of Membership, and Measuring Progress.

SOCIAL DEPRIVATION

'The two basic needs of the human being – besides the physical one of survival – are the needs for self respect and for "belonging", the acceptance of the "I" and the "You", the finding of the bridge between two' (Konopka, 1963).

Josephine Klein (1961) has suggested that it is in the family group that we first learn to value ourselves. She writes that expectation of satisfactions from group membership derives to a large extent from the primacy of the family in the individual's experience. The continuing need for interdependence will remain, and the person will need to live his life in the context of small groups of others. Assurance of individual worth is a reciprocal process gained through membership of groups whose members behave in ways acceptable to the group.

Many of the clients of a Family Service Unit seem never to have known any feelings of worth, and the families in which they grew up tended not to have fostered the kind of reciprocal satisfaction of basic social or emotional needs necessary for future emotional growth. They also fail to regard as worthwhile any skills which they may have acquired, and this undervaluing of themselves is reinforced by the rest of society. Neighbours regard them as nuisances, officials misunderstand their inability to make appropriate use of services, and they are categorised as 'scroungers', 'layabouts', 'delinquents', labels which the individuals concerned accept and 'live down' to.

Group experience, supplementing individual casework, can prove effective in helping to provide the kind of basic experience which was lacking in childhood. To some extent this is done through the one-to-one casework relationship, but casework alone can lead to too great a dependence on the social worker, and does not help the client to relate to others or to learn to evaluate himself in the kind of interdependency which a satisfactory family background would have provided.

Clients of the FSU often lack the ability to express themselves clearly, or to control their use of language. This seems to be closely linked to lack of a sense of worth, as is the inability to make satisfying relationships, and fear and suspicion of authority figures. In many cases clients will have been referred for help in acquiring competence in home and child care and budgeting. Having received casework help prior to joining the group they will all be aware of their weak areas and will see the group as another means of helping them, though this 'help' will often be rationalised as 'getting us away from our homes for a break', or 'having a rest from the children'.

Irvine (1970) stressed the immaturity of such clients and their need for nurture. Certainly 'feeding' in both the literal and metaphoric sense seem to be needed, but the concept of the group worker taking the role of 'mother' and eventually 'weaning' the members of the group from their dependency needs has not proved a completely satisfactory one in practice. As group worker I provide a kind of mothering to new members, but all the time I am looking for new ways of helping other members to provide the necessary nurture. Berne's (1961, 1964) transactional concept of Child/Parent/Adult seems to me a more profitable way of viewing group members. In this way one is watching for all three role transactions and rewarding the Adult behaviour. For instance, when Jim's wife died from an overdose during a group meeting group members were able to parent him far better than any social worker. They took turns to sit with him for the first few evenings, and one went to the funeral. When Linda attacked the male group worker in a hysterical outburst he set the adult pattern by not retaliating or appearing 'thrown'.

My present view is that although one wants to give group members warm, secure, dependable experiences, the more practice they can get of behaving in adult ways and seeing for themselves the greater effectiveness of such behaviour when tested on, for example, school teachers and officials, the more quickly they will grow into more competent adults.

DEFENCES IN GROUPS

When I commenced group work I had assumed that women who were barely literate would be unable to communicate verbally, but would be prepared to demonstrate any skills they might possess and acquire skills such as child care, cooking, sewing, etc. (Walker, 1970). I did not allow for the fact that the members of *any* new group would be cautious about exposing themselves in what has now come to be termed the 'preaffiliation' stage (Garland *et al.*, 1972), and that people who had received consistent negative feedback during their lives would be even more careful to guard against exposure the little they had. The fact that they all talked at once and nobody seemed prepared to listen (Walker, 1970) was not an inability to communicate but a defence mechanism. I have since come to recognise a recurring pattern within successive groups – first, an extremely wary approach which may take the form of withdrawn silence or defensive, sometimes embarrassed verbosity, and/or irregular attendance. Next come unrealistic idealised accounts of themselves and their families – usually not borne out by their unkempt appearance. With increasing feelings of security in the group they present equally unreal negative images, and only after these have been accepted without judgement do new members then begin to reveal skills and discuss problems at a deeper, more realistic level. Some members need a long time (twelve months is not unusual) to achieve the latter stage, and sometimes it is not until group membership has changed considerably and they are in a position to compare themselves favourably with newcomers that they begin to allow themselves to shine.

FORMATION AND CONTINUITY

The type of group I am about to describe seems to have the advantages of both open and closed groups. It is open in the sense that new members are accepted at any time, and may leave at any time. It is closed in the sense that it serves a limited pre-selected membership, i.e. FSU clients who already have ties and loyalties to the agency and its workers, and who know that ceasing to be a member of the group is not necessarily synonymous with severing the relationship with an individual caseworker and the agency.

It has been postulated that open groups are more creative than closed groups because of the continuing influx of new ideas, beliefs and values (Ziller, 1965). This is certainly so with groups for the socially deprived, because individual members have so few personal resources. The group can very easily get caught on a treadmill of depression when, as one member expressed it, 'The more we talk the worse it seems to get'. In our case the need to avoid such depressed inward-looking situations overrides a disadvantage of open groups – that they tend to be in a constant state of flux and unable to plan ahead. FSU clients are unused to planning ahead in any case, but the long-term nature of most members' involvement with the group does produce a degree of stability, and makes possible the handing on of traditions. One hears comments such as 'We come because we want to learn to stand on our own feet', or 'Will you call for me if I come on the bus because I've got to get over my fear of riding on buses?' (said to another member). One of the traditions is that members aim to get themselves and their children to the group instead of relying on transport being provided.

Another one is that school age children who are unable to attend school are not allowed to attend the group, and the mother is 'expected' to stay at home with the child. The more self-centred the mother the harder this rule seems; but it has been discovered that several school age children can disrupt everything, and the membership is not strong enough to be able to allow exceptions. Seeing this rule in its positive sense of caring for the child's needs only occurs much later when there has been considerable emotional development.

Looking back over the records of the past ten years, there have been distinct groups in spite of the overlapping of membership. Possibly *because* of the overlapping, traditions are not easily discarded, a feature which most forcibly impressed me three years ago and which gave rise to the present style of group. At that time the group appeared to have come to a natural end just prior to the school summer vacation. I wanted to try out a new style of group, since for several years the pattern had been an afternoon meeting with discussion and sporadic outbursts of activity–usually focused on such things as embroidery, rug making or very simple dressmaking. This pattern did not allow for flexibility and tended to inhibit physical movement, thus making it easy for a member to remain in a passive, non-participatory role. Also there was a tendency for the group to get caught up in a sterile recital of woes – the 'treadmill of depression'. I wanted to see what would happen if members could move around in interacting subgroups, and if they could be provided with opportunities for organising group activities themselves. I had seen and been impressed by a group of similarly deprived clients whose main activity was preparation of a midday meal, and I wished to experiment on similar lines. The new scheme was for the group to meet during the morning, prepare lunch and have a meal together, and finish up with a 'post-prandial' discussion. I changed the meeting day from Tuesday to Thursday to emphasise the new style, and mothers on the Unit caseload were invited to join. Four mothers came and showed complete indifference to the idea of preparing lunch, preferring to buy themselves a sandwich. No one else applied to join, but meanwhile the two remaining members of the previous Tuesday group continued to turn up on Tuesday afternoons, and could not be persuaded to try the Thursday group. Their group began to grow and the Thursday one fizzled out, at which point I accepted that tradition was stronger than I was and moved back to the Tuesday group and watched it continue evolving at its own pace.

RECRUITMENT

In this case the two members from the previous group, Alma and June, carried on the traditions, and recruited new members from clients whom they met in the Unit on other occasions – when they came to purchase second-hand clothing, for instance. Two of these were husbands who had wanted to come with their wives. In all previous groups caseworkers had recruited from their own caseloads. This time it was left entirely to the group, and Alma and June assumed leadership from the start. It was interesting to watch Alma's developing self-confidence, because in previous group settings she had been timid and silent. June became the 'historian', describing incidents and activities from previous groups, but above all she was able to offer hope and consolation to newer, depressed members by recalling her own past. 'Don't worry if you don't say anything, I came for a year and never opened my mouth!' 'Didn't change me jumper and skirt for a month!' This comment carried more weight because she was clean and smartly dressed and wearing make-up.

New members seemed more motivated towards change because they had chosen to join the group. For one thing there was little demand for help with transport – a fact which caused the social workers to wonder whether in the past they had not been too eager to offer transport which once begun was not so easy to discontinue.

Another phenomenon of this self-selected group was that they got down to talking about their real problems at an earlier stage than previous groups. In fact one member suggested we should have a second meeting in the week for games – 'To get away from our troubles!'

Since the Unit clientele were for the most part young parents in their twenties, age discrepancy presented no problem. The chief difficulty lay in a reluctance to limit numbers. They found it hard to refuse anybody who they felt would fit into the group, and at times I had to be firm about not exceeding a membership of twelve, a number which ensured an average attendance of eight given the crises and illness to which the families were prone. Eight seems to be the optimum for a group of this kind, as anything above this too easily disintegrates into a crowd, which precludes the kind of deeper sharing and learning from one another which is the chief purpose of the group. It is also useful to have pressure from would-be recruits to remind members that they cannot stay in the group indefinitely.

Fears that the group might invite the seriously neurotic or psychotic proved on the whole to be unfounded, though sometimes sympathy did override their better judgement, as was the case with Shirley, a very damaged, restless person. Lax as most of the members were about child care, they were horrified at Shirley's indifference towards her child, and tried hard to help her with feeding and nappy changing. Shirley was quite willing to hand the baby over while she curled up in a chair and snored through the meeting. She dropped out of the group shortly before giving birth to another child, and there was no attempt by members to encourage her back.

Experience has confirmed that unsuitable members do drop out fairly soon, but it is necessary for the group worker to help the other members to recognise their hostile feelings and to deal positively with the unacceptable member. They avoid confrontation, even when the offending member is disrupting the group, and it is hard for the group worker to resist pressure to tackle the offender. However, the result of the group worker's standing firm on these issues has led to a list of rules being drawn up and pinned to the door, and I am sure they were not the first group to have hidden behind the objectivity of the written word. Because this document needed a signature, three committee members were elected and given the additional task of enforcing the rules when necessary. This does actually work, though direct confrontation still tends to be avoided.

The current group consists of seven mothers and five fathers, which includes four married couples. Admitting fathers to the group had been resisted until three years ago when the Tuesday group resurrected itself. I think the change of attitude to some extent reflects a change in society's attitude towards men. There is slightly more tolerance of the unemployed man if this is due to social or personal handicap, and one of our current members, Jim, is an unsupported father who receives a good deal of support from group members, some of whom are unsupported mothers. It is important that the men are not in too much of a minority, which could lead to identity problems, but their numbers do fluctuate as they go in and out of jobs. On the positive side they provide a balance when domestic or matrimonial matters are being discussed, and I have noticed far less tendency for the mothers to project blame for all their troubles on to their husbands. A mixed sex group shows less tendency to wallow in depression – a bawdy joke or two soon lightens the atmosphere!

On the negative side there is a risk of liaisons forming and leading to complications. For instance, Jim, the widower in the group, became involved with Marie, an unsupported mother also in the group, much to everyone's disapproval because the group as a whole had great difficulty in tolerating Marie's destructive behaviour. Jim knew the group disapproved of his alliance, but this did not deter him; the outcome was unhappy, but Jim has remained in the group, and through his doing so there would seem to be more chance of his being helped towards a more realistic facing of himself and his problems. Marie has removed herself from the group for the time being, but the door is open should she be able to make more use of the group at a later stage.

RESOURCES

(1) *Material.* Occasionally a visiting social worker, intending to form a group such as ours, asks 'What are the most important things I shall need?', and members invariably reply, 'You will need a room with comfortable chairs, a playroom with toys and sand for the children, and a kitchen where you can at least make tea'. These are the basic requirements, and anything else can be added later. Our members have collected items in this way, and it helps the group to cohere and feel a sense of possession. Money is useful to subsidise parties and outings, and members' contributions provide added satisfaction in 'paying their own way'.

(2) *Leadership.* Although it is possible for one group worker to run a group of this kind, two is preferable. Two workers support each other and the task becomes much less arduous, given that much of the interaction within the group is on a non-verbal level. Small incidents or nuances missed by one worker will be noticed by the other; differences of opinion can be shown as positive and not destructive; planning becomes easier when two are involved. There are pitfalls, not the least being a tendency for the group to split the leadership into 'good' and 'bad', but handled properly this can provide a demonstration that everyone has both qualities.

DECIDING GOALS

The group worker will have goals both for the group and for individual members, and these will need to be conveyed to members and recapped from time to time. Konopka (1963) distinguishes three goal determinants: 'the members' expressed needs; the agency's purpose; the group worker's understanding. These may coincide, supplement or contradict each other.'

Severely deprived people will express very limited needs. They will want to get away from their homes, and have a respite from their children. Even finding friendship or enjoying the experience will at first be hedged by doubts and fears. The agency's purpose is to develop and extend the work already being done by the caseworkers on an individual level, and this is to some extent recognised by those group members who talk about wanting to stand on their own feet. Linked to this, however, is the fear that 'success' will involve separating from the security and nurture provided by the agency, so there is an inbuilt resistance to growth in themselves unless and until they are convinced that support will not disappear before they are ready for independence.

In such a group the group worker will recognise three basic goals: *an increase in individual self-confidence and skills*; *competence in social interaction*; *competence in planning ahead and organising*. Obviously at the beginning of a group and with the admittance of new members there will be coincidence between the agency's purpose and the group worker's understanding, while both will contradict the members' expressed needs.

However, if one starts from the premise that the basic value of social work is the value of the individual (Parsloe, 1969), then in the group experience members will learn to value themselves and thus move closer to an understanding of agency and group worker's goals, until with increasing self-confidence they will be found helping new members towards those same goals – and reinforcing their own developing feelings of worth.

ACHIEVING GOALS

One feature of the self-generated group was members' stronger motivation toward change in themselves, and a shorter period than formerly of 'idealism'. It was noted that within four months June was practising talking and improving in fluency and coherence; also that Alma was reflecting before speaking, whereas previously she had tended to stammer and look embarrassed.

Lack of verbal skill is not the same thing as inability to communicate. Communication can be very direct and expressive at a non-verbal level – as for instance the member who always kept her coat on when depressed. By contrast verbal fluency can disguise feelings.

Most members seem to believe that they lack the ability to express themselves, and though this may often be a realistic appraisal it is involved with their total poor self-image. This leads to 'acting out' behaviour rather than talking. Once they feel secure enough it is possible to help them by means of questions which cause them to reflect and try again. Tape-recorders have been invaluable; people listen to themselves and each other on a playback and are able to be critical by means of jokes and teasing. For example, Kate remained unaware of her loud stentorian voice, in spite of Jim's legpulling, until she heard herself on tape. After that she consciously and effectively decreased the volume.

There is always a stock of magazines in the sitting room, and those not engaged in cooking will often use articles in these as opening gambits for discussion. The more secure the group the more likely members are to ask for explanations of phrases or words. It is also useful to run through the latest 'official' pamphlets. I have found that these are often unintelligible to the group, with words such as 'domiciled' or 'inhabited' conveying nothing to them but mystery. When they receive official communications, instead of hiding them behind the clock they will now bring them to the group, and this helps everybody.

Bowlby (1973) has suggested that the secure base to which one can retreat is the prime condition for extending one's experience. This certainly seems to be the principle activating group members to extend themselves. An example was Barry who had had numerous short-lived jobs lost because of a quick temper and hostility to authority. Having acquired some insight through casework he joined the group and talked at length about his problem, linking it up with his experiences in care during most of his childhood. Most of the group could share his feelings about the experience of being in care, and gave him encouragement and support, with the result that within four weeks of joining the group he had found another job and came to group meeting the following week (sacrificing sleep as he was on night shift) to talk about the job and receive further encouragement.

The more withdrawn members will find it easier to develop self-expression through an activity. They will talk unselfconsciously while doing something, and if it is shared activity such as cooking a meal there has to be communication.

Ironically, in view of my abortive efforts with the Thursday group (above), the Tuesday group seemed from the first to want to include a meal in their programme. They progressed rapidly from sandwiches to pie and peas, which necessitated one of them putting peas into steep on the previous day, another one cooking them and someone else buying the meat pies. This arrangement lasted for eighteen months by which time initiative seemed to have waned and the group had regressed to the 'depression treadmill'. With hindsight I think the group worker could have intervened earlier to suggest that we invite an FSU mothers' group from a neighbouring town to one of our meetings. The suggestion was received with interest if not enthusiasm, but that visit marked a watershed for the group.

The visitors were markedly unimpressed by our offering of pie and peas, and boasted about their meals. They issued a return invitation, and no effort was spared to impress us. Our members were mortified, but rose to the challenge and decided that there would be a return match! From that day planning and preparation of lunch became a central feature of the group's activity, and they were keen to use the knowledge of a student teacher who was later on placement at the Unit on Tuesdays.

Cooking a meal provides opportunities of achievement in all three basic goals. Individuals improve their skills through interest and practice. The group worker is careful to encourage individual effort and to praise whenever possible. Members who have usually received little positive feedback in their lives are quick to recognise its value and to copy the group worker's example. The day Kate and Linda were cooks for the first time the group nearly overdid the praise, considering they had eaten sloppy shepherd's pie, and Angel Delight which had finished up as chocolate water!

Cooking a meal is an activity which helps social interaction; concensus decisions have to be arrived at if they are to eat. Sharing the shopping and the cost is a social activity calling for forbearance if someone spends too much – which in turn is a means for individual learning. Learning to follow recipes; discovering that stewing meat is more tender if it has a long cooking time, or that fresh vegetables in season are cheaper and tastier than tinned or prepacked; learning what constitutes a balanced meal for the children and adults; all these are individual learning experiences, mediated through one another and the whole operation becomes an exercise in planning ahead and organising. Alma, Tom, Jim and Beryl, the current natural leaders, have all taken turns to organise the group in respect of deciding the next week's menu and who is to bring what and how much.

The rewards came not only through the enjoyment of the meals and the sense of achievement, but also when we gave a return invitation to the rival FSU group, and later by a visit from a local authority group whom we shook out of their rut in much the same way as we had been. Experience has demonstrated that pressure from peers within a group, and pressures by one group on another are highly effective stimuli for the examination of group goals.

Possibly the one most important achievement of group meal preparation was an increased ability to plan ahead by individuals habitually living hand to mouth. Having mastered the ability to look one week ahead they began in October planning and saving up for a Christmas party. They needed the help of the student teacher in deciding quantities and cost, but they made good use of this, and the following year were able to begin saving up from September and to carry through all the preparations, including baking and icing a Christmas cake, without any help whatsoever. The party was an even bigger success, as they said, 'Because we did it all ourselves'.

Plans are the means by which goals are attained, and the group worker will be constantly making and revising plans by which he hopes to help the group and individuals to recognise needs and achieve goals. Bringing in the student teacher was a way of focusing a particular activity, leaving both group workers free to concentrate on other needs. Inviting the other group was the group worker's plan but the second time members themselves planned the visit and contacted the group. In group work as in casework the aim must be for clients to become increasingly able to do and plan on their own behalf. As Foulkes and Anthony (1965) put it: 'Good leadership will develop forces in the group which will take over the leader's original function and free him to work at a higher level.'

In all groups, but especially in growth oriented groups, goals for the group and for the individual are adopted through example and approval. At first it is the group worker's approval, then the approval of fellow members, and at a later, more advanced stage success becomes the spur and is its own reward. At this stage group members are likely to outdo the leader in goal setting. For instance, the second Christmas party was such a success that the group decided to hold a monthly social.

As goals apply at both individual and group level, at any one time there will be individuals at varying stages of achievement, and the group will be at a particular stage. New members who happen to join at a point where the group is experiencing the headiness of success will have the advantage of witnessing the group goals achieved, but soon after – when the competent members have left – the remaining members have to take over the struggle. Their plans and their ultimate achievements will be different as, for instance, they might decide on a summer outing or a weekend camp instead of a Christmas party.

Naturally the group worker's ultimate goal for the group is that members should carry their new knowledge and skill into the home and work situation. Barry's inability to hold down a job arose from his quick temper and over-sensitivity to authority. After getting a job he continued to attend group meetings on the weeks he was working night shift, because he realised that he had to learn to tolerate others and to control his feelings. Barry was intelligent enough to gain and use insight. Tom provided a different example. He had become unemployed because of failing eyesight, and this undermined his already weak self-assertiveness. Alma, who had joined the group some months before her husband, made significant gains in confidence and self-expression and became the dominant partner. After several months in the group Tom became more assertive, and discovered that Alma was prepared to let him be the dominant one. The result was Tom taking firmer control of their eight children, freeing Alma's energy for coping more satisfactorily with the physical care of home and children. This was an example of learning more effective behaviour through group feedback and applying it to the home situation. Jim was able to use the group for learning skills in cooking and catering which helped him to cope with the role of unsupported father.

These members found an additional incentive through the appreciation shown by their families. Such positive feedback was lacking in Beryl's case, so that although she had status in the group both as cook and organiser, at home she was consistently undermined by her husband and received little appreciation from her children who were confused by constant arguments between the parents. Consequently Beryl's care of the home remained chaotic, but she did improve in budgeting and brought her family out of debt. Some members seemed to prefer a double standard, leaving the Unit kitchen spotless but returning to dirt and chaos at home. However, the group worker has to be aware of the enormous length of time needed by some members. For instance, June had been coming to the group over six years for block periods of a few months interspersed with periods of depression, and had also been receiving casework help all that time before it was felt that she was coping adequately at home and taking more interest in life in general, though still with an intractable marital problem.

UNDER FIVES

While the parents are engaged in their activities their young children are busy with sand and water play, painting or singing rhymes, in a separate room. Once the children are used to the play group they tend to stay there with only occasional sorties to show parents something they have made. Newcomers, both parents and children, need frequent contact with each other, and this is tolerated for several weeks by the group. After that, if separation is still a problem, pressure from the group increases, and only in a few cases does the group worker need to reinforce this pressure. Kate, quite unconsciously, was preventing her child from settling in his group. The others pointed this out, and mirrored it back to her one day when she blatantly called back her child as he was returning to his play group. Once aware of her behaviour she began to check herself.

Work with the children is as important as with their parents, and ideally one needs a trained pre-school play group leader, with at least one other helper, both prepared to give a full year's commitment. The ideal is seldom attainable, but when we have been fortunate in having this kind of leadership in the play group there have been obvious gains to the children. A succession of new faces reinforces the children's insecurity, and in some cases repeats a pattern which is already evident in their home environment. Continuity of leadership produces a contented group, whose toddler members are eager to learn and experiment, and even at the very low provision of one day a week there are gains in speech development and co-ordination. Untrained child minders are very much a second best, but not to be rejected if these are the only ones available, as there is always a chance that one of them might become interested enough to attend a training course. Male helpers, though rarer, are always appreciated by the children, many of whom lack positive male relationships even when fathers are still in the family.

When choosing the next week's menu the children's needs are borne in mind, and parents learn almost unconsciously how to balance and serve a child's meal. Some mothers grossly overfeed their children, others pander to food fads, but this is controlled in the group situation. I overheard Kate say, 'My children don't like rhubarb', and Beryl reply, 'They are having it, Auntie Beryl says so'. One of them came back for seconds! The mothers (or fathers) feed their own children while the helpers have a break.

The parents' low standards of child care are seldom entirely due to lack of knowledge. It seems truer to say that the children are caught up in the total family sense of worthlessness and failure. The children become visible examples of this. Kate's baby was her sixth child, and even allowing for below-average intelligence it is obviously an oversimplification to say that she still did not know how to feed and make comfortable her children. She had apparently given up trying, and needed peer influence as well as social work. The group followed the group worker's example in praising her at any opportunity; they also became parents and scolded her. As her self-confidence increased she and the children turned up looking cleaner and better dressed, and the children were more content and obviously better fed.

The door between the kitchen and playroom is usually open, so that before lunch there is an opportunity for parents to see their children at play. I have noticed that the men seem to have more idea of play than their wives, but I can only speculate as to why this is so, and I have no knowledge of any relevant studies. I have not recorded any great success in getting mothers to become more positively involved with their children's play, the biggest obstacle being the mother's own attention needs. However, if one assumes that a low level of parental participation in children's play has its roots in working class culture (Newson, 1968), then one needs to be cautious about trying to produce change. Consequently I have tended to concentrate on physical child care and interpretation of children's behaviour rather than attempting to involve parents actively with their children. There is room for more experiment and study in this whole area.

CONFLICT AND TRAUMA

One way of assessing the progress of a group is by examining the way it resolves conflict (Konopka, 1963). A characteristic of deprived people is impulsive behaviour, which in a conflict situation leads them into displays of verbal abuse, or at worst physical violence. In the group situation what they do about conflict depends to a large extent on the frame of reference in which the group sees itself (Garland *et al.*, 1972) or, if the group is in a stage of preaffiliation, on the frames of reference in which individual members see the group. An example of the latter occurred when some members thought they were contributing more than others, particularly with regard to washing up, and it was a clash between older and newer members. The older ones who were beginning to develop an 'us' frame of reference suggested a rota, but Linda, a very unstable young woman, flew into a hysterical outburst which she directed towards the male group worker, her frame of reference being the institution of 'us and them'. Linda's contemporaries gave her half-hearted support and the meeting ended fairly abruptly. During the squabble Kate neglected to attend to her baby's needs, which resulted in a pile of faeces on the floor.

I think it is important following conflict to allow the group a cooling off period and not to expect conflicts to be dealt with at a time when feelings are high. In this way members learn the value of not acting impulsively. It is also important for the group worker to be aware of the 'hidden agenda' in a group meeting. In the case mentioned the established members were feeling resentful of the newer ones, and this general tension had split into a power struggle between Tom and Jim; a challenge to both from Fred (Linda's husband and a 'new boy'); a 'troika' leadership by Beryl, Alma and Tom – which sometimes admitted Jim but not always; Kate oscillating between trying to behave like a responsible 'elder' and regressing to pair off with Linda; and group resentment because I was absent. Kate's allowing her baby to make a mess was a visible sign of anger, but there were many other non-verbal messages flying about, so that it was important for the group worker as well as members to have a cooling off period in order that both group workers could examine the dynamics and make plans for helping members to resolve their problems. To have treated the incident merely as a childish squabble about washing up would have been to miss an opportunity of fostering growth in individuals and in the group. The following week Linda prevented face-to-face discussion by taking charge of the kitchen and the cooking – presenting herself as the 'good girl'. Kate was taken to task by Jim for having supported Linda. Kate denied it and burst into tears, but three weeks later when Linda and Fred had missed two group meetings Kate asked if she could become a committee member in place of Linda. I saw this as Kate making a real choice to join the elders, who demonstrated maturity by insisting that one of them must first visit Linda to inquire why she was absent.

Occasionally emotional build-ups occur which are not the result of conflict. I recall an occasion when one of the members, overwhelmed by recent events in her family, in the course of which two of her brothers had been arrested for murder, poured out all her anxiety, shame and fear. The group, shocked, listened patiently, giving her the needed opportunity to verbalise and thus try to come to grips with the situation. They also gave sympathy and understanding of her feelings, thus alleviating her fear that no one would now want to know her. After a while someone remarked, 'Oh, it's raining and I've left my washing out', and I picked this up – sensing that the group had given as much as they could – and added that ordinary life has to continue in spite of the tragedies.

In my experience groups can deal with intense emotion, provided the group worker remains calm and is prepared to intervene at a critical point. Jim and his wife Jean had only been attending the group a few weeks when Jean collapsed from an overdose during the meeting, and was dead on arrival at hospital. We were all suffering from shock and one or two began crying, but that did not prevent Alma and Beryl from arranging support for Jim. The following week, and for several weeks, the group needed to talk about the incident over and over again. As well as our own guilt – had we done the right things? could we have saved her? could we have prevented it? – there were more fundamental questions centring round drug taking, and one's responsibilities as a wife and mother. It was interesting that Helen, who had for some time seemed trapped in black despair about her marital and home situation, seemed to be shaken into facing up to her life.

Her appearance improved, and there was a spectacular improvement in home care and treatment of her children. In the group she became a rival for leadership against Alma and Tom, and six months later, after a spell of brushing up her cookery, she dropped out of the group, saying she had too much to do at home. A year later she had maintained the improvement. Two members dropped out of the group following the incident – both were withdrawn, disturbed characters, unable to cope with shock at that level, but on balance we were able to use the experience positively. A strong bond was formed between Alma, Tom, Jim and Beryl which has resulted in emotional growth in all four, and is helping Jim through his present difficulties (mentioned earlier).

Following an experience of this kind a closed group might have become too inward looking and dependent on each other. An open group forces members to look towards the future (Ziller, 1965), and in this case by the time the trauma had been worked and talked through new members were joining and forcing the older ones to concentrate on the present and the future.

TERMINATION

Membership of the group may be needed for several years before the individual achieves sufficient confidence and social maturity to hold his own in the larger community, but it is important not to lose sight of the fact that this is the ultimate aim, and, just as with casework, the termination process can be a positive stage of the group work experience (Bywaters, 1975). A good time to focus this is during the weeks leading up to the school summer vacation, because a break of six weeks represents a minor or intermediate ending, and is the time when the biggest exodus of members takes place. Inevitably the group when it reconvenes in the autumn will seem different.

Signs of outgrowing the group are irritation and a feeling of impatience with what is felt to be slowness and triviality. The problem facing the member who wants to move on is lack of suitable alternatives, but here the situation has improved over recent years, and in addition to the working men's clubs (most of which admit women nowadays) community development schemes of one sort or another can absorb ex-members into, for instance, tenants' associations or hobby groups, while the adult education movement is beginning to concentrate more on providing informal education groups on some of the inner city housing estates. Some ex-members take up paid employment, perhaps for the first time.

MEASURING PROGRESS

I have already quoted examples of members who have shown obvious gains, but it must be remembered that, with the exception of Barry – who in any case may yet slip back before his new self-confidence is thoroughly established – such gains have been made gradually over a long time. Without careful records one can miss subtle changes. In my recording I note any modifications I need to make in respect of goals; I note whether last week's plans have been practicable, and make further plans for the next meeting. There are goals and plans for each individual and for the group as a whole, and in assessing individual needs I draw upon the Stages of Growth theory of Erikson (1950 and 1968), and Bales' (1950) Interaction Process Analysis. Sociograms are useful aids to looking at individual and group dynamics, as in Louis Lowy's (1972) chapter on 'Goal Formulation in Social Work with Groups'. The 'Model for Stages of Development in Social Work Groups' (Garland *et al.*, 1972) is also useful when looking at the group as a whole. If one is looking systematically at the group and its members there is no need for long detailed accounts.

Caseworkers involved with individual members can provide the group worker with valuable feedback as to progress, or otherwise. It is important to have frequent reciprocal feedback between group worker and caseworkers, not least for the support it gives to the group worker, especially a single-handed one.

Thus progress is measured by experiencing with the group, i.e. being part of it; recording of it, i.e. part of one's self being free to observe the group; and, third, by additional feedback from the group via the caseworker. In this way one's subjective impressions are corrected by the discipline of recording, and by the more objective view from outside.

SUMMARY

The socially deprived person was defined as one who is isolated in infantile self-centredness, and lacks any sense of personal worth. In order to learn to relate to others, or to evaluate himself, he needs to experience the kind of interdependency which provides reciprocal satisfaction of social and emotional needs, and which can be provided through group experience.

The view of the group worker's task as being to provide primary nurture for immature individuals has been found to be inadequate, and it is suggested that Berne's Transactional Analysis theory provides a more satisfactory framework. Earlier expectations concerning communication and self-exposure have been modified by observations, and reinforced by subsequent developments in theories of group dynamics.

Group formation is dependent on two factors: (1) the group is open ended, (2) membership is limited to FSU clients.

Some of the advantages and disadvantages of open groups were considered and reasons given for preferring an open group.

The group exists on a minimum of material resources, and at times there has only been one leader. Two however is preferable.

The process of determining goals was examined from the standpoint of the agency, the group worker and the group member. The group worker recognises three basic goals: (1) an increase in individual self-confidence, (2) competence in social interaction, (3) competence in planning ahead and organising. These aims spring from the premise that the basic value of social work is the value of the individual.

Goals are achieved through (1) developing self-expression and verbal ability, (2) group activities which require communication, planning and sharing.

It was stressed that a secure base to which one can retreat is the prime condition for extending one's experience.

The distinction was drawn between goals and plans, and mention made of some of the factors affecting the carry over of newly acquired confidence into the home and work situation.

The linked under fives play group was described, and mention made of some of the problems of leadership. Parental involvement is encouraged within a structure which has been built into the programme, and is used as a means of diagnosis and education.

One way of assessing the progress of a group is by examining the way it resolves conflict. Examples were given of incidents of conflict and trauma and how they were dealt with.

Consideration was given to some of the problems of termination and separation peculiar to a long-term open group which is concerned primarily with emotional growth.

In order to measure the slow progress of individuals in the group, records must be kept and information exchanged with social workers involved in a one-to-one relationship with group members. Constant revision of goals and plans helps to delineate progress, and mention was made of some theoretical models which have been found helpful.

Chapter 11

GROUP WORK IN A HOSTEL FOR THE MENTALLY HANDICAPPED

Alice Breslin and Sheila Sturton

RESIDENTIAL GROUP WORK

In a residential institution no one functions in true isolation. Through the process of giving and receiving care, and the sheer proximity of communal living, residents and staff are drawn together as members of a total group. This situation is often regarded as essentially destructive, leading to loss of individuality and all the deadening effects of institutionalisation. However, a more hopeful interpretation is possible, and is essential if residential care is to develop. Life in an institution can be seen as a kind of corporate enterprise based on mutual need and interdependence, to which all can contribute with dignity and from which all can derive comfort. Membership of the residential group may actually enhance rather than diminish the quality of life for both residents and staff.

The authors of the discussion document *Training for Residential Work* take this approach, setting out a challenging and heartening philosophy of residential care (Central Council for Education and Training in Social Work, 1973):

> In ideal terms, the residential experience . . . becomes a privileged opportunity for enrichment, and contributing to the experience of others, rather than 'time out of life' . . . We explicitly reject the tendency to categorize people according to their problems of handicap, and therefore to set sterile and limited goals of achievement for them.
>
> In our view, good residential care involves a collaboration between residents and staff, to establish their capacities and needs, and to define the objectives of work . . . for maximum effectiveness, efficiency and economy, all the resources of a residential society need to be utilized: those of residents as well as those of staff.

If we accept this view of residential living we must encourage the necessary collaboration between residents and staff. In the everyday life of an institution there are many informal ways of involving the residents and stimulating the contribution they can make to the well-being of the total group. Structured opportunities for involvement are important as well, to reinforce what can be achieved informally. Group work provides such an opportunity, through the planned use of group discussions for residents and staff. Clearly formal meetings can never replace more spontaneous channels of communication; but there is probably no substitute for regular, known occasions when the whole residential group can talk over their experience of life together.

Of course some doubt may be felt about the feasibility of group work for all forms of residential care. Community meetings are a recognised part of life in many rehabilitation hostels for the mentally ill, and occasionally are also offered to residents in old people's homes with encouraging results. But can the same method help people who are mentally handicapped, have considerable problems in communicating, and do not readily understand the nature of group membership? It would be easy to reject the idea of formal group work untried. Yet if residents who are mentally handicapped could learn to make use of group discussion they would be much better equipped to benefit from the group living situation in which they find themselves.

At a conference held in 1972 for mentally handicapped people, the delegates expressed a wish for just those opportunities that group work can offer – a greater say in running their own lives, shared meetings with staff (Campaign for the Mentally Handicapped, 1972). When our clients are asking for greater responsibility and a chance to participate, and group meetings would be a possible vehicle for achieving this, we should surely be prepared to risk some experiments in the use of group methods.

This article describes one such experiment, carried out in a local authority hostel for mentally handicapped women. In October 1972 the staff decided to set up regular group meetings with the residents, and invited their department's group work consultant to take part. This account covers the first six months of the group. It may seem premature to evaluate the project at this stage, but the initial results are so encouraging that we did not want to delay in sharing them with a wider audience.

THE HOSTEL

Originally the hostel was intended to provide places for women who could be rehabilitated into a work situation and move into lodgings. In recent years, however, there has been a great demand for accommodation for people whose degree of mental handicap makes this sort of rehabilitation impossible. At the moment there are twenty-seven residents, with ages ranging from 18 to 78, and only two of them are working.* Apart from two who are retired the remainder attend the local adult training centre. If there

* Since this paper was written in the summer of 1973, the situation has changed – the majority are now working.

were a labour shortage, some of these residents would probably be able to find and hold down work in the community; others are severely mentally handicapped and for them the training centre is most suitable. The residents come to the hostel from widely varying backgrounds: some have been discharged from large subnormality hospitals after years of strictly regulated institutional life; others have come from family situations which have broken down.

Rehabilitation obviously has a limited meaning for many of the residents, since they cannot hope to live unsupported in the community. For the most handicapped the hostel will be a permanent home, although they are of course helped to develop their potential to the full within the hostel setting. Others may be able to move out to unstaffed hostel accommodation where they have the support of a small group of friends and can turn to the hostel staff for help if necessary. Two group homes have been set up near the hostel on this basis – one for working women and one for people at the training centre – and have proved most successful.

From the point of view of group work, the most important aspect of the hostel is the range of ability displayed by the residents. Some are capable and articulate, and can reflect well on their situation; others are very handicapped and dependent, with only a few words at their command. With such differences in ability within the residential group, the viability of group work was well tested.

PLANNING THE GROUP

The staff have always believed that the feelings and ideas of mentally handicapped people should be valued and respected. This belief underpins the whole programme of care in the hostel: residents are encouraged to develop a sense of self-worth, to think for themselves as far as possible, and to be sensitive to each other's needs.

The idea of setting up a group grew naturally out of this caring philosophy. The staff thought a group might have a favourable effect on life in the hostel in a number of ways. Joint discussions for residents and staff would be a good medium for involving everyone in the running of the hostel: issues could be raised and talked over, and decisions made within the group. The staff recognised that their responsibility in some areas would remain, but could be shared with the residents in others. They also hoped the group would provide an open forum where people could express their feelings about living together, and learn of the impact they have on each other. Achievements and sorrows could be shared, and conflicts resolved openly and with dignity. In this way relationships within the hostel could be strengthened, and residents might develop social skills. Above all, the staff hoped that group discussion, if properly handled, would increase each individual's self-esteem, because everyone would feel they had a place in the group and a contribution to make.

Although the staff had high expectations of the group, they were also apprehensive. Without specific training in group work they were unwilling to hold group discussions on their own – hence the invitation to the group worker. The group worker had her own apprehensions too. To hold sensible meetings of twenty-five or so people is never easy; to do so when the participants have considerable difficulties in verbal communication, a short span of concentration, and are intellectually limited seemed almost impossible. How would the residents react to a stranger visiting just for group meetings? Would they grasp the purpose of the group at all?

From the outset staff and group worker co-operated as a team. The staff had specialised knowledge of mentally handicapped people, and of course were familiar with all aspects of life in the hostel; the group worker lacked this understanding but was experienced in group methods. Between us we had enough experience and skills to compensate for any individual deficiencies, so it was obviously important to use a team approach.

The residents were introduced to the group worker at a preliminary session, and were asked by the staff if they would like to meet regularly. They agreed, and this initial agreement has been reinforced by the very high level of attendance at each meeting. Residents come voluntarily, and staff are careful not to press anyone to take part, but usually almost everyone is present. The group meets fortnightly in the evenings, and all the staff on duty join in.

It is possible to analyse the development of the group in two main ways: the content of the discussions, and the form they took. At first the form of the meetings preoccupied staff, group worker and residents; later, when the group was functioning better, the subjects raised became the more significant feature of the meetings.

INTERACTION WITHIN THE GROUP

We began by giving clear statements about how the group might be used – to talk about what people had been doing, what had been going on in the hostel, to share worries, and so on – and encourage everyone to participate.

This is usually sufficient to get a group 'off the ground' with people of normal intelligence. In this case it was clearly not enough. Initially meetings were chaotic. The residents were shy, and unsure how to take part; silences or embarrassed giggles alternated with outbursts of comment, with people talking against each other. Remarks were either directed to the staff and group worker – as though they were the only people in the group worth talking to – or made to a subgroup when someone else was capturing the staff's attention. Topics might be raised, but were quickly abandoned, so there was no continuity to the discussions. Laughter was often used to cover the discomfiture people felt at participating in a puzzling exercise.

We realised that a lot of work would have to be done on the basic issue of how the group was to function. Without dampening the wish to participate we had to discourage the residents from talking all at once or splintering into subgroups. They too appreciated that something was wrong: apart from staff, no one responded to their contributions, and they were bored by disconnected discussion which they could not follow. We talked about ways of improving the situation. Could they talk one at a time? Could they speak not just to staff and group worker but the whole group? Could someone else in the group give an answer sometimes? The residents agreed to try these tactics, and we illustrated what was needed by our own behaviour in the meetings, since they clearly required a 'model' of group membership to copy. At times a very explicit demonstration of what we meant was necessary. A resident might come up to the group worker to show her brooch or a photo, or might lean over to whisper a comment in the ear of a member of staff. We would thank her for contributing and then, without destroying her wish to communicate, would gently turn her round to the whole group, suggesting she show everyone, tell everyone her ideas. It would then be important to encourage the rest of the residents to look at what was being offered, or comment on the ideas put forward.

Gradually the meetings improved. After the first stage, when we had to put tremendous efforts into simply making communications within the group possible, the residents began to work at this themselves. To begin with they quietened each other when staff were speaking; later this courtesy was extended to other residents as well. They no longer talked just to us, but to the whole group, and increasingly ventured responses to each other's comments. Now the group functions well by any standards. People are usually listened to with attention; and even the very shy or inarticulate enjoy making an occasional contribution, encouraged by the rest of the group. Residents are ready before the session starts, and have often planned what they want to say. In response to a query from the group worker about how best to cope with meeting in a large room on scattered chairs, the residents now rearrange the seats into a close circle. There is a much wider spread of involvement during the discussions. At first a vociferous few did most of the talking; now participating is more evenly shared among the whole group.

After the meetings are over residents often stay behind to talk to the group worker. Sometimes this is simply to tell her about some incident well known to everyone else already, and therefore not raised in the group – such as getting a birthday card or finishing off some knitting. Occasionally residents will want to express a worry which they were anxious to bring out in the group. These 'marginal' discussions afterward help to remind us that people are still inhibited in the meetings, or can easily be overlooked, especially if they find it hard to talk at all. It is important fo us to be aware of the Mongol resident struggling to put thoughts into words, or the woman depressed and silent in the corner; we cannot, of course, make people talk if they would rather not, but a word of inquiry and encouragement in a pause in the group discussion can often bring out someone's particular worry.

We feel that the way the meetings function is crucial. Not everyone is verbally competent: many stumble, and cannot contribute with much relevance. It is not merely good group work to value each person's contribution and encourage group discipline so that all are listened to with sympathy and respect, and given some appropriate response. It is a reflection of the philosophy behind the whole programme of care. To say we want all to participate, and not to help the residents make this participation possible; to say we value individuals, but let them be ignored by the whole group – this would lead to a contradiction between the group sessions and our philosophy. Residents who were less able could sink to the bottom in the group, and have their feelings of worthlessness reinforced. Vigorous and sustained efforts to prevent this happening are obviously an essential feature of group work with mentally handicapped people.

THE CONTENT OF THE DISCUSSIONS

The residents came to accept and want a group which functioned in an orderly and sensitive fashion. Apart from this, how free have they felt to make full use of the meetings by raising matters of individual or general concern? The staff had a very wide brief for the group, and hoped that the residents would share personal worries or achievements and also discuss relationships with each other and aspects of hostel management. They were quite prepared to hear conflicts aired or complaints levelled at themselves.

The residents did not accept this brief to begin with. Suggestions from the staff that they might like to talk about quarrels, or suggest changes in the hostel, were met with embarrassed laughter and indications that 'It's not for us to decide things'. Scarcely surprisingly, the meetings initially stayed on safer topics – work at the training centre, recent films seen, who was going out at the weekends. Residents showed sewing they were doing, and talked about hobbies. Even in these areas they needed a lot of encouragement, and some direct questioning, to talk at all.

Remarks tended to mean 'I am here, notice me, I have something to say', and we responded appropriately with praise, while trying to extend the contributions into a general discussion – who else was packing boxes at the training centre, what sort of films did the others like, was anyone else going out soon? Everyone was on best behaviour, apparently anxious to show themselves and the hostel as a whole in a good light to the stranger. We can only speculate how this early phase of the group might have gone had no outsider been present.

After three meetings the first significant change occurred. The residents wanted to plan their own Christmas party, and brought this idea to the meeting. The staff welcomed the plan, while firmly placing responsibility for the party with the residents. We discussed the probable expenditure, the various tasks involved, and who might be invited. One resident said she would like to have a live pop group to play at the party, instead of the usual records. There was an outburst of enthusiasm for this, followed by some realism from the more thoughtful residents – it would cost too much! We talked about this, and a member of staff offered to see if a local group she knew would agree to come and play.

The party took place as planned, and was a great success. Boyfriends came; so did the pop group; and so did the group worker. The food was well prepared, and the residents were beautifully dressed – some in long dresses which transformed them. Not everyone felt comfortable in a party situation, but with guidance from the staff and each other soon learned how to be hostesses to their guests.

The tangible success of the party helped to convince the residents that the group really was a place for planning activities. They saw that the discussion was not empty, but had an impact on their lives. From then on, the meetings seemed to be charged with greater significance, and the issues raised were often painful ones which had been avoided before. Although people continued to make contributions of the 'I am here, I have something to say' variety, comments were increasingly made of a different kind: 'I have a concern to raise, I would like a response from someone.' The staff's hopes for the group began to be realised.

The first really difficult issue brought to the group arose from a change within the hostel. Five of the residents were to move out to a new unstaffed house nearby – with their agreement, of course. The following record of part of the meeting where this was discussed was written by the group worker.

> When I arrived at the hostel Ann approached me to say that she and four of the others would be moving out at the weekend into the new unstaffed hostel. I encouraged her to raise this in the meeting . . . Before the session began there was an incident in the office when Doris rushed in demanding that a member of staff wash her hair for her. She was told quite firmly that she was capable of doing this herself. She became very upset and went off crying. I gathered that she was another of the candidates for the unstaffed hostel, and was reacting to the prospect of moving out (though she had opted for the move) by making excessive demands on the staff . . .
>
> I went into the meeting room ahead of the staff, to find everyone assembled and listening in silence to Doris, who was crying noisily and saying something between sobs. She stopped talking when she saw me

but went on crying. There was a pause, and I encouraged her to continue. She explained she was not going to the house after all – she'd changed her mind. It took a lot of work to sort out why. At intervals she would revert to sobs again, and I appealed to the others to help her say what was troubling her, if they knew. Gradually the problem emerged: Doris' friend, Muriel, who was not moving out, was 'being mean' to Doris. The rest of the group confirmed this. Doris could not stand being tormented – she would rather stay at the hostel.

Unfortunately Muriel was out for the evening, so could not defend herself. The feeling against her mounted higher, and it seemed she was being scapegoated for the others' anxieties and jealousies. Eventually Iris shouted out, 'You are all being unfair to Muriel', and burst into tears herself. A few others began to cry too. I said to Iris, 'It seems you are saying the change in the hostel is hard on Muriel as well as Doris – maybe Muriel is upset too'. Iris agreed. We went on to discuss, bit by bit, all the feelings involved. How did those who were moving out feel? Pride, fear, excitement in general were identified. Mrs Breslin, who was in the meeting by now, helped the five concerned talk about their plans for the house – the tasks they would have, how they would do the cooking, and so on. She was firm in getting each individual resident to speak for herself, since the more managing ones of the five tended to take over and allot the less pleasant jobs to the weaker residents, in anticipation. A calmer atmosphere permeated the meeting. We went on to encourage the residents who were staying behind to say how they felt. Jealousy, indifference, relief at not being faced with this challenging change – all these feelings seemed to be present. Discussion was slow, and there was a lot of silence.

We tried to suggest there was a connection between some of them being 'mean' to each other, and all these feelings they had. It was hard to judge how much of this was understood, but Doris, who had been the focus for distress in the group, said she would go to the hostel after all.

This meeting demonstrated to the residents that deep and disturbing feelings could be shared and to some extent relieved within the group. The five set up house successfully, and there were no major difficulties around their departure. We learnt something about helping the group handle sensitive areas of emotion through this session and subsequent ones. The residents often seemed to be caught up in conflicting feelings, only one of which they could put a name to. It was therefore important to help them recognise and define all their emotions, and work out the causes of distress where possible. A patient process of unravelling the meanings behind tears or anger or silence must take place. It is vital too to involve the rest of the group in this, because often they have the clues to the disturbance or can recognise what is happening from their own experience. Encouraging the group to think about an individual's problem and identify feelings and worries helps to develop the greater sensitivity towards others that the staff were hoping for. Of course these techniques are used in group work with other clients, but it seems especially important in this setting. To let the residents flit uneasily and superficially over a range of ill-defined feelings leads to frustration, sometimes masked by apparent boredom or withdrawal.

Since the session described above, the meetings have covered many topics, painful and joyful. Residents have talked of their feelings at being abandoned or ignored by their families, and have shared their sense of loss over having to leave home when a parent or relative died. Relationships with boyfriends, and the implications of marriage, have also been discussed, though with some inhibition. Conflicts between residents have come into the open. The main irritant seems to be the unavoidable sharing of rooms – disagreements become almost intolerable in this situation. Sometimes it is possible to arrange a swap to help the tension; sometimes alterations in sleeping arrangements are impossible, or have been tried many times before. In the end the group may be left with no alternative but to reflect on how hard it is to live en masse, after noting the conflict and ensuring that each party has had her say. This in itself seems to ease the tension.

The meetings have also been used to plan further activities, or discuss possible outings. We are careful to follow through and ask for reports on how people found the outings – were they enjoyable, could different plans have been made? Occasionally a resident is unable to take part in something strenuous, like swimming, because of a disability or a tendency to have fits: the group shows great understanding in these instances. A few suggestions have been made about changes within the hostel, and where feasible these have been put into practice. The staff welcome such suggestions, and are careful to explain why some ideas are impractical or are too expensive.

THE IMPACT ON THE HOSTEL

A residential group has value proportional to its effect on institutional life outside the actual meetings. This is often hard, of course, to evaluate, and it may be tempting to make claims for the group when changes are really due to other causes. With this proviso, there is every indication that the meetings have made a helpful contribution to the residents' lives.

The residents themselves clearly enjoy the discussions, and invest a lot in them. If someone is absent or late, it is usually to demonstrate depression or anger, rather than indifference. Roles taken in the group tend to reflect patterns of influence or friendship within the hostel as a whole; and the changes in the meetings, with more people actively taking part and less dominance by the articulate few, have been echoed in relationships outside.

The staff are extremely enthusiastic about the group. They think that the residents now hold more informal discussions among themselves than they used to, and some residents are apparently improving their communication skills. They believe there is less tension and unresolved conflict; and fewer residents run to them with tales to tell! Problems raised in the meetings do seem to be sorted out, since they do not recur again later. The staff feel that the residents are less dependent on them now for advice and support, because they have learnt to make use of their peers and gain support from a group.

It would seem that the group has begun to realise the original expectations held by the staff. The total residential group – residents and staff – have an increased sense of well-being as a result of the meetings, and this suggests that the experiment is on the right lines and need be labelled experiment no longer. We recognise, of course, that the group still has a long way to go. The residents do not seem to be as forthcoming about suggesting improvements to the hostel as they might be – perhaps they need more encouragement over this. Weekly meetings instead of fortnightly ones might hasten progress, but at the moment the group worker is unable to attend more frequently, and the staff are still reluctant to run the sessions solo. We have realised there are many areas where the group's potential can be developed further, but at least there is no lack of enthusiasm – among residents as well as staff – for further effort.

CONCLUSIONS

We have described an attempt to make use of formal group work methods in a hostel for mentally handicapped women. These methods have been successful, despite the size of the group and the degree of mental handicap involved. We feel that it is important to include everyone in gatherings of the total community, rather than to take the easier path of stimulating small group discussions, and the results we obtained seem to justify this approach. There is nothing unique about the hostel, or very sophisticated about our group methods, so we hope that staff in other residential settings for the mentally handicapped will be encouraged to try group meetings along similar lines.

POSTSCRIPT: FOUR CONSUMER COMMENTS

'Well, in the group we can say what we want to say.'
'It gives us a chance to have a good natter!'
'The staff listen to us.'
'In the group we can decide what we want to do.'

We would like to thank Herbert Laming, Deputy Director, Hertfordshire

County Council Social Services Department, who supported this group work experiment and encouraged us to write it up. We would also like to thank the Editor of *Social Work Today* who gave us permission to reprint this paper which originally appeared in *Social Work Today*, 21 February 1974, vol. 4, no. 23.

Chapter 12

FAMILY THERAPY: THE FAMILY GROUP AS THE MEDIUM FOR CHANGE

Rosemary Whiffen

INTRODUCTION

'Eels get used to skinning,' was one of my grandmother's many vivid sayings. Years later when I observed (as a family therapist) the skill with which the family scapegoat continually put him or herself in the same vulnerable position, where he must surely 'be skinned', I at last understood what she meant.

For family therapists, the knowledge and experience drawn from their own family life will always be an important source of learning. They are also influenced by many areas of professional knowledge and skill. Psychoanalytic theories and psychodynamic understanding from various sources, group dynamic, systems and communication theories are only a few of the conceptual frameworks which are drawn upon. From these sources the theory and practice of family therapy has emerged.

The family therapist, drawing on this rich and complex inheritance, has to decide which approach he will use, where to focus his therapeutic interventions and what area to choose for the medium for change. These decisions will be dictated by a variety of considerations. Some will depend on the problem the family brings to the therapist, some on the type of family and, to a certain extent, on the individuality of the therapist.

In some instances, groups of therapists working together may develop one particular way of working and come to be known for that approach. In the Philadelphia Child Guidance Clinic, for instance, Structural Family Therapy has been developed and widely taught and written about over the past few years (Minuchin, 1974).

There is an important conceptual leap to be made when moving from working with individual family members to the family as a whole. It may take many months or even years to arrive at this new vantage point, the essence of which is contained in the notion that the group is more than the sum total of its parts. In the words of John Donne, 'no man is an island entire unto himself', least of all in the complex interpersonal, interfamily, intergenerational ebb and flow of family life.

AIMS

The family group exerts a power the effects of which the individual member is unable to avoid; nor is it easy for the individual to stand up to them alone, or to alter them. Family therapy aims to understand and alleviate the damaging pressures which the family may exert on the individual and to liberate and enhance its nurturing and creative forces. It helps the family to create an environment where individuals can have support, be dependent, have room to grow, individuate and finally separate, before becoming founders of their own families. Rather than help the individual to change the group, family therapy aims to help the group to change so as to give space to the individual.

In all kinds of groups each member receives pressure from the other members to hold certain roles and fulfil certain functions. This is particularly subtle and powerful in family groups because of the complicated delineation of roles, sexes, ages, generations and life tasks. Where you find a child who is always the one in trouble, the awkward, acting out, or 'bad' one, his counterpart will usually be found in the same family. The counterpart is the 'apple of everyone's eye', the adults' pet but often the butt of his peers. Similarly, where you find an 'ineffectual', 'incompetent' mother, you will frequently find a capable, managing grandmother who allows her daughter to opt out of her effective mothering role. Both sides contribute to this state of affairs, one serving the needs of the other and both colluding in maintaining the status quo.

ROLE OF THE DESIGNATED PATIENT

One of the key concepts to be considered in family therapy is the position of the designated patient or client. He or she is the member of the family who is deemed to be the one in need of help and brought to the agency as the one in trouble. Often he is the scapegoated one who is described as the most difficult, disturbed, disruptive member of the family. All therapists, however, who have tried to dislodge him or her from this position will be familiar with the difficulty of trying to beat the designated patient at his own game. He will invariably cling to his habitual ways of behaving. This, after all, is his modus vivendi in this family and he may know of no other way of relating. Without the angry acknowledgement of his presence by his elders, he feels he would have no place in the family. No wonder he desperately fights for his known position, however painful. But his pain is a signal to the outside world that all is not well in the family. It is neither functioning as it could as a group nor offering the best opportunities for the individuals within it.

The family therapist, having responded to this signal, frequently finds that those who have not had the capacity to send out signals are often the more vulnerable members of the family. It is not unusual to find the quiet, 'good' child carrying the sadness and depression on behalf of all the family members. This child does not make the imperceptive family feel uncomfortable, nor does he have the psychic energy to signal for help, this energy being used in an attempt to hold the depression at bay.

This was evident in the Smith family, who came into therapy following the mother's admission to a hospital for several weeks. Two years earlier, the father had finally left the family and the mother had managed to look after the three children with the help of her parents. On her return home from hospital, Caroline, aged 10 years, had become acutely self-conscious and anxious about a not very noticeable birthmark on her neck, which was minimally disfiguring. Her mother also recognised a more generalised anxiety-state in both herself and her daughter and willingly agreed to bring the whole family to the clinic. Caroline's anxiety quickly moved on to an open expression of anger about the whole family situation, which manifested itself particularly in her relationship with her mother. John, aged 8, on the other hand was quiet, compliant and drew busily and with great skill and precision throughout the first two sessions. We finally realised, however, that he was quite depressed and then learned that he had a severe sleeping problem with head-banging symptoms. It was important also to include Emma, 5 years, who had not been so involved in the violence between her parents. Due to the good substitute parenting of her grandparents she had been less traumatised by the break up of the family. She was more serene and outgoing than her sister and brother but was, however, in trouble with them, for they were well aware of her greater potential capacity to have her needs met and to face the vicissitudes of life.

ROLE OF THE FAMILY AS A GROUP

Once one has seen the importance of the pattern and rhythm of family group behaviour, it becomes virtually impossible to reach an understanding of a family and their way of functioning and their particular strengths and difficulties, unless the therapist can meet and experience all of the actors in the drama.

In order to reach adequate understanding, therefore, and hopefully to initiate change, it is necessary to see all the important members involved. This does not mean that family therapists always work with the whole family throughout the period of therapy. Systems theory suggests that if you are able to change a sub-system, this will in turn affect the whole system (see Goldstein, 1973, Ch. 4 and Vickery, 1974). So having started work with all the family members, it not infrequently becomes advantageous at various stages to work with subgroups, for instance the marital subgroup, the mother/child subgroup, or the grandmother/mother/granddaughter subgroup. But this must always be done in agreement with the rest of the family, and the subgroup must be reintegrated in the family sessions before terminating therapy.

THE FAMILY AND THE ECOLOGICAL SYSTEM

A further implication of the concept, that changing one part of a system will affect the whole, requires that one perceives the family as one system interacting with many others. In other words, it is part of an ecological system. The importance of this was first explored by Auerswald (1968). The family exists amidst a complex web of other groups, some of which may be perceived by them as helpful and some as persecutory. The extended family system, the school, work, and the community groups and political factions all influence the way the family as a group responds to the outside world and vice versa. To work with one part of the ecological system may be enough to help a family to progress. More often, however, it is necessary to work with both the family and the outside agents, in much the same way as we take cognisance of the inner and outer worlds of the individuals within the family.

The Brown family is an example of this sort of approach. William was referred by his school. He had a very real problem in being an exceptionally large and well-developed boy for his twelve years, so that his well-aimed punch could only too easily put another twelve-year-old in hospital with a broken jaw or ribs. Finally the school had to suspend him and referred the family to the clinic for help.

The family originally came from Glasgow and William was an only child. His father owned a greengrocer shop, like his father-in-law a street away. Mrs Brown acted as bookkeeper for her husband and had a part-time office job in the Civil Service. William was always in trouble at school and in the neighbourhood and was frequently observed to provoke the violence he received and then returned. He was a regular 'punch-bag' and other boys knew they could always get a rise from him. At home his maternal grandparents were his allies, but his mother was still greatly influenced by her mother's high expectations of her as well as of the opinions of other relatives and neighbours. William persisted, in her eyes, in letting her down. He was untidy, unbiddable, rude and obsessed with accidents and violence of all kinds and was himself very accident-prone.

His father, a powerful man himself, nevertheless had less high expectations of William and would often side with him in their triangular, fraught family life. When this happened mother would feel blamed and a failure, and she would become angry, depressed and isolated.

As Aponte (1976) maintains in a detailed analysis of concurrent work with a school and a family, a child with a problem cannot be seen as the sole repository of his problem, nor necessarily should his family. So from the beginning I worked with the school and with the family, having combined meetings with William and his family and with all those closely concerned with him at school, including the Head of Junior School, the Year Head, his form teacher and the Educational Welfare Officer. In the family sessions I involved the maternal grandparents and we carved out areas of work to be negotiated with his mother. His bedroom became his arena for independence; in there he could do as he liked away from his mother's houseproud eyes. She, however, was allowed in once a week to clean the room.

William returned to school after a few weeks and managed to stay out of any serious fights for four or five months. Although he continued to do exceptionally well in his scout troop, he was again suspended from school for violence. It was decided that he needed a less stimulating and more structured school environment. After further work with the school and the family and with William's agreement, a special school was found for him where he is still struggling to improve his social relationships, and meeting with increasing success.

At home there was a dramatic realignment of family members. The mother angrily withdrew for a while from taking any responsibility for William, and his father took over the disciplining of him, visiting schools, helping him with his work for his home tutor and also with his relationships with boy and girl friends. Mrs Brown, having been initially depressed about her new position, began to find some definite gains in her changed relationship with her two men. Her husband began to make demands on her to share more activities with him; and William also began to try to woo her and win back some of her attention. At the same time he and his father began to go to football matches together and finally the whole family decided to take up their former interest in dog racing. Mother is now back as a partner to her husband in looking after William and helping in decision making, but without 'over-owning' her son. Stierlin (1976) describes this concept of family life in his article on the dynamics of owning, disowning and over-owning among family members.

THE SOLUTION TO A PROBLEM AS THE MEDIUM FOR CHANGE

It is interesting to follow our professional thinking about family problems and to note the changes which have taken place over the years. There was a time when discipline was considered the answer for children who stole, lied, disobeyed or did whatever was perceived as antisocial in their particular group. Many parents still hold this view. Over the years, professionals have become more concerned about the reasons which lie behind the child's problem than about the problem itself. The causes for children lying and stealing are numerous and varied. Some reasons can be readily understood, but many are deeply buried in the complicated structure of the personality and the individual's past and present life experiences. So a further shift has taken place in our thinking. Rather than focusing on the reasons for the problems, although these may be understood, some family therapists increasingly find it more relevant to focus on the way the family seeks to find solutions to their problems.

I do not believe that, in some families, therapy should stop short here; many families can benefit greatly from understanding more about themselves and from finding out where their patterns of behaviour originate. However, for other families who have a multitude of problems which they present to the therapist, deliberations on the reasons behind these difficulties can escalate the pathology in the family. Narrowing the focus to the exploration of the way the family has attempted to deal with one specific problem with discussion and encouragement to think about other and new ways, can be both containing to the family and manifestly effective. One reason for this is that the way the family deals with a problem is often more available to change than the problem itself. Moreover, an alteration in the approach to problem solving will almost inevitably bring about some change in the functioning of the family and subsequently in the symptom of the individual or individuals. As Weakland *et al.* (1974) maintain in their article describing the results of brief therapy and focused problem resolution, the kinds of problems brought to therapy *persist* only if they are maintained by on-going current behaviour of the patient and others with whom he interacts. If this behaviour is changed in an appropriate way the problems will be resolved or disappear.

A straightforward approach to problem solving, however, may not at times bear fruit. All family therapists are familiar with the hopeless reiteration by family members that they have tried everything and nothing makes any difference. Any suggestion is greeted with a litany of the uselessness of any suggested approach. At this point it is fruitless to push against the family resistance. One example of a technique for overcoming resistance was used in the therapy of a family with a young adolescent girl of 15 years. Her mother maintained that her daughter would not be able to come to sessions because she would be sure to get lost on the way from her school to the clinic. It was not possible for the family to pick her up by car with the rest of the family. However, this girl was the centre of the family's discomfort and the therapist persisted in her request that she should come to the sessions. As predicted, at the next family meeting the girl rang thirty minutes after the session had started to say she was lost on the underground. The therapist took the call and commented on how well she carried out the expectations of her mother and asked her to join the group as soon as she could. No further directions were given but within fifteen minutes the girl arrived. Discussion soon centred around the girl's persistent refusal to come in at night at the agreed-upon time. Using a paradoxical approach again, the therapist commented on how well the girl conformed to the expectations of her parents, who seemed no longer to *expect* her to be in on time. The therapist suggested there must be some sphere in which she did not want to comply with her parents' expectations of her. All adolescents need some area where they can exercise their own choice and make their own decisions. Soon it transpired that she would like to go camping with some friends this summer, rather than go on a family holiday. This then became the focus of dissension and tension between the girl and her parents, with the therapist supporting the girl at this juncture. If coming home late remained a problem, some negotiating between the parties was encouraged, using the girl's wish to go to camp with her friends as a bargaining point. The paradoxical approach, which avoids direct confrontation with the resistant members of the family, and task negotation are techniques of paramount importance when working with the adolescent in his struggle to span the two worlds of the child and the adult. Although these techniques are complex and controversial and require skill and good timing, they may prove to be more effective in these circumstances than the more readily understood, straightforward approach.

THE FAMILY'S LIFE STYLE AS THE MEDIUM FOR CHANGE

A family's life style can be perceived as a tapestry of variegated behaviour patterns. When the therapist joins a family unit, particularly at a time of transition or crisis, changes may occur in which new patterns are formed and a new balance of family interaction is created. An example of this is the Davies family.

The family was referred to the clinic by the school who had become concerned over Megan, an 11-year-old girl, in her first term at secondary school, who was unable to stay in any classroom for more than half-an-hour but instead wandered around the school enveloped in a nylon fur coat and carrying an enormous handbag. Her nickname in the school became 'the Lone Ranger'. Two years earlier her sister Wendy, also at the age of 11, had been burnt to death in tragic circumstances in an accident in their home.

The family came from a poor neighbourhood in Wales where the father had been brought up in an orphanage, never knowing his father, his mother unable to care for the family of three boys on her own. Family life for this man, therefore, was an almost sacred ritual, and he and his wife, who came from a large family, had successfully raised their four children in a fairly rigid and authoritarian way. The two older boys, Brian and Hugh, aged 15 and 16, were doing well in school and had many friends.

When I first met the family it did not take long to discover the great weight of guilt carried by each member of the family for the death of Wendy. A series of tragic but coincidental circumstances had led each member to believe that they had been partly responsible for her death. All except the father and Megan were able to talk about this in an oblique way and share their feelings of guilt, grief and sorrow. Wendy had been the favourite of her father. He would not allow his daughter's name to be mentioned in the family, and over the past two years had become increasingly morose and withdrawn, obsessed with litigation, trying to pin the blame for his daughter's death on to a builder and claim compensation from him.

Megan had tried to take her sister's place in her father's affections and had partly succeeded, but only at the expense of her own unfolding individuality. She had been very close to her elder sister, and as she approached the same age as Wendy had been when she died, her anxiety and the struggle to replace her became too much and she showed her distress by her restlessness at school. The mother, unable to comfort her husband or understand her daughter's behaviour, became increasingly perplexed, overactive and anxious. This was a family in crisis.

The first move in therapy was to try and help the father acknowledge his grief. Verbal discussion helped the rest of the family but the father remained aloof and impassive through two or three family sessions. Explaining to them that I wanted to understand more about their family life, I introduced the idea of family sculpting. This requires each member in turn to place the family members into positions which portray their perception of the emotional structure of the family. They make up a tableau which demonstrates who is closest to whom, which member is nearest to the centre of the family and who is on the outside, and so on. The family joined in with alacrity, and when the father placed Megan on his knee, the eldest boy, Hugh, burst out, 'That is where Wendy always sat'. There was a moment's silence, Megan moved off her father's knee and the ice was broken. Remaining alone and very sad-looking, the father sat through a torrent of family reminiscences about the time when Wendy was still a living member of the family and the fun they had had. The boys demonstrated how they would ride the two younger girls on their shoulders and have jousting matches, and so on.

The following session the mother brought photographs of Wendy and letters the family had received on her death, and at last the father was able to join in. On a subsequent home visit he was able to show me the dress she was wearing the day she died and share other things of intense meaning to him.

From then on the family was able to change their pattern of behaviour and to begin to create a new tapestry of family life. Hugh, in many ways the most accessible member of the family, was encouraged to work out his differences with his mother and spend more time with his father, tinkering together with his motor-bike which he had bought with the wages earned by his evening job at the supermarket. As his mother became less provoked by Hugh, she had energy left to make efforts to show her husband more overt affection. Sessions were held with the parents without the children, in which they not only expressed their disappointment in their marriage but also what they would still like to receive from each other. As a result of these sessions Mrs Davies went to the Family Planning Association for advice on contraception so as to become a more active sexual partner to her husband again. In many ways, she moved in to take a more relaxed and effective role as wife and mother.

Gradually the pressure on Megan relaxed and she made a knight-like move, as in chess, one step forward in finding a close girl friend in her new school, and two steps sideways away from her father's knee. Despite the efforts of the family and the therapist, the father remained the most isolated and sad member of the group, but he contained his grief more within himself and not at the expense of another family member. He gave up his restless search to find someone to blame for Wendy's death. As John Byng-Hall (1976) points out in his paper on handling family safety mechanisms in relation to family myths and dramas, to move from a sense of blame to a sense of pain is one of the most powerful tools of therapy.

SIMILARITIES BETWEEN FAMILY AND GROUP PHENOMENA

Since the days when scapegoating was a ritualised event of the Bedouin tribes in the desert, at which time a live goat was driven into the wilderness to die, symbolically carrying with it the unacceptable and disowned attributes of the tribe, the phenomena of scapegoating individuals or groups has been observed as a common dynamic in the life of small groups and families and affecting inter-group relations in society. In family therapy one must take into account both the pressures on the individuals in the family and the pressures on minority groups in a community.

In our society, the newly arrived ethnic group in a neighbourhood is often expected to be noisy, disruptive, strange and different. Every manifestation of differentness is exaggerated and confirms these expectations. Once labelled noisy and disruptive, this is often the way the new group makes its presence and needs felt. It may soon become the only way of communicating with the other groups around them. There is 'justification', therefore, for the community to start disciplinary measures against them, and 'justification' for the weary growth of prejudices with the familiar progression of scapegoating leading to expulsion into a 'wilderness' of isolation, denigration and discrimination. And all through this process the indigenous groups can remain the benign virtuous ones with 'high standards', their badness all projected outwards on to the minority group. It will be appreciated that the same phenomena can be seen in the scapegoated family member. The quandary in which the family member or group find themselves is that the system leaves them little or no alternative but to behave in the way that is expected of them, and provides some understanding of why eels appear to 'get used to skinning'. As with individuals it is the way the neighbourhood seeks to integrate the differences within their midst, rather than the differences themselves, that leads to difficulties.

Cultural pressures too play a part in this phenomenon. The pressures are often incomprehensible to outsiders, and to many insiders the meanings of customs are often lost in the mists of time, even to those whose inheritance gives them access to this esoteric knowledge. Potock in his superb novels (1967, 1969, 1972) illustrates the intensity of the struggle of a modern Hasidic Jewish boy in his attempts to break away from the expectations of his Hasidic Jewish inheritance, against a backcloth of cross-cultural conflicting influences and his own needs as a unique individual.

SUMMARY

In this chapter I have tried to outline some of the many and varied choices open to family therapists in deciding on methods of intervention and the selection of a focal system. The choice of working with intra-family conflicts, or with some system pressing heavily on the family, or both, has been explored.

I have tried to indicate some of the wider implications of family therapy and to present it not just as another method or technique for helping people in trouble, but as a way of understanding systems and how to intervene in them, thereby changing individual behaviour.

There have been many articles and books written about these methods of working with families, including two books recently published by British writers, S. Walrond-Skinner (1976) and R. Skynner (1976). Many of the points I have covered in this chapter are expanded in these first excellent British texts both written by practitioners.

Chapter 13

JOURNEY INTO THE ACTING COMMUNITY: EXPERIENCES OF LEARNING AND CHANGE IN COMMUNITY GROUPS*

David N. Thomas

The language of community work conveys *movement*–the word 'community' often prefaces words like 'work', 'development', 'change', 'action' and 'organisation'. Community work is concerned with the movement of resources, service functions, decision-making power (Perlman and Gurin, 1972, p. 57) and opportunities. It is also about movement in people who join neighbourhood groups–such as tenants' associations, playground committees, parent-run play groups, and care groups. I shall consider two aspects of movement concerning people: first, the major phases of a process that Haggstrom has called 'the migration of marginal groups into the acting community' (1970, p. 102); second, the changes that occur to and within individuals–for instance, in their values, attitudes, knowledge, skills and confidence.

But, first, a word of caution: the paper draws upon my experiences as a community worker, the scarce writings of fellow community workers, and the work of others, like community teachers, who have written about their projects. I have seen local people change and develop through the time of their membership of neighbourhood groups–groups which achieved substantial material benefits for their constituents; other community workers and adult educators have also witnessed such changes–see, for instance, the accounts by Sidney Jacobs (1976, ch. 11) and Tom Lovett (1975, ch. 4). But the community worker's own testament to change in group members is not hard-nosed evidence. I cannot be *certain* that people changed through involvement in community action, even though they themselves might testify to it. Such changes may have begun before their participation in neighbourhood groups (and thus explain *why* they became participants), or they may have been wrought by other factors in the neighbourhood, family or work situations of group members of which I was not aware. The reader should know that there have been very few systematic investigations that enable us to be conclusive about the fact of individual change through community action, or about the nature and the

* I am grateful to Margaret Theodore, Paul Henderson, David Jones and Jack Rothman for their help with this paper.

extent of such changes. What little evidence is available from social science research findings may be found in Rothman, 1974 (see pts 5 and 6).

THE INTERNAL REVOLUTION

Community work is concerned with *product* and *process* – the first refers to the interest of workers in specific, tangible and material products from the efforts of groups; and process goals are 'to do with the worker's perceptions of, hopes for, and relationships with the people who constitute the action system'. These process, interactional, educational or relationship goals 'refer to the enhancement and strengthening of the competence of participants' (Kramer and Specht, 1969, p. 9).

There is considerable disagreement amongst practitioners and writers as to the appropriate emphasis to be given to process goals. Biddle and Biddle, for instance, argue that 'community development is a social process by which human beings can become more competent to live with and gain some control over local aspects of a frustrating and changing world. It is a group method for expediting personality growth' (1966, p. 78). This conception of community work has been criticised by Khinduka who suggests, 'It is just this preoccupation with process and with personality that keeps community development from becoming an effective instrument for large-scale institutional change' (1975, p. 180).

An interest in process also characterises the radical left in community work, which is as often preoccupied with educational and interactional goals, and as often dismissive of the material gains aspired to by local people for their neighbourhoods. Here, the language of process is that of increasing political consciousness and awareness, or developing political capacity and understanding. The development of a critical consciousness helps people better to understand the factors and processes that oppress their daily lives; this is 'conscientisation' – a learning that enables one 'to perceive social, political and economic contradictions, and to take action against the oppressive elements of reality' (Freire, 1972, p. 15). Conscientisation includes an enabling process to train the working class. This training occurs at three levels: political training to enable men to participate in power at all levels; economic training to take up roles as the producers, distributors and consumers of products; and social training to enhance men's awareness of their duties and responsibilities as members of the working class (Alfero, 1972, pp. 7–8).

The work and thoughts of Paulo Freire on education as a 'practice for freedom' have done much to re-emphasise process goals even amongst those pursuing community work as a radical alternative, who had no stomach for the personality growth values of writers like Biddle and Biddle. There have been other influences beside Freire, and two are worth mentioning. First, the integration of community work and adult education activities in developments like the Liverpool Educational Priority Area Project and the appointment of community workers to adult education institutes, and as link people between schools and local communities. Second, the influence of radical philosophy, particularly that of Pateman (1975), who, in discussing obstacles to revolutionary change, identifies the importance of communicational activities, and hence that of process and educational goals, in political change and, I would argue, in community work. Pateman suggests that certain cognitive and linguistic behaviours perpetuate oppression and these have to be changed if people are to understand and confront the world for what it is in order to change it.

MOVEMENT INTO THE ACTING COMMUNITY

Communities, suggests Haggstrom, have two guises: first, there is the community as *object*–'it is an interdependent system of neighbourhoods, bureaucratic work organisations, interest groups, political parties and other sub-systems, tied together by processes such as transportation, communication and the circulation of money'. Second, there is the community as an *acting community*–'an entity that engages in collective action and embarks on one or more social journeys'. A group in the acting community participates in identifying community needs and problems, and participates in decision making and often the implementation of these decisions. A group in the object community is acted upon, whereas a group in the acting community acts for itself and upon others.

People and groups have differential access to the acting community, an access that is determined by factors like class and economic position, race, stigma and educational opportunities. Groups who seldom get into the acting community, and are more usually the objects of others' actions, include immigrants, single parents, children, the mentally ill, the poor and the homeless. These people comprise Haggstrom's 'marginal groups'. The community worker can help such groups and neighbourhoods to create organisations to make the journey into the acting community. The making of this journey to, and entry into, the acting community provides the major opportunities for growth and learning for individuals in community groups–I act, therefore I am.

The learning of the individual on this social journey, through which acting brings about an affirmation of being, affects his capacities for *reflection, vision, planning* and *action.* In practice, learning occurs simultaneously in these areas, and we find that they are interlocking and mutually supporting. This is particularly true of reflection and action: Alfero has described reflection as 'a structural factor, inseparable from practice', because it generates new actions and supports that which has already been accomplished (1972). Aneurin Bevan put it very succinctly: 'action and thought go hand-in-hand in reciprocal revelation' (1952, p. 18).

I think that the dialectic between reflection, vision, planning and action is embodied within Goodenough's concept of 'culture' – which he takes to consist 'of standards for deciding what is, standards for deciding what can be, standards for deciding how one feels about it, standards for deciding what to do about it, and standards for deciding how to go about it' (1963, pp. 258–9). Goodenough suggests that successful outcomes in community development may be contingent on local people making changes in their individual cultures. He describes the complex interplay between social and economic change in a community and changes in the private cultures of individuals.

People in marginal groups will remain powerless where their private and subgroup cultures (in Goodenough's sense) are inappropriate, inoperative or unvalued in the acting community. The responses of the people described by Dennis to the threat of demolition by the local authority of their homes (e.g. 'I went to the Town Hall about it, but they want it, so that's the end of it. There's nothing more we can do . . .') are good examples of individual private cultures that need to be changed if people are to deal with threats to their well-being that emanate from one system (the local authority) in the acting community (1970, p. 346). The community worker must work with people to achieve private and group cultures that will be as effective as possible when up against the norms and procedures of the acting community. The revitalisation of reflective faculties is a first step in the development of an effective operating culture.

REFLECTION

Reflection, meaning an internal process of contemplation and reasoning, is a means through which people and groups overcome what Rowbotham has called a 'paralysis of consciousness' (1974) and become able to understand, conceptualise and articulate what goes on around them and impinges on their social, economic and political lives. Reflection of this kind may produce an understanding of how to intervene to affect these forces, and to predict, control and overcome them. The importance of this reflective process is that people, if they are to undertake a social and political journey that will not be without its costs, need to be aware that the journey is, first, necessary and, second, that it will have benefits for themselves and relevant others.

The community worker will work with people to develop a critical awareness of themselves in their local situation in respect of an issue or problem around which a group is forming. Group members will come to grasp, first, a sense of their own marginality in the community and in society at large, and a linked understanding of the futility of individual efforts to achieve the goals they have in mind. Secondly, reflection produces an understanding of the dynamics and power of the acting community, and an appreciation that there are people and agencies within the acting community who need to be changed in order to achieve something. Thirdly, there develops in reflection a sense of individual and group worth and the beginnings of an understanding of the varied potentials of people in a group, and the potential powerfulness of group action. Here, too, the individual begins to conceive of himself as part of a system acting with others for change, and to recognise new roles and responsibilities.

Reflection is part of the process through which local people achieve the changes in identity or self-image that are often fundamental to success in community work. These changes are fundamental because a good deal of community work involves populations where there is often considerable apathy and resignation, little confidence, and no sense of personal and collective worth. Despite a wealth of indigenous talents, the organiser often finds that there is no desire to change when people view their selves and their situations as impossible to change. Specific techniques have been suggested by Clinard for use by community development workers in facilitating changes in self-image (1966, pp. 301–8).

Reflection, then, should help individuals to give up defining themselves as powerless, and their own or neighbourhood situation as a constant, immutable given. There are, in principle, no limits to the objects that may be reflected upon, and eventually the community worker may find an awareness in individuals about wider, structural issues in society. There are, however, a number of obstacles to learning in the reflective process and these include:

(1) the confidence that people have in the validity of their own perceptions is, as Dennis has claimed, often 'systematically and powerfully under attack by opponents . . . decked in all the paraphernalia of prestige and scientific professionalism' (1975, p. 146);
(2) the complexity and breadth of a person's reflections on the reality that confronts him, his neighbourhood and his class may depend in part upon possession of an elaborate language code with which to name and conceptualise the world (Bernstein, 1971). Pateman (1975, p. 34) and Rowbotham (1974, ch. 3) have also suggested other conceptual and verbal factors which may explain limitations in the development of our critical consciousness;
(3) reflection, and dialogue between group members, and between them and the community worker, may be impaired by certain communicational activities and conventions. These, according to Pateman, include idle and repressive forms of discourse and evasions of argument. Pateman argues that 'If widespread through a population, and pervasive in their influence, . . . evasions . . . can be of considerable political significance. For such evasions sustain, in

practice, all existing social institutions, since they stand in the way of any critical (reflective) consciousness' (1975, p. 47).

Techniques to facilitate reflection have been developed and used by community workers. Alinsky, in particular, is well known for his repertoire of interventions designed to stimulate people into a thinking awareness of their situation. Much of his writing emphasises the importance of reflection and he argues, for instance, that 'the function of the organiser is to raise questions that agitate, that break through the accepted pattern . . . [to raise] . . . the internal questions within individuals that are so essential for the revolution which is external to the individual' (1971, pp. 72–3). He provides a very vivid example of stimulating 'internal questions':

Organizer: Do you live over in that slummy building?
Answer: Yeah. What about it?
Organizer: What the hell do you live there for?
Answer: What do you mean, what do I live there for? Where else am I going to live? I'm on welfare.
Organizer: Oh, you mean you pay rent in that place?
Answer: Come on, is this a put-on? Very funny! You know where you can live for free?
Organizer: Hmm. That place looks like it's crawling with rats and bugs.
Answer: It sure is.
Organizer: Did you ever try to get that landlord to do anything about it?
Answer: Try to get him to do anything about anything! If you don't like it, get out. That's all he has to say. There are plenty more waiting.
Organizer: What if you didn't pay your rent?
Answer: They'd throw us out in ten minutes.
Organizer: Hmm. What if nobody in that building paid their rent?
Answer: Well, they'd start to throw . . . Hey, you know, they'd have trouble throwing everybody out, wouldn't they?
Organizer: Yeah, I guess they would.
Answer: Hey, you know, maybe you got something – say, I'd like you to meet some of my friends. How about a drink?

British community workers have also described their techniques for promoting reflection (see, for instance, Mitton and Morrison, 1972, p. 30). One of these techniques that is being used more and more as an educational, consciousness-raising tool in community work is video. Equipment and techniques in video, and an analysis of its strengths and limitations in community work, are discussed in a handbook produced by Inter-Action Trust (Inter-Action Advisory Service, 1975).

Besides dialogical and other techniques used by the community worker, significant developments in reflection may also occur for individuals as a result of events and decisions in the wider community. For instance, a tenant may become more aware of his marginality, and more motivated to take the chairmanship of a group, when he experiences uncaring behaviour from 'putter-offers' at the Town Hall.

VISION

Reflection enables men to understand the situations that limit them and to attempt to overcome them. Vision follows on from reflection – increased consciousness of me-in-this-situation can lead (but so seldom does for marginal people) to a vision of me-in-another-situation in the future.

Effective action is contingent upon local people being able to conceive of themselves as 'new' people – a conception of themselves working at tasks, taking on roles, and exercising skills and knowledge in ways previously unimaginable to them. The community worker's task is to facilitate people's ability to articulate a desired future state of affairs (such as better housing, a new playground), and then to work with them to realise it. The challenge facing the community worker, however, is that before, and at the outset of people becoming organised, group members are often not visionary. They may perceive something is wrong, but often they do not know what they want to do by way of improving the situation, or how to go about it. The community worker's task, then, is to develop in people a capacity for visionary thought, to help them cross 'the frontier which separates being from being more' (Freire, 1972, p. 71).

The process of becoming able to articulate alternative visions about themselves and their neighbourhood situations may itself be a growth experience for local people. Haggstrom has described a 'psychological conflict' that occurs in marginal people at the outside of joining an organisation – conflict between an image of themselves as inferior beings that has been internalised from the definitions and stigmas of the acting community; and the beginnings of a vision of themselves as being as competent and able as anyone else. Growth occurs as 'marginal people ward off the definitions of their inferiority and act on the basis of assumptions about their potential equality within the acting community' (1970, p. 105). Previously apathetic or uninterested members become 'galvanised into action'. This galvanisation, which seems to come from a synthesis of reflection on the here-and-now and vision about what might be, is a significant point of development for people in local groups. Alinsky has described its sustaining, almost therapeutic qualities very vividly: 'If people are organised with a dream of the future ahead of them, the critical planning that takes place in organising and the hopes and the fears for the future give them just as much inner satisfaction as does their actual achievement' (1969, p. 49).

The community worker will often be purposively catalytic in galvanising group members to cross the frontier between 'being and being more'. The worker can do this by using his own vision of a better world to inspire group members. Haggstrom has written beautifully of the mobilising effects of the community worker's vision:

> An organiser must not only perceive how people are, but it is also essential that he be *unrealistic* in that he perceives people as they can be. Noting what is possible, the organiser projects this possibility and moves people to accept it and to seek to realise it. The organiser helps people to develop and live in an alternative reality in which their image of themselves and their abilities is enhanced . . . People are moved to accept the new world of which they catch a glimpse because it appears to be attainable in practice and intrinsically superior to the world in which they have been living. (Haggstrom, 1970, p. 106)

But moving people to accept this new world, to migrate into the acting community, requires at least three things of the community worker. First, that he works with group members to develop an appropriate organisation and decision-making processes; second, that he works with the group to transform visionary statements into operational goals; and, third, that he helps people to see leadership as located not just in himself but in themselves and other members of the group. This facilitates the development of a leadership nucleus, a leadership that represents both the aspiration and the means to a slowly forming alternative reality. How does this leadership nucleus emerge? At one level, the community worker struggles to shift basic assumption activity (Bion, 1961) in the group from dependence (on himself or the imagined magical potency of the group) to controlled pairing (between members, or between himself and the chairman or secretary). At other levels, the leadership nucleus that best embodies the group's collective vision emerges in response to events in the community like a meeting with a prestigous decision maker, or the setting up of a cinch fight by the community worker, and through constant dialogue and disputation within the group and between it and its opponents in the acting community.

PLANNING

As the vision establishes itself the means to realise it become important concerns to the members, and the community worker seeks to stimulate an awareness in the group about the need for planning – the need for conscious, intentional and purposeful decisions and activities that take the group forward to the achievement of its goals. Many group members have to be weaned away from relying on familiar but inappropriate methods of organisation and decision making. Mitton and Morrison have pointed out that taking action in groups to tackle a problem was in itself an unfamiliar experience to the mothers with whom they worked; a consequence is that people 'do not develop skills in organising themselves collectively, making group decisions, handling group funds and so on. The traditional ways of doing things, such as keeping accounts in one's head or passing information on the grapevine, are suited to everyday tasks but were not always adequate for playgroup business' (1972, p. 156). It has also been suggested by Rainwater that working-class people are suspicious of and hostile to participation in organisations and this hinders the community worker's attempts to involve them (1968).

Daniel Schler has described four areas in which local people must learn a planning or social technology in order to push forward the interests of neighbourhood groups (1970, p. 126). People need to acquire and improve their skills in:

(1) rational goal setting, so that the activities of individual members are more likely to be focused on collectively agreed tasks and targets;
(2) identifying, acquiring and planning the use of resources in and outside the group so as best to achieve the goals of the group;
(3) rational processes of dividing up labour, in order, for instance, that no one person becomes overburdened with the group's work;
(4) administering and co-ordinating the various subgroups and activities within the ambit of the neighbourhood group.

Planning also involves the formulation of strategies and tactics on the part of neighbourhood groups, and here again members need to acquire competence and confidence. According to Brager and Specht there are five areas in which the group needs to become skilled. They are:

(a) the development of a tactical game plan – involving the identification of the essential players in the game, and an anticipation of their likely moves;
(b) researching the target – the group must acquire knowledge of the weaknesses and strengths of the target system;
(c) empathising with the target – 'to observe, hear and understand the target permits more informed tactical judgements and increased tactical options';
(d) image management – learning to choose the image that is most appropriate for the tactics of the group;
(e) timing the action – groups need to learn that the sequence and timing of events influence outcomes (Brager and Specht, 1973, pp. 272*ff*).

ACTING

Membership of neighbourhood groups demands of individuals that they learn new skills and knowledge, and extend what they already bring to the group. This is particularly the case with those who take up leadership roles such as chairman, secretary and treasurer. Several writers have made the point that, in relation to the size of their constituency or neighbourhood, the number of people who significantly develop in this way is quite small.

People are called upon to expand their skills in both task performance and group maintenance, both of which require that group members gain *technical* and *interactional* skills and knowledge. There have been many recent descriptions written by community workers of the need for local people to acquire these skills: for instance, Mitton and Morrison, 1972; Benington, 1975; Thomas, 1975, 1976; and Jacobs, 1976. Many of the texts already referred to in this paper also contain analyses of the technical and interactional skills required of both community workers and members of neighbourhood groups. And several attempts to list the knowledge and skills that community workers need to have (for example, Naish and Filkin, 1974; Association of Community Workers, 1975) can be seen also to describe many of the areas in which local people need to acquire competence.

(1) *Technical Skills and Knowledge*

There are a variety of jobs to do in a neighbourhood group, and they will vary with the nature of the group's concerns. But in most groups individuals have to develop civic or committee skills to some degree or other – drawing up agendas, writing minutes, implementing decisions, keeping financial accounts, printing and distributing a newsletter, using a telephone and writing letters. The writing of letters is usually one of the first significant explorations of personal skill and confidence by group members, and writers have drawn attention both to its importance in the process of personal change, and to its limitations as an instrument of negotiation in social change (see, for example, Benington, 1975). Members in many groups have also to master techniques involved, for instance, in doing a survey, getting round a petition, arranging a deputation to the Town Hall, holding a press conference, and organising a rent strike or demonstration.

People are also likely to improve their knowledge, in pursuit of the group's goals and the interests of its constituency, in matters like personal, work and welfare rights; aspects of social problems and issues; legislation and conventions that impinge on the work of the group (in housing, health, play and planning, for instance); resources in the neighbourhood and wider community; political processes and the workings of private and public bureaucracies; tribunals and public inquiries; and the knowledge and roles of specialists in the community, like the planner, the health inspector, the community worker and the solicitor.

(2) *Interactional Skills and Knowledge*
These are of two kinds: first, political skills and competence; and, second, caring and supportive capacities within the neighbourhood group.

Group members need to become adept in political transactions within the group, and between the group and the constituency that it represents. The group also has to develop skills in managing its relationships with systems in its environment – the Town Hall, service agencies, potential resource people and groups, the press and television, other neighbourhood groups, councillors, MPs, trade unions and private and public industries. Relationships with all these systems require broad political skills in representing, and negotiating for, the interests of the groups. It also includes competence in executing and evaluating chosen strategies and tactics.

People who take leadership roles in neighbourhood groups also need to be caretakers of the emotional life of the group, and to be aware of the effects of people's intra- and inter-personal relationships (within or outside the group) on the group's work, as well as events in their social and economic lives. Caring for the group also involves 'training' members for leadership roles, sharing the burden of the work, and attending to the recruitment of new members. The community worker and officers need to understand, and mobilise in the group's interest, the original and changing motivations for membership of the group, and to be sensitive to the effect of behaviour in the group like scapegoating. A fuller discussion of group behaviours has been provided for community workers by McCaughan (1977a).

LEVELS OF APPLICATION OF CHANGE

People in neighbourhood groups thus change and develop their operating cultures in the four areas of reflection, vision, planning and action. But what is the significance and the extent of this change as it occurs and is applied within and outside the community group? I think there are three levels of application of change, and I shall look at these below.

Primary Application
The individual develops in ways that are of immediate and prior application within the context of the skills, knowledge and confidence needed to perform assigned roles and responsibilities within the community group; and between the group and those in its environment with whom it must interact.

Secondary Application
The effects of the changes may be felt in the individual's transactions in his life outside the community group – at home, in the neighbourhood and at work. It is often hoped that learning acquired within the group will enable individuals to become more aware of, and more effective in (1) their civic (including trade union) responsibilities, and (2) sectional or class responsibilities in pursuing structural change.

There may be ways in which membership of a community group enables an individual 'better' to function within his family and social life. Schler has argued that membership of community groups is *intrapsychically* beneficial: 'individuals are encouraged to think and express their feelings towards the community . . . and to divert those feelings into constructive actions . . . which may lead to gratifying accomplishments rather than to failure, frustration, apathy or alienation' (1970, p. 125).

The mere act of involvement in a neighbourhood group can provide relief from, and support in, domestic and work situations. Membership provides opportunities for friendship, support, ventilation, a legitimate outlet for anti-authoritarian/anti-establishment feelings, the use of previously unused talents and energies, a sense of creativity and fulfilment, and the excitement of discussion and controversy. It also provides an 'escape' from domestic problems like overcrowding, loneliness and isolation, routinisation and marital stress. Group membership can provide *relief* through expression, and *restoration* through participation and acceptance: 'Being a respected and effective member of the group, being accepted, being able to share, to participate, belong to the basic constructive experiences in human life' (Foulkes and Anthony, 1965, pp. 15, 27–8). Participation in a group leads, too, to a sense of worth and accomplishment that is gained through being able to help others.

Involvement in community groups can also lead to greater *interpersonal competence*: 'individuals may learn more about how to take others into account and to negotiate for consensus and common goals, rather than seek to dominate through positions of power, authority or status . . . continuous participation in such groups provides the individual with recurring opportunities to experiment with improving his own group performance as well as aiding other individuals in their improvement (Schler, 1970, p. 25). This interpersonal competence in the group is carried over, it is suggested, into relationships with others in the home and work situation. Mitton and Morrison have provided two examples of this kind of 'carry-over'. In the first, a husband describes the effect on his wife of her involvement in a community group:

> At night time she would trot off and be gone for an hour or two and the next day you'd be discussing what had been discussed the night before

> and she really did this thinking she was doing some good. She was a person who had been content to do the housework and sit about and go from one day to another, and this certainly made a different woman of her. She met new people, people who I had never met before . . . They all come round to have a chat with her and it really excites her to have these conversations. (Mitton and Morrison, 1972, p. 154)

The second example is a quotation from a general practitioner describing one of the consequences of a community worker's intervention:

> At the time of her work here, the number of families who always used to attend surgery began to drop. I've seen women become very independent, expressive people able to organise, able to get information and feel that they were doing something constructive. (1972, p. 160)

Women often experience some liberation from traditional and oppressive sex roles as they take up leadership in community groups, and this has an effect on their relationships with their husbands and family.

Finally, it is important to note that participation in neighbourhood groups helps some people to become more ambitious about the direction of their lives, and thus to try, sometimes successfully, to develop more competence in traditional roles like spouse, parent and breadwinner. Local people improve their jobs, 'go straight', acquire mortgages and houses, attend training courses, and aspire to and take on jobs like welfare rights workers and play group leaders.

Tertiary Application

The acquisition and internalisation of knowledge and expertise becomes especially clear when local people pass on their new-found competence to others within the group, their families and to people in the wider community. The role of group members as educators becomes apparent when they feel able and confident enough to participate in activities like advising other neighbourhood groups; attending inter-group meetings in the community; taking community work students on placement; giving lectures and talks to college students; representing constituents at tribunals; getting up petitions; using the press and the television; and producing newsletters. Internalisation of changes is particularly well advanced when local people are able to challenge and modify the views of the original 'trainer' – the community worker.

HOW LEARNING TAKES PLACE

Little seems to be understood, or written, by community workers (and others, for that matter) about just how people do learn and grow through their membership of community groups, though much that is relevant may be found in accounts of experiments and projects in the fields of adult education, group dynamics and social psychology.

The community worker's task is to help create a climate in a group in which people want to learn *in order to realise the vision they have for themselves and the neighbourhood.* This is the single fact that most helps the worker in his concern with the educational aspects of his work – that 'knowledge . . . becomes an arsenal of weapons in the battle against injustice and degradation. It is no longer learning for learning's sake, but learning for a real reason, a purpose' (Alinsky, 1969, p. 173). Adults learn best where they have problems to solve, and especially problems that impinge upon their own day-to-day existences (see Knowles, 1972).

One of the most potent forms of learning in community groups is learning through doing – 'a skill is learned by practice . . . practice is not possible until there is some confidence . . . confidence develops from observing demonstrations of skill by others, over a fairly long period' (Mitton and Morrison, 1972, p. 43). Many community workers have ir their minds, and are on the look-out for, especially at the start of the life of a group, a sequence of events and decisions that will incrementally build up the confidence and abilities within the group.

Learning also proceeds through dialogue, conversation, argument conflict and disputation both inside and outside the group. Direct tuition i also possible – for instance, where local people and community workers gc on day courses together or where 'experts' are invited to talk about som aspect of the group's work or interests. But some of the most endurin learning takes place through modelling. Local people change and develo values, attitudes, relationships, behaviour, etc. through modellin themselves on someone like the community worker, another professiona who is helping the group or a more experienced or able group member. have described elsewhere some of the possible drawbacks of this kind o learning (1976, p. 162).

CONCLUSION

I expect that some readers will be cynical and wary about some of the clain I have made about individual change in neighbourhood work. This may b caused by the paucity of substantive evidence, and also by a suspicion that have romanticised the working class, and made it appear that communi action was either a kind of people's university, or a growth experienc Perhaps, then, it is well to remember that in the groups in which I worke there were many individuals who did not change, or changed very littl through their experience of community action; who were oft overwhelmed and defeated by the demands made of their skills, energi and time (and just as often bounced back); who dropped out of groups; ar who expressed and acted out the feelings of despair and hopelessness that we all experienced in the work. To the extent that they carried this projective burden, they freed other group members to seek and 'to do the truth' through neighbourhood activities, winning important material benefits for their constituents and the community.

Chapter 14

PROGRAMME ACTIVITIES IN SOCIAL GROUP WORK

Catherine Briscoe

Social work groups are established for many different purposes; purposes which are determined initially by the group worker and his agency anc often negotiated and modified with the group as it meets. In helping th group to work towards the achievement of the group purposes the worke has three main tools at his disposal: his own skill at using himself t influence group interaction and the actions of the members; the interactio of the group itself and its impact on individual members; and the activity o programme content of the group or what the group actually does during it meetings. This paper will focus on the last of these three, the programm content of groups, the contribution activities can make to achieving grou purposes and the factors affecting their selection.

Programme activities provide the vehicle whereby the interaction of grou members and group worker takes place (Middleman, 1968). By a carefu choice and structuring of activities, that interaction can be influenced an guided to move towards the accomplishment of group purposes.

The extent to which this choice and structuring are seen a responsibilities of the worker or as being responsibilities shared betwee worker and group depends in part on the worker's perception of his ro and objectives, and in part on the purposes of the group and th characteristics of its members. While the manner of choosing and plannin programme activities will vary from group to group and worker to worke it is possible to see that in all groups the actual choice may contribute to hinder the accomplishment of a range of group tasks. These tasks a common to all groups, though the emphasis given to each of them varie They relate to the different stages of development of a group, with differe tasks assuming particular importance at each stage.

GROUP DEVELOPMENT AND RELATED TASKS

Group theorists have worked out schemes for the stages of development groups (Sarri and Galinsky, 1974; Tuckman, 1965), and while these diff to a certain extent most agree that groups move from beginni exploratory and testing stages to a phase of intimacy where work is most productive and finally to ending stages where the work of the group is finished. Progression through these stages is not smooth and continuous. The group may move backwards and forwards at different moments in the group's history. It is, however, possible to identify these stages and to see the tasks described above as being emphasised at different moments in the group's development.

Table 3

Stage of Development of the group	*Group Tasks*
Beginning stages	Diagnosis and goal setting The building of group cohesion
Stage of intimacy and productive work	Work on implicit needs and goals of group members Work on explicitly agreed group goals
Ending stages	Assessment and evaluation Moving the members on

Group tasks associated with those stages can be seen in Table 3. Activities can contribute to the accomplishment of each of these tasks, and the timing of activities can either help or hinder the movement of the group.

(1) *Diagnosis and goal setting*
Both the group worker and group members usually come to the first meeting of a group with some idea, though it may often be vague, as to what it is they are to work on together. The interaction of the group clarifies the needs, the concerns and the strengths of each member and helps the worker and/or the group plan realistic goals for individuals and for the group as a whole. Activities can be planned to reveal different aspects of group nembers to themselves and to other members of the group so that material which might otherwise remain concealed is brought into the group content o be acknowledged and worked upon.

In planning activities for diagnostic purposes the worker must be clear as o what information will be helpful to the work of the group and how it may est be elicited. For some groups discussion of the way in which a particular roblem affects each member may be the most helpful. For others activities vith physical materials such as paint, plasticine, clay, or pencils and paper rovide information both on co-ordinative skills and on emotional states f mind. Activities requiring interaction and co-operation such as games or hared crafts can focus on the social skills of members, while trips in a car or elaxed activities such as preparing food and eating together provide pportunities for informal discussion of interests and concerns.

(2) *Building Group Cohesion*

Group cohesion, a complex concept comprising the sense of identity and belonging felt by members of a group, has been recognised as a powerful curative factor in group psychotherapy (Yalom, 1970). Social group workers acknowledge that the development of such a sense of cohesion, which keeps members coming to the group and involved in its work, is a primary task for a group in its early stages as the group members test out the group situation. Three elements appear important in developing group bond:

the interest, use or enjoyment offered by the group content;
trust in the worker by the members;
trust and liking among the group members themselves.

The interest, use and/or enjoyment of the group is a powerful attraction factor for members. In some groups where the hopes and interest of the members focus on the solution or easing of clearly defined problems, the extent to which the group seems likely to help with these problems will be important and activities can focus directly on the problems and on working towards coping with them. Discussion speakers, films, planning individual and group assignments and providing for feedback on and evaluation of these are some activities which could help in keeping such a group engaged.

For other groups, particularly in work with children and adolescents, activities which are fun and which offer popular facilities not easily accessible to members outside the group may be important. The chance to take part in activities such as skating or bowling which require more than one or two people to be fun, the provision of transport to more distant places or the use of craft materials and games equipment all help to draw members to the group.

For a group of mothers with young children, fun and active programming might not be as interesting as the chance to sit and chat with others without interruption while someone else looks after the children.

At later stages of the group activities, emphasising comfort, belonging enjoyment or achievement in the group may also be briefly important, for example after the completion of a particular task, in a waiting or slow period of the group, or where the group has gone through a difficult or challenging experience (Churchill, 1959).

Trust in the worker that enables the group to engage with him can also be promoted through activities which are useful and enjoyable. With some groups the worker's understanding and knowledge of their concerns and his ability to offer practical help is important, and activities can allow the worker to demonstrate these. In other groups the worker must place more emphasis on activities that show him to be someone with whom it is worth engaging. Providing food, materials to make attractive objects, transport and entry to facilities such as swimming pools or football games, and teaching desirable skills such as swimming, dancing or sewing can help members to engage with the worker. Some groups in the early stages of engagement prefer to plan reasonably familiar activities and to assess the worker on his ability to make them possible and on his willingness to participate in them. They may not at first accept any suggestions from him of unfamiliar or more adventurous nature.

In the initial stages of a group the worker can be tested out by group members, and particularly in working with younger groups needs to plan activities where this can be done safely without danger of harm to group members or to property. Activities which are potentially dangerous in themselves or in the materials and tools they require can at this stage mean that the worker will be forced to spend considerable energy attempting to control testing out behaviour to safeguard the members or their environment. Planning activities which require the minimum enforcement of rules and finding settings for these activities which are similarly free of prohibitions eases the establishing of relationships between the worker and the group.

Activities can be a tool for the worker in developing relationships with the group, but cannot in themselves ensure that the members will trust or engage themselves with him. That depends on their perception of his attitudes and interest in them. However, the activities can offer an incentive to consider the worker's possibilities and not to reject him out of hand.

Trust and liking among the members helps to motivate the members to come to the group and to feel able to expose their concerns and interests to one another and work together. Some groups develop a sense of identity through the verbal sharing of problems and concerns which show them all as having common interests and an investment in the purposes of the group. Others where such links are not readily apparent develop relationships among members through sharing enjoyable activities such as eating and preparing food together or going on outings.

Activities planned to help members develop relationships among themselves should allow for equal sharing of the enjoyment by all members and no competition for available rewards, otherwise the activity may develop divisions rather than cohesion in the group.

(3) *Work on the implicit needs and goals of group members*

This is actually important throughout the life of the group, though it can be focused on most productively in the stage of intimacy when group members are more able to give to one another.

Any individual joining a group brings with him a more or less unconscious personal agenda of hopes, purposes and needs centred around his need for recognition and self-confirmation from his fellow men. Those who have had positive social experiences in belonging to other social groups such as the family and peer groups have developed some social skills to relate to others in groups and to win themselves positive confirmations of their human identity. Social work clients frequently have a history of negative social experiences and do not have the social skills to relate easily in groups and meet their emotional needs through interaction.

Social work groups are often formed to focus upon the correcting of these negative experiences and the learning of social skills. In other groups where these are not the main focus, the social needs of the individual members still can exert a powerful influence upon the group interaction, and if not taken into account in the structuring of activities may hinder work on the group's actual purpose. Whatever the main aim of the group, the worker has to be alert to member needs for acceptance and for receiving expressions of affection and caring.

In the beginning stages of the group the worker may have to meet many of these needs himself. The participation of the worker in activities and the helping of members to participate may show acceptance, while the worker's offering of food or serving of tea may demonstrate caring (Walker, undated) and provide a model for group members in learning to offer such support to one another.

As the group develops intimacy the members become less intent on their own needs and more able to offer to others.

Activities at this stage can offer members *the chance to give to one another or to others outside the group* to promote confidence and self-appreciation (Yalom, 1970). Group members can share skills, knowledge and perceptions with each other, can do things for each other or for the group as a whole or can plan and carry out service projects outside the group. The latter also offer opportunities for recognition from the outside world.

Other personal needs can also be met through activities. *Recognition and status*, both within the group and outside it, can be earned for individual members through activities which allow them to show their particular skills. This can be done in the group by choosing activities at which quieter or scapegoated members have particular skills and making sure these are acknowledged (Churchill, 1959), or through helping the group put on activities for the outside world in which each member has a significant role to play and is important in the accomplishment of the activity.

Self-expression: activities can also encourage the expression of suppressed feelings such as anger, fear and affection. Dramatic skits, story telling or puppet theatre allow members to put their own feelings into the mouths of others and to act them out (Wilson and Ryland, 1949). The use of craft materials such as clay, paint or wood and a hammer and nails can allow the pictorial representation of feelings or the violent use of the materials through hitting, pummelling and sweeping movements, both giving a release to feelings and a chance to recognise their presence and force.

Developing the self-confidence of members in their ability to face authority figures and to take some control of their own environment can be helped in the group through the planning of occasions where the group negotiates about rules or resources (Shulman, 1968, p. 27) or invites visitors with resources into meetings. For group members with very little faith in their ability to alter or to achieve anything successful, planning and negotiation can be an important part of learning. *Achievement* on an individual basis is important too, and activities should allow for the successful accomplishment of, for example, crafts or games and the learning of new skills within the capacities of the individual member.

More adventurous and unfamiliar activities which offer group members chances for new learning and for increased achievement and self-confidence will only be undertaken willingly at the stage of intimacy where group members feel supported and at ease in the group.

Work on the explicitly agreed group goals is usually emphasised and most productive once the group has reached the stage of intimacy, though some groups focus on work-related activities from their start. Activities for such tasks could include discussion of problems and of the investment of the members in change, the planning of group and individual strategies and assignments, the exchange of ideas, experiences and opinions. The rehearsing of new roles or behaviours, the actual carrying through of planned assignments and the assessment afterwards of performance and achievement all contribute to work on group goals.

Group members may also be involved in *data gathering* (Shulman, 1971) to help in planning and developing their work, through activities such as films, inviting speakers, doing surveys or library work or interviewing relevant people. They may *learn specific skills* such as sewing or cooking as part of their agreed work. *The planning of future activities* and making decisions about their content and form may also be a part of the explicit work of the group.

Finding ways of *entry into difficult areas* (Shulman, 1971) for discussion through, for example, introducing a film or a speaker or attempting to help members feel comfortable in working on agreed goals can also be the focus of activity. Providing younger group members with craft materials or pencils and paper to use may help them to enter into discussion or stay silent without feeling pressured (Churchill, 1974). Involving older group members in washing up after demanding discussion may also allow them to bring out concerns they could not in the formal session (Broadbent and Lovelock, 1975).

Assessment and evaluation may well be emphasised throughout the life of the group, but may be given particular attention as an activity in itself after the group has completed any major piece of work to evaluate events, programmes or tasks which the group have planned and undertaken. This helps the group to recognise group progress and achievement and to maximise learning from any experience. It may be used to help the group towards closing by acknowledging the accomplishment of their purposes, or may be a tool for the worker and the group to see where they have moved to. For some groups, assessment and feedback on progress may be a regular part of the group's activity providing the link between one phase of the group's work and the next. For other groups, the worker may need to plan activities which will reveal any change in the members' behaviour and reactions. For example, a group of children working on their behaviour might show their progress in developing internal controls by taking part in an outing which demands a certain degree of conformity to external rules (Churchill, 1959). A group of adolescents which has planned and organised a party might use the meeting after the party to look at what went well and what went badly and their own impact on the party's events.

Activities throughout the life of the group can of course provide the worker with information as to the development and changes in each member. Activities planned specifically for this task may be used to provide information on particular behaviour or to bring assessment and evaluation into the conscious work of the group and to the attention of members.

TERMINATING THE GROUP

Moving through endings and separation is one of the more difficult tasks of a group. Activities may be planned which provide a ceremonial end to the group with a final party or some kind of ending ritual. This kind of procedure is often used with camps or groups which have a visible time limit. For other groups it is possible to develop activities which require an increasing degree of separate activity on the part of the members, as opposed to the co-operative and integrating activity which may have helped to build group cohesion (Churchill, 1974). In other groups individual members may need encouragement to move out although the group continues. Activities can include visits to places where members may become attached, such as youth clubs or new residential settings.

Termination normally belongs to the later stages of the group when the work of the group is completed. However, in particular groups, for example patients in hospital, members may move out of the group without the group itself coming to an end, and both the group and the member may need activities which focus on the member leaving and acknowledge his and the group's feelings about this (Frey, 1966).

The phases and their tasks described above are not distinct and separate, and it is evident that any given activity may be contributing to one or several of them at the same time. The tasks overlap with one another, and in pursuing the achievement of one the worker and the group may also be achieving others. It is only useful to separate them to help the worker recognise which tasks he may be focusing upon at any one meeting of a group, and to make provision for activities which will contribute to and not hinder those tasks.

In different groups different degrees of emphasis need to be given to the different tasks. In some groups activities will focus on one kind of task throughout the group. In others there will be movement from one to another. The degree to which the tasks described need to be emphasised in activity planning for any particular group at any phase of development depends on factors related to the nature of the group.

THE NATURE OF THE GROUP

The group purposes are the first and most important determinants from which others will follow. The worker in his initial planning for and with the group will have to consider what goals the group is designed to accomplish and to plan or suggest activities accordingly.

For a group which is to work on specific problems or situations, as in groups of prospective adoptive parents or of patients with long-term illnesses or disabilities, activities will focus around ways of helping members identify their particular concerns and work towards explicitly agreed goals. For a group which is organised to offer social skill development in a supportive setting, for example with deprived and isolated mothers, activities will be sought which help to build a setting for mutual support and help where members can work together on their implicit needs.

The group contract, or the agreement and understanding shared by the group members and the worker about the group purposes, also affects the choice and emphasis of activities. Each group develops some form of understanding with the worker as to why the group is there and the worker's role in it. This may be clear to all from the start of the group, may develop gradually during the course of the group or may be grasped only dimly, if at all, by group members. This depends partly on the nature and purpose of the group and partly upon the worker's perception of his and the group's function. Focusing upon the nature and purpose of the group rather than the stance of the worker as the major determinant of the form of the group contract, it is possible to see a continuum ranging from groups where contracts are clear, to groups where contracts are exploratory, to those where the worker may be struggling to establish any form of contract at all. Table 4 attempts to show examples of groups at different points on this continuum.

Looking at this continuum it is possible to make some generalisation about the length of different stages, and the task focus in groups at different points along the continuum, and about the activities which will contribute to the task focus. In groups towards the end of the continuum, where purposes are relatively clear and defined for both members and worker, the main focus of the group would be on the explicitly agreed group tasks. Diagnosis and goal setting would be a part of those tasks, allowing group

Table 4 *Group Contracts*

clear ←		exploratory		→ undefined
Problem-centred groups	*Situation-centred groups*	*Involuntary groups*	*Exploratory groups*	*Outreach groups*
e.g. couples with marital problems; parents of children with behaviour problems.	e.g. single parents; patients with serious illness or handicap; parents of handicapped children.	e.g. probationers, prisoners.	e.g. mothers from multi-problem families; children referred by schools, court or home.	e.g. youth in a neighbourhood.

members to explore individual members' investment and potential contribution to change. Group cohesion would develop through the members' perception of the group's usefulness in helping with their needs. The beginning stages of exploration and testing out would focus more on whether the group could offer useful work on its stated goals than on activities designed to promote liking and enjoyment.

Further along the continuum more attention has to be given to activities which encourage the group and the worker to explore one another and the situation of the group members in order to decide whether work together is likely to be possible or productive. The less group members have any feeling of shared problems or any recognised wish to change themselves or their situation, the more prolonged will be the stage in which the worker concentrates on activities which establish him as a useful and resource-holding person, and the group as a setting where it is possible to enjoy doing things together. A comparison of the account by Goetschius (1967) of outreach work to unattached youth with the account by Rose (1969) of work with parents having problems with their children show such differences in activity emphasis clearly. On Rose's account the group clients came to the agency requesting help and their needs were clarified before they arrived in the group. The group focused exclusively on activities which contributed to the agreed group purpose of working on those needs. The unattached youth in Goetschius' account had not requested any help, they were defined from the outside as having problems, and the focus of the worker was on how they perceived those problems and on attempting to establish relationships with potential group members to help them work on their perceived concerns.

Work on the implicit goals of group members also requires greater attention in groups where the content is less defined, although the extent to which this is emphasised in any group is also dependent on other variables such as age and needs of the group members. In groups where contracts are being explored or where the worker is reaching out, members will be drawn to the group, and their willingness to work with one another will be influenced by the extent to which they see the group as offering them emotional satisfaction, chances to win recognition and status, and feelings of being wanted and useful in the group. Activities which offer opportunities for all members to experience gratification and individual meeting of needs in the group will help the group members to see themselves as people who can work together.

The actual activities which will contribute to a particular task for any one group vary. The worker in choosing activities for a group will have to match the characteristics and needs of the group members with the components and demands of the various activities.

THE CHARACTERISTICS OF THE GROUP MEMBERS

The ages and abilities of the group members will affect considerably their reactions to and their gains from any particular activity. These variables will help to decide which activities will contribute, for instance, to the building of group cohesion for group members, which will provide a stimulating challenge once the group members have some trust in the group and in the worker, and which will simply prove frustrating and unattainable. Group workers with children should be particularly alert to the interests, concentration span and physical endurance of children at different ages (Piaget, 1951 and 1954) and to their limited abilities to communicate verbally (Konopka, 1954).

Each individual develops at a different pace and it is not possible to make definite rules for the capacities of every 8-year-old or every 15-year-old, but it is useful to know, for example, that any single activity normally should have a short time span for younger children, and that the younger the child the more he needs opportunities for individual and parallel activities with only brief periods of co-operative group play.

Other kinds of group members also have their particular characteristics and needs. The physically and mentally handicapped need imaginative programming which will enable them to gain maximum satisfaction without underlining their disabilities and differences. The elderly too can enjoy a range of activities which may be unfamiliar and different but which do not make too heavy demands for such fading powers as co-ordination or physical movement. They can enjoy unfamiliar activities such as painting or craft work which reveal new talents to themselves, or in more task-centred groups can take a strong part in changing their own situation and influencing public opinion.

Restraints on group members' abilities come not only from age and physical and mental constraints but also from their experience in life. Skills are only learnt if the opportunity has been offered. Children, or for that matter adults, may be more than usually inarticulate in discussions because they have no experience of verbalising their own feelings and thoughts.

Reading or number recognition required for some activities may also be outside the members' possibilities. Even imitating animals, trains or boats in dramatic play may pose difficulties for the child who had never seen even a picture of them.

The interests of group members and their normal patterns of activity outside the group will affect their response to activities within the group. Interests can be picked up from group members by the alert worker from scraps and hints of conversation and from reactions to activities already undertaken. Group members may have a very limited experience of potential activities, and when asked may opt for the most familiar and safe. They will sometimes need to be led into new possibilities through seeing examples, through watching the worker or other groups demonstrate the activity, or through careful introduction by the worker. Spergel (1966) cites the case of a juvenile gang member who stole oil paints and an easel in a burglary where more easily disposable materials were also available, and the worker recognised an interest in art which led to a visit to an art gallery for the whole group, painting lessons for the individual member and a recognition by the group of his newly discovered talent. Not all workers will receive this kind of indication, but group members will reveal interests which can be picked up and developed to contribute to the development both of individuals and the group.

THE CHARACTERISTICS AND COMPONENTS OF ACTIVITIES

The nature of an activity itself and the demands it makes of group members will affect very strongly the effect it has on the group and the contribution it makes to the various tasks. Vinter (1967) has developed a framework for analysis of activities which appears the most helpful available (compare Middleman, 1968). This framework has been described (Davies, 1975), used and developed (Whittaker, 1974) to look at different popular activities. The framework describes components and characteristics which may be studied and compared for different activities. These may be altered by the organisation and structure of the activity if the worker wishes to increase or decrease the effect of a particular characteristic. The components and characteristics Vinter selects are:

(1) *Prescriptiveness*–that is, the extent to which an activity prescribes the required behaviours and bodily movements of participants. Some games, for example, have very strict movement rules and allow players only to follow the movements of a leader or to move when told to do so. Craft activities or story telling also restrict movement since they cannot be carried out without stillness and bodily control.

(2) *The source and nature of controls* exercised over participants during an activity. The agent of control and the source of control vary from activity to activity. Some offer opportunities to participants to exercise

control either individually as in games with a controlling 'it' role, or in turn as in changing leader games. Learning specific skills such as sewing, cooking or carpentry tends to place control in the hands of the teacher, though it emanates from the nature of the material being used. Teachers can pass some control to participants in allowing them choice as to the final product and the details of production. Plasticine and clay modelling have greater flexibility and require less control on the part of the worker or activity organiser to ensure a successful end product. Organised sports, the use of potentially dangerous equipment or outings to places requiring conformity to certain rules, such as libraries or museums, also by their nature require considerable control. This control can be enforced by officials such as referees and umpires, by agents of social rules such as attendants, and for some activities with careful planning and structuring by the group members.

(3) *Provision for physical movement*. Some activities, such as swimming or running games like tag, require constant movement engaging the whole body in an unconfined area. Other activities confine movement to just the hands, as in crafts, or restrict the body movements to a limited space at a desk or table.

(4) *The competence and skill level needed* to participate even minimally in the activity. Some activities may require skills such as reading or number recognition. Arts and crafts may require sufficient motor co-ordination to wield scissors, fold paper or paint between straight lines. More complex skills may be needed for water skiing, rock climbing or playing some forms of musical instrument, while free swimming, hill walking or group singing require relatively low levels of skill for participation. Most activities can be made more demanding or less so. Swimming can be made more difficult by adding ball games or races in the water. Group singing can be choral and highly organised.

(5) *Provision for participant interactiveness*. Different activities and their pattern of organisation allow for, provoke or require different forms of interaction. Craft activity around one table sharing some materials will provoke interaction which may be friendly or productive, or where members have difficulty sharing may lead to dissension and anger. Some games limit interaction to commands and responses, others encourage both verbal and physical interaction. Acting in skits or improvising scenes requires interaction to produce a joint effect.

(6) *Reward structures* – that is, the extent to which rewards are available from a particular activity and their distribution. Some activities provide abundant rewards for all members. Eating together, holding a jointly planned party or going on a weekend's camp will offer some rewards to all members, while a competitive game offers most reward to the winner. Craft programmes may offer rewards of achievements or the acquisition of a desirable object. Singing may offer enjoyment to all, but soloists in a

group concert will gain the highest level of reward if they perform well.

Davies (1975) in describing this framework stresses another useful element touched upon by Vinter, which is the extent to which the activity allows for creativity and variation by the group members. Some activities limit their performance rigidly while others allow for diversity and initiative. For example, colouring outlines already drawn may allow choice of colour but otherwise restrain creativity, while free drawing allows more choice and requires more self-expression from the participant.

In looking at these activity components and characteristics it is possible to decide which of them are desirable in the activities of a particular group at any given time in order to fulfil the goals of the group.

THE RESOURCES AVAILABLE

Understanding of the factors described above can help the worker in developing programme plans and suggestions for different groups. However, the choice of activity open to him does not depend solely on the needs and characteristics of his group. This range of choice will be limited or extended by the resources available to him. Resources for activities are available from

the worker
the agency
the community

The worker of limited experience with groups may not feel that he has many personal resources. Konopka (1954) stresses that the worker should be able to offer the greatest possible variety of activity skills, but particularly for the casework-trained worker this is a counsel of perfection. Once the worker is aware, however, of the contribution which can be made to groups by the use of a variety of activities he can start looking for programme ideas. Libraries have shelves on recreation usually including games and crafts. The National Associations for Youth Clubs and Boys Clubs and the YMCA and YWCA are also sources of ideas and literature. Writings on the theatre and dramatic exercises and techniques can be fruitful, and books are available on making puppets and on other kinds of scrap crafts. Pictures and newspaper articles can serve as stimulus for group discussions, and films or television programmes can be hired for group use.

The group may offer activity resources too. In a mothers' group one member may be good at dressmaking or cooking and sooner or later may feel able to share this with the group. Young people may be able to teach each other and the worker dance-steps or songs. Group members may also have relatives or contacts with special skills and may be proud to be able to bring them into the group.

The agency resources are important, and many a good programme idea has foundered because the agency has not budgeted for buying equipment or materials or for subsidising activity costs. The worker needs to know exactly what is available in the agency in the way of activity spaces, transport, materials and equipment, and funds. Where all or any of these are limited or unavailable they may require hunting for outside the agency or some intensive negotiating within the agency.

The community may be liberally supplied with activity resources within manageable distance such as swimming pools, skating rinks, sports centres, libraries, restaurants for outings, bowling alleys, etc. or it may be singularly devoid of any of these. Where they are present the worker needs to be aware of opening hours, rules and entry fees and to plan their use carefully according to the needs and likely reactions of group members. Getting banned from such facilities for bad behaviour or being made to feel unwelcome is not generally a positive experience, and the worker may need to prepare the ground with both the group and with the community facility. In a community lacking in such resources the worker will be thrown back upon his own and the group's resources in developing entertainment within the group. Community residents may also provide help in teaching skills and new activities and can sometimes be found through night classes or events reported in local papers.

CONCLUSION

It is important that the worker recognise the importance of thought and planning for programming well before the beginning of a group. He must develop an idea of what activities will contribute to the various tasks of his group based on his understanding of (1) the nature and aims of his group, (2) the characteristics and needs of the group members, (3) the components and characteristics of different activities and (4) the resources available to him.

REFERENCES

Advisory Council on Child Care (1971) 'Discussion paper 6: Supervision in field practice', in *Fieldwork Training for Social Work* (London: HMSO).

Alfero, L. A. (1972) 'Conscientization', a paper presented at the XVIth International Schools of Social Work, 8–11 August, The Hague, Netherlands.

Alinsky, S. D. (1969) *Reveille for Radicals* (New York: Vintage Books).

Alinsky, S. D. (1971) *Rules for Radicals* (New York: Random House).

Aponte, H. (1976) 'The family-school interview: An eco-structural approach', *Family Process*, vol. 15, no. 3, pp. 303–11.

Armstrong, R. and Davies, C. T. (1975) 'The educational element in community work in Britain', *Community Development Journal*, October.

Ashcroft, B. and Jackson, K. (1974) 'Adult education and community action', in D. Jones and M. Mayo (eds), *Community Work One* (London: Routledge & Kegan Paul).

Association of Community Workers (1975) *Knowledge and Skills for Community Workers* (London: ACW).

Auerswald, E. (1968) 'Interdisciplinary versus ecological approach', *Family Process*, vol. 7, no. 2, pp. 202–15. Also (1972) in C. J. Sager and H. Singer Kaplan (eds), *Progress in Group and Family Therapy* (New York: Brunner/Mazel; London: Butterworth).

Bales, R. F. (1950) *Interaction Process Analysis* (Reading, Mass.: Addison-Wesley Publishing Co.). Quoted in M. E. Hartford, *Groups in Social Work* (New York: Columbia University Press, 1972).

Barnett, H. O. (1919) *Canon Barnett, his Life, Work and Friends* (London: Murray).

Batten, T. R. (1967) *The Non-Directive Approach in Group and Community Work* (London: Oxford University Press).

Bavelas, A. (1968) 'Communication patterns in task-oriented groups', in D. Cartwright and A. Zander (eds), *Group Dynamics: Research and Theory*, 3rd edn (London: Tavistock Publications).

Beedell, C. (1970–1) 'Provision for playgroups in a reception centre', in *Groups*, Annual Review of the Residential Child Care Association, vol. 18, pp. 107–34.

Bell, E. H. C. Moberly (1942) *Octavia Hill* (London: Constable).

Benington, J. (1975) 'Gosford Green Residents' Association: A case study', in P. Leonard (ed.), *The Sociology of Community Action* (Keele: University of Keele).

Bennis, W. G. and Shepard, H. A. (1956) 'A theory of group development', *Human Relations*, vol. 9, no. 4, pp. 415–57.

Berne, E. (1961) *Transactional Analysis in Psychotherapy* (London: Souvenir Press)

Berne, E. (1964) *The Games People Play* (London: Penguin).

Bernstein, B. (1971) *Class, Codes and Control*, vol. 1, *Theoretical Studies towards a Sociology of Language* (London: Routledge & Kegan Paul).

Bertcher, H. and Maple, F. with Wallace, H. (1974) *Group Composition* (Ann Arbor: Campus Publishers).

Bevan, A. (1952) *In Place of Fear* (London: Heinemann).

Beveridge, Lord William H. (1948) *Voluntary Action* (London: Allen & Unwin).

Biddle, W. W. and Biddle, L. J. (1966) *The Community Development Process: The Rediscovery of Local Initiative* (New York: Holt, Rinehart & Winston).

Bigge, M. L. (1964) *Learning Theories for Teachers* (New York: Harper & Row).

Bion, W. R. (1961) *Experiences in Groups* (London: Tavistock Publications).

Bion, W. R. (1962) 'A theory of thinking', *International Journal of Psychoanalysis*, vol. 43, pp. 306–10.

Boehm, W. (ed.) (1959) *Curriculum Study* (New York: Council on Social Work Education).

Bowlby, J. (1973) *Separation–Anxiety and Anger* (London: Hogarth Press).

Bradford, L. P. and Gibb, J. R. (eds) (1964) *Theories of T-group Training* (New York: John Wiley).

Brager, G. and Specht, H. (1973) *Community Organising* (New York: Columbia University Press).

Broadbent, M. and Lovelock, R. (1975) *Group Work Theory in Practice* (London: Invalid Children's Aid Association).

Burns, M. E. and Glasser, P. H. (1963) 'Similarities and differences in casework and groupwork practice', *Social Service Review*, vol. 37, no. 4, pp. 416–28.

Button, L. (1974) *Developmental Group Work with Adolescents* (London: University of London Press).

Byng-Hall, J. (1976) 'Renovating unstable family safety mechanisms by re-editing family myths and dramas' (unpublished paper).

Byrne, D. (1969) 'Attitudes and attraction', in L. Berkowitz (ed.), *Advances in Experimental Social Psychology*, vol. 4 (New York: Academic Press).

Bywaters, P. (1975) 'Ending casework relationships', *Social Work Today*, vol. 6, nos. 10 and 11, pp. 301–4.

Campaign for the Mentally Handicapped (1972) *Our Life*, Report on the Conference (London: CMH).

Central Council for Education and Training in Social Work (1973) Discussion Document: *Training for Residential Work* (London: CCETSW).

Central Training Council in Child Care (1971) *Staff Development and In-service Study for the Staff of Children's Departments*, Paper No. 3 (London: CTCCC).

Churchill, R. (1959) 'Prestructuring group content', *American Journal of Social Work*, vol. 4, no. 3, pp. 52–9.

Churchill, S. R. (1974) 'Preventive short-term groups for siblings of child mental hospital patients', in P. Glasser, R. Sarri and R. Vinter (eds), *Individual Change through Small Groups* (New York: Free Press).

Clinard, M. B. (1966) *Slums and Community Development: Experiments in Self-Help* (London: Collier-Macmillan).

Collins, B. E. and Hoyt, M. F. (1972) 'Personal responsibility for the consequences: An integration and extension of the "forced compliance" literature', *Journal of Experimental Social Psychology*, vol. 81, pp. 558–92.

Colman, A. D. and Bexton, W. H. (eds) (1975) *Group Relations Reader* (California: GREX).

Cooper, C. L. (1969) 'The influence of the trainer on participant change in T-groups', *Human Relations*, vol. 22, pp. 515–30.

Curnock, K. (1975) *Student Units in Social Work Education* (London: Central Council for Education and Training in Social Work).

Danziger, K. (1971) *Socialisation* (London: Penguin).

Davies, B. (1975) *The Use of Groups in Social Work Practice* (London: Routledge & Kegan Paul).

Davies, E. (1973) 'The use of T groups in training of social workers', *British Journal of Social Work*, vol. 3, no. 1, pp. 65–77.

Davies, H. and Taylor, P. (1973) 'Two agency placements in social work training', *Social Work Today*, vol. 4, no. 8, pp. 245–50.

Dennis, N. (1970) *People and Planning* (London: Faber & Faber).

Dennis, N. (1975) 'Community action, quasi-community action and anti-community action', in P. Leonard (ed.), *The Sociology of Community Action* (Keele: University of Keele).

Douglas, T. (1970) *A Decade of Small Group Theory 1960–1970* (London: Bookstall Publications).

Douglas, T. (1976) *Group Work Practice* (London: Tavistock Publications).

Erikson, E. H. (1950) *Childhood and Society* (New York: Norton).

Erikson, E. H. (1968) *Identity, Youth and Crisis* (London: Faber & Faber).

Festinger, L. (1954) 'A theory of social comparison processes', *Human Relations*, vol. 7, pp. 117–40.

Follet, M. (1918) *The New State* (London: Longmans).

Foulkes, S. H. and Anthony, E. J. (1968) *Group Psychotherapy: The Psychoanalytic Approach* (London: Pelican).

Freire, P. (1972) *Pedagogy of the Oppressed* (London: Penguin).

Frey, L. (1966) 'Group work with hospitalized children', in L. Frey (ed.), *Use of Groups in the Health Field* (New York: National Association of Social Workers).

FSU Publications (1974) *Families and Groups: A Unit at Work* (London: Bookstall Publications).

FSU Publications (1975) *Time to Consider* (London: Bedford Square Press).

Garland, J. A., Jones, H. E. and Kolodny, R. L. (1972) 'Model for stages of development in social work groups', in S. Bernstein (ed.), *Explorations in Group Work* (London: Bookstall Publications).

Gifford, C. G. (1968) 'Sensitivity training and social work', *Social Work*, vol. 13, no. 2, pp. 78, 86.

Goetschius, G. W. and Tash Goon, M. (1967) *Working with Unattached Youth* (London: Routledge & Kegan Paul).

Golding, W. (1954) *Lord of the Flies* (London: Faber & Faber).

Goldstein, H. (1973) *Social Work Practice: A Unitary Approach* (South Carolina: University of South Carolina).

Goodenough, W. H. (1963) *Cooperation in Change: An Anthropoligical Approach to Community Development* (New York: Russell Sage).

Grinberg, L., Sor, D. and de Bianchedi, E. T. (1975) *Introduction to the Work of Bion* (Strath Tay, Perthshire: Clunie Press).

Haggstrom, W. C. (1970) 'The psychological implications of the community development process', in L. J. Cary (ed.), *Community Development as a Process* (Columbia: University of Missouri Press).

Haines, J. (1975) *Skills and Methods in Social Work* (London: Constable).

Harper, J. (1969) 'Group supervision of students', *Social Work*, vol. 26, no. 4, pp. 18–22.

Harrison, J. (1974) 'Community work and adult education', *Studies in Adult Education*, April, pp. 50–67.

Harrow, H., Astrachan, B. M., Tucker, G. J., Klein, E. B. and Miller, J. C. (1971) 'The T-group and study group laboratory experiences', *Journal of Social Psychology*, vol. 85, pp. 225–37.

Hartford, M. E. (1972) *Groups in Social Work* (New York: Columbia University Press).

Haythorn, W. (1956) 'The effects of varying combinations of authoritarian and equalitarian leaders and followers', *Journal of Abnormal and Social Psychology*, vol. 52, pp. 210–19.

Hilgard, E. R. and Bower, G. H. (1966) *Theories of Learning*, 3rd edn (New York: Appleton-Century Crofts).

Hollander, E. P. (1960) 'Competence and conformity in the acceptance of influence', *Journal of Abnormal and Social Psychology*, vol. 61, pp. 365–9.

Hollander, E. P. and Julian, J. W. (1970) 'Studies in leader legitimacy, influence and innovation', in L. Berkowitz (ed.), *Advances in Experimental Social Psychology*, vol. 5 (New York: Academic Press).

Hollander, E. P. and Willis, R. H. (1967) 'Some current issues in the psychology of conformity and non-conformity', *Psychological Bulletin*, vol. 68, pp. 62–76.

Hunt, L., Harrison, K. and Armstrong, M. (1974) 'Integrating group dynamics training and the educating and development of social work students', *British Journal of Social Work*, vol. 4, no. 4, pp. 405–23.

Illich, I. D. (1971) *Deschooling Society* (London: Calder and Boyers).

Inter-Action Advisory Service (1975) *Basic Video in Community Work*, Handbook no. 5 (London: Inter-Action Imprint). See also 'Video: Can it help?' in *Community Action*, June–July 1975.

Irvine, E. E. (1970) 'Helping the immature to grow up', Preface to *Groupwork with the Inarticulate* (London: Family Service Units).

Jacobs, S. (1976) *The Right to a Decent House* (London: Routledge & Kegan Paul).

Jacques, E. (1970) *Work, Creativity and Social Justice* (London: Heinemann).

Jerman, B. (1971) *Do Something* (London: Garnstone Press).

Jones, M. (1968) *Beyond the Therapeutic Community* (London: Yale University Press).

Kelman, H. C. (1958) 'Compliance, identification and internalisation', *Journal of Conflict Resolution*, vol. 2, pp. 51–60.

Kelman, H. C. (1963) 'The role of the group in the induction of therapeutic change', *International Journal of Group Psychotherapy*, vol. 13, pp. 399–432.

Khinduka, S. K. (1975) 'Community development: Potential and limitations', in R. M. Kramer and H. Specht (eds), *Readings in Community Organisation Practice*, 2nd edn (New Jersey: Prentice-Hall).

Kierkegaard, S. (1938) *The Journals of Kierkegaard*, ed. and trans. A. Dru (London: Oxford University Press).

Klein, E. B. and Astrachan, B. M. (1971) 'Learning in groups: A comparison of study groups and T-groups', *Journal of Applied Behavioural Science*, vol. 7, pp. 659–83.

Klein, J. (1961) *Working with Groups* (London: Hutchinson University Library).

Knowles, M. S. (1972) 'Innovations in teaching styles and approaches based upon adult learning', *Journal of Education for Social Work*, vol. 8, no. 2, pp. 32–9.

Konopka, G. (1954) *Group Work in the Institution* (New York: Association Press).

Konopka, G. (1963) *Social Group Work: A Helping Process* (New Jersey: Prentice-Hall).

Kramer, R. M. and Specht, H. (1969) *Readings in Community Organisation Practice*, 2nd edn (New Jersey: Prentice-Hall).

Kreeger, L. (ed.) (1975) *The Large Group: Dynamics and Therapy* (London: Constable).

Kuenstler, P. (ed.) (1954) *Social Group Work* (London: Faber & Faber).

Lakin, M. (1969) 'Some ethical issues in sensitivity training', *American Psychologist*, vol. 24, pp. 923–8.

Lawrence, G. (1972) 'Some dangers in group training', *Social Work Today*, vol. 3, no. 4, p. 10.

Lippit, R., Watson, J. and Westley, B. (1958) *The Dynamics of Planned Change* (New York: Harcourt, Brace and World).

Lomas, P. (1973) *True and False Experience* (London: Allen Lane).

Lovett, T. (1975) *Adult Education, Community Development and the Working Class* (London: Ward Lock).

Lowin, A. and Craig, J. R. (1968) 'The influence of level of performance on managerial style: An object lesson in the ambiguity of correlational data', *Organisational Behavior and Human Performance*, vol. 3, pp. 440–58.

Lowy, L. (1972) 'Goal formulation in social work with groups', in S. Bernstein (ed.), *Explorations in Group Work* (London: Bookstall Publications).

McCaughan, N. (1977a) 'Group behaviour: Some theories for practice', in C. Briscoe and D. N. Thomas (eds), *Community Work: Learning and Supervision* (London: Allen & Unwin).

McCaughan, N. (1977b) 'Social group work in the United Kingdom', in H. Specht and A. Vickery (eds), *Integrating Social Work Methods* (London: Allen & Unwin).

McCullough, M. K. and Ely, P. J. (1968) *Social Work with Groups* (London: Routledge & Kegan Paul).

Maier, H. W. (1965) 'The social group method and residential treatment', in H. W. Maier (ed.), *Group Work as part of Residential Treatment* (New York: National Association of Social Work).

Mann, R. D. (1967) *Interpersonal Styles and Group Development* (New York: John Wiley).

Meyer, H. J., Borgatta, A. F. and Jones, W. C. (1965) *Girls at Vocational High* (New York: Russell Sage).

Middleman, R. R. (1968) *The Non-Verbal Method in Working with Groups* (New York: Association Press).

Middleman, R. and Goldberg, G. (1974) *Social Service Delivery: A Structural Approach to Social Work Practice* (New York: Columbia University Press).

Miles, M. B. (1971) *Learning to Work in Groups* (New York: Teachers College Press, Columbia University).

Milgram, S. (1974) *Obedience to Authority* (London: Tavistock Publications).

Miller, E. J. (ed.) (1976) *Task and Organisation* (London: John Wiley).
Miller, E. J. and Rice, A. K. (1967) *Systems of Organization* (London: Tavistock Publications).
Millham, S., Bullock, R. and Chessett, P. (1975) *After Grace-Teeth: A Comparative Study of the Residential Experience of Boys in Approved Schools* (London: Human Context Books).
Milson, F. (1973) *An Introduction to Group Work Skill* (London: Routledge & Kegan Paul).
Minuchin, S. (1974) *Families and Family Therapy* (Cambridge, Mass.: Harvard University Press).
Mitton, R. and Morrison, E. (1972) *A Community Project in Notting Dale* (London: Penguin).
More, H. (undated) 'Hints on how to run a Sunday School', in A. F. Young and E. T. Ashton (eds), *British Social Work in the Nineteenth Century* (London: Routledge & Kegan Paul, 1956).
Moscovici, S. and Faucheux, C. (1972) 'Social influence, conformity bias and the study of active minorities', in L. Berkowitz (ed.), *Advances in Experimental Social Psychology*, vol. 6 (New York: Academic Press).
Murstein, B. (ed.) (1971) *Theories of Attraction and Love* (New York: Springer).
Naish, M. and Filkin, E. (1974) *What does a Community Worker need to know? What does a Community Worker need to be able to do?* (London: Goldsmiths College).
National Council of Social Service (1967) *Caring for People: Staffing Residential Homes*, report of the Committee of Inquiry (Chairman: Gertrude Williams) (London: Allen & Unwin).
Neill, A. S. (1962) *Summerhill* (London: Gollancz).
Newcomb, T. (1961) *The Acquaintance Process* (New York: Holt, Rinehart & Winston).
Newson, J. and E. (1968) *Four Years Old in an Urban Community* (London: Allen & Unwin).
Northen, H. (1969) *Social Work with Groups* (New York: Columbia University Press).
Owen, D. (1965) *English Philanthropy, 1660–1960* (London: Oxford University Press).
Paley, J. and Thorpe, D. (1974) *Children: Handle with Care* (Leicester: National Youth Bureau).
Palmer, B. W. M. (1973) 'Thinking about thought', *Human Relations*, vol. 26, no. 1, pp. 127–41.
Palmer, B. W. M. and Reed, B. D. (1972) *An Introduction to Organisational Behaviour* (London: The Grubb Institute, duplicated).
Papell, C. P. (1972) 'Sensitivity training: Relevance for social work education', *Journal of Education for Social Work*, vol. 8, no. 1, pp. 42–55.
Papell, C. P. and Rothman, B. (1966) 'Social group work models: Possession and heritage', *Journal of Education for Social Work*, vol. 2, no. 2, pp. 66–77.
Parsloe, P. (1969) 'Some thoughts on social group work', *British Journal of Psychiatric Social Work*, vol. 10, no. 1, pp. 3–11.
Pateman, T. (1975) *Language, Truth and Politics* (Sidmouth: Stroud and Pateman).

Perlman, R. and Gurin, A. (1972) *Community Organisation and Social Planning* (New York: John Wiley).

Piaget, J. (1951) *Play, Dreams and Invitation in Childhood* (New York: Norton).

Piaget, J. (1954) *The Construction of Reality in the Child* (New York: Basic Books).

Pincus, A. and Minahan, A. (1970) 'Toward a model for teaching a basic first-year course in methods of social work practice', in L. Ripple (ed.), *Innovations in Teaching Social Work Practice* (New York: Council of Social Work Education).

Pincus, A. and Minahan, A. (1973) *Social Work Practice: Model and Method* (Illinois: Peacock Publishers).

Polanyi, M. (1973) *Personal Knowledge* (London: Routledge & Kegan Paul, paperback edn).

Potock, C. (1967) *The Chosen* (Greenwich, Conn.: Fawcett Publications).

Potock, C. (1969) *The Promise* (Greenwich, Conn.: Fawcett Publications).

Potock, C. (1972) *My Name is Asher Lev* (Greenwich, Conn.: Fawcett Publications).

Rainwater, L. (1968) 'Neighbourhood action and lower class life-styles', in J. B. Turner (ed.), *Neighbourhood Organisation for Community Action* (New York: National Association of Social Workers).

Reynolds, B. C. (1965) *Learning and Teaching in the Practice of Social Work*, 2nd edn (New York: Russell & Russell).

Rice, A. K. (1963) *The Enterprise and its Environment* (London: Tavistock Publications).

Rice, A. K. (1965) *Learning for Leadership* (London: Tavistock Publications).

Rose, S. D. (1969) 'A behavioural approach to the group treatment of parents', *American Journal of Social Work*, vol. 14, no. 3, pp. 21–9.

Rothman, J. (1974) *Planning and Organising for Social Change* (New York: Columbia University Press).

Rowbotham, S. (1974) *Women's Consciousness, Man's World* (London: Penguin).

Sales, E. and Navarre, E. (1970) *Individual and Group Supervision in Field Instruction–A Research Report* (Ann Arbor: School of Social Work, University of Michigan).

Sarri, R. C. and Galinsky, M. J. (1962) *A Conceptual Framework for Teaching of Social Group Methods* (New York: Council on Social Work Education).

Sarri, R. C. and Galinsky, M. J. (1974) 'A conceptual framework for group development', in P. Glasser, R. C. Sarri and R. Vinter (eds), *Individual Change through Small Groups* (New York: Free Press).

Schler, D. J. (1970) 'The community development process', in L. J. Cary (ed.), *Community Development as a Process* (Columbia: University of Missouri Press).

Schutz, W. C. (1967) *Joy: Expanding Human Awareness* (New York: Grove Press).

Schwartz, W. and Zalba, S. (1971) *The Practice of Group Work* (New York: Columbia University Press).

Seed, P. (1973) *The Expansion of Social Work in Britain* (London: Routledge & Kegan Paul).

Selby, L. (1968) 'Helping students in field practice identify and modify blocks of learning', in E. Younghusband (ed.), *Education for Social Work, Readings in Social Work*, vol. IV (London: Allen & Unwin).

Sherwood, M. (1964) 'Bion's experiences in groups: A critical evaluation', *Human Relations*, vol. 17, pp. 113–30.

Shulman, L. (1968) *A Casebook of Social Work with Groups: The Mediating Model* (New York: Council on Social Work Education).

Shulman, L. (1971) '"Program" in group work: Another look', in W. Schwartz and S. R. Zalba (eds), *The Practice of Group Work* (New York: Columbia University Press).

Skynner, R. (1976) *One Flesh: Separate Persons* (London: Constable).

Smith, C. S., Farrant, M. R. and Marchant, H. J. (1972) *Wincroft Youth Project* (London: Tavistock Publications).

Smith, D. M. (1972) 'Group supervision: An experience', *Social Work Today*, vol. 3, no. 8, pp. 13–15.

Smith, P. B. (1973) *Groups within Organisations: Applications of Social Psychology to Organisational Behaviour* (London: Harper & Row).

Smith, P. B. (1974) 'Group composition as a determinant of Kelman's social influence modes', *European Journal of Social Psychology*, vol. 4, pp. 261–77.

Smith, P. B. (1975) 'Controlled studies of the outcome of sensitivity training', *Psychological Bulletin*, vol. 82, no. 4, pp. 597–622.

Smith, P. B. (1976) 'Social influence processes and the outcome of sensitivity training', manuscript submitted for publication, 1976.

Smith, P. B. and Linton, M. J. (1975) 'Group composition and changes in self-actualisation in T-groups', *Human Relations*, vol. 28, pp. 811–23.

Sociological Review (1962) *The Canford Families*, Monograph no. 6 (Keele: University of Keele).

Somers, M. L. (1968) 'The small group in learning and teaching', in E. Younghusband (ed.), *Education for Social Work, Readings in Social Work*, vol. IV (London: Allen & Unwin).

Somers, M. L. (1969) 'Contributions of learning and teaching theories to the explication of the role of the teacher in social work education', *Journal of Education for Social Work*, vol. 5, no. 2, pp. 61–73.

Sparrow, J. (1976) *Diary of a Delinquent Episode* (London: Routledge & Kegan Paul).

Spergel, I. A. (1966) *Street Gang Work: Theory and Practice* (Reading, Mass.: Addison-Wesley Publishing Co.).

Stierlin, H. (1976) 'The dynamics of owning and disowning: Psychoanalytic and family perspectives', *Family Process*, vol. 15, no. 3, pp. 277–88.

Stock Whitaker, D. and Lieberman, M. A. (1964) *Psychotherapy through the Group Process* (London: Prentice-Hall).

Tavistock Institute of Human Relations and The Tavistock Clinic (1975) *Annotated List of Publications 1946–1975* (London: Tavistock Joint Library).

Thomas, D. N. (1975) 'Chaucer House Tenants' Association: A case study', in P. Leonard (ed.), *The Sociology of Community Action* (Keele: University of Keele).

Thomas, D. N. (1976) *Organising for Social Change: A Study in the Theory and Practice of Community Work* (London: Allen & Unwin).

Towle, C. (1963) 'The place of help in supervision', *Social Service Review*, vol. 38, no. 4, pp. 403–15.

Trecker, H. B. (1972) *Social Group Work*, revised edn (New York: Association Press).

Trist, E. L. and Sofer, C. (1959) *Explorations in Group Relations* (Leicester: Leicester University Press).

Tuckman, B. W. (1965) 'Developmental sequence in small groups', *Psychological Bulletin*, vol. 63, no. 6, pp. 384–99.

Tutt, N. (1974) *Care or Custody? Community Homes and the Treatment of Delinquents* (London: Darton, Longman and Todd).

Vickery, A. (1974) 'A systems approach to social work intervention: Its uses for work with individuals and families', *British Journal of Social Work*, vol. 4, no. 4, pp. 389–404.

Vinter, R. (1967) 'Program activities: An analysis of their effects on participant behaviour', in P. Glasser, R. C. Sarri and R. Vinter (eds), *Individual Change through Small Groups* (New York: Free Press).

Walker, L. (1970) *Groupwork with the Inarticulate* (London: Family Service Units).

Walrond-Skinner, S. (1976) *Family Therapy. The Treatment of Natural Systems* (London: Routledge & Kegan Paul).

Warren, R. (1963) *The Community in America* (Chicago: Rand McNally & Co.).

Weakland, J., Fisch, R., Watzlawick, P. and Bodin, A. (1974) 'Brief therapy: focused problem resolution', *Family Process*, vol. 13, no. 2, pp. 141–68.

White, R. and Lippitt, R. (1968) 'Leader behaviour and member reaction in three "social climates"', in D. Cartwright and A. Zander (eds), *Group Dynamics: Research and Theory*, 3rd edn (London: Tavistock Publications).

Whitaker, D. S. (1976) 'Some conditions for effective work with groups', *British Journal of Social Work*, vol. 5, no. 4, pp. 423–39.

Whitehead, A. N. (1962) *Aims of Education* (London: Benn).

Whittaker, J. K. (1974) 'Program activities: Their selection and use in a therapeutic milieu', in P. Glasser, R. Sarri and R. Vinter (eds), *Individual Change through Small Groups* (New York: Free Press).

Wills, D. W. (1964) *Homer Lane: A Biography* (London: Allen & Unwin).

Wills, D. W. (1970) *A Place like Home* (London: Allen & Unwin).

Wills, D. W. (1971) *Spare the Child* (London: Penguin).

Wilson, G. and Ryland, G. (1949) *Social Group Work Practice* (Cambridge, Mass.: Houghton Mifflin Riverside Press).

Woodroofe, K. (1962) *From Charity to Social Work* (London: Routledge & Kegan Paul).

Yalom, I. D. (1970) *The Theory and Practice of Group Psychotherapy* (New York: Basic Books).

Young, A. F. and Ashton, E. T. (1956) *British Social Work in the Nineteenth Century* (London: Routledge & Kegan Paul).

Ziller, R. C. (1965) 'Towards a theory of open and closed groups', *Psychological Bulletin*, vol. 64, no. 3, pp. 164–82.

INDEX